THE LAUGHING SWAMIS

THE LAUGHING SWAMIS

*Australian Sannyasin Disciples of
Swami Satyananda Saraswati and
Osho Rajneesh*

HARRY AVELING

MOTILAL BANARSIDASS PUBLISHERS
PRIVATE LIMITED ● DELHI

First Edition: Delhi, 1994
Reprint: Delhi, 1996

© MOTILAL BANARSIDASS PUBLISHERS PRIVATE LIMITED

ISBN: 81-208-1118-6

Also available at:

MOTILAL BANARSIDASS
41 U.A. Bungalow Road, Jawahar Nagar, Delhi 110 007
120 Royapettah High Road, Mylapore, Madras 600 004
16 St. Mark's Road, Bangalore 560 001
8 Camac Street, Calcutta 700 017
Ashok Rajpath, Patna 800 004
Chowk, Varanasi 221 001

PRINTED IN INDIA
BY JAINENDRA PRAKASH JAIN AT SHRI JAINENDRA PRESS,
A-45 NARAINA, PHASE I, NEW DELHI 110 028
AND PUBLISHED BY NARENDRA PRAKASH JAIN FOR
MOTILAL BANARSIDASS PUBLISHERS PRIVATE LIMITED,
BUNGALOW ROAD, DELHI 110 007

CONTENTS

PREFACE TO THE SECOND PRINTING

This is an unaltered reprint of the 1994 edition. The book describes the two movements as I understood them to be at the beginning of the Nineties. There have been some changes since then Osho has indeed become a major sage and his teachings are widely distributed, in India at least, through books, videos and television—possibly, however, at some distance from the movement he founded. Paramahamsa Niranjan has sought to transform the Satyananda movement into a newer and tighter organisation, in which the differences between Full Sannyasins and Householder Sannyasins are more definite than before. If Guru's grace allows, it would be fascinating to write another study of these newer religious movements at the end of this decade.

HARRY AVELING

PREFACE

This book aims to study the reinterpretation of the ancient Indian tradition of world-renunciation, *sannyasa*, by two contemporary teachers, Swami Satyananda (b. 1923), and Osho (1931-1990) otherwise known as Bhagwan Shree Rajneesh.

The major focus of the study is on Australians who were disciples of these teachers during the seventies and eighties. In particular, the work seeks to describe the cultural settings for renunciation both in India and in Australia after 1965; and to explore the motives, understandings and lifestyles of the Australians who became *sannyasin* disciples of these two teachers. In this Preface I would like to provide an overview of the whole work.

The study is based on a wide range of texts, including classical scriptures, ethnographies, talks in which Satyananda and Rajneesh explained their position on renunciation, and the replies to a 'Questionnaire on Sannyasa' provided by sixty-seven respondents: twenty full *sannyasin* initiates and twenty-two 'householder *sannyasin*' disciples of Swami Satyananda, as well as twenty-five neo-*sannyasin* disciples of Rajneesh. Part One serves as an introduction to the volume and deals with the methodology used—an analysis of 'discourses', and the problems related to the distribution of the questionnaire to a dispersed, uncodified, self-protective population.

Part Two presents the traditional Indian theory and practice of renunciation. *Sannyasa* was considered the last of four life-stages. It has been interpreted in various ways in the scriptures: as a continuous state of divine ecstasy outside the conventional society, by the *Vedas*; as a form of self-control based on knowledge of the Self (*atman*) and God (*Brahman*, the Ground of Being), in the *Upanishads*; as a defined code of practice, with specific external insignia, grades and obligations, in the *sannyasa upanishads*; and as a state of inner detachment from the consequences of one's action (*karma*), in the *Bhagavad Gita*.

Contemporary sociological research suggests that renunciates in India are expected to wear the insignia of their order; to be characterised by the quality of 'holiness'; to have some knowledge of Sanskrit texts, and skill in ritual or devotional leadership; and to follow a distinctive lifestyle based on asceticism and physical restraint (including sexual celibacy). Most renunciates derive from small joint families of the *Brahmin* caste, particularly those engaged in farming. Most are also illiterate, and rely on begging for their food and other needs. Although some *sannyasins* are initiated before the age of thirty, most are initiated after this age and many after the age of sixty. For most, a desire to lead a spiritual life is less important than the opportunity to follow a convenient and respectable existence. Some Europeans have joined orders of mainly Western renunciates which seek to maintain a lifestyle similar to those of Indian renunciates. These include the disciples of Swami Vishnu Devananda in Canada, and the devotees of the Hare Krishna movement. Unlike their Indian counterparts, these Western renunciates have been aged in their twenties at the time of first joining, been well-educated (often to tertiary level), were single or divorced, and have expressed a strong need to understand the world in religious terms.

Part Three deals with the lives and teachings of Satyananda and Osho. By concentrating on the 'inner essence' of *sannyasa*, both have sought to justify the extension of renunciation to non-Indians, non-Hindus, and women. Of the two teachers, Rajneesh was the more radical, in that he sought to use the inner essence of *sannyasa* as a means of attacking what he considered to be the abuses of contemporary renunciate lifestyles in India.

Part Four deals with the experiences of Australian renunciates, and forms the major part of the study.

Chapter Six shows the limited position of religion in the Australian society, and the unusual place of Asian-based religions in a Christian, materialist and racist society. Such religions are most likely to appeal to those who are not well-integrated into the mainstream of society and are available to the adoption of new and unusual identities. The rise of the 'counter-culture' in the late 1960s and throughout the seventies created such a situation. Chapter Seven presents the main features of the counter-culture, beginning with the opposition to the war in Vietnam, and moving to more personal issues such as feminism, new arrangements of shared accommodation, new concepts of 'personal power', particularly as developed in the 'growth movement' which was a part of Humanistic Psychology, the use of drugs, and the rise of movements devoted to 'eastern mysticism' including the practice of *yoga*.

Australians attracted to a commitment to either Swami Satyananda or Osho had backgrounds similar to those of the other Western renunciates described above. They were usually under the age of thirty, well educated, with some religious background in a mainstream Christian denomination, and often single or recently divorced. The demographic details of the respondents are summarised in Chapter Eight. In this chapter it is suggested that three cohorts can be distinguished among each of the group of full *sannyasins*, householder *sannyasins* and neo-*sannyasins*. The first cohort took initiation in the seventies, often in India, and were closest to the values of the counter-culture. The second cohort, who took initiation in the early to mid-eighties, moved into a known and defined situation, and spent less or no time in India. The third cohort have joined after the major collapse of both movements in the later part of the eighties, and exhibit distinctively individual reasons for joining. Members of the second and third cohorts show less attachment to the values of the counter-culture than do members of the first cohort. Nevertheless, all belong to what Mannheim (1952:306) has described as a 'generational unit', a group of persons with a common psychological and emotional perception of the world, and characteristic way of behaving.

Chapters Nine, Ten and Eleven describe each group in detail by turn. The chapters follow a similar pattern, beginning with the life of a representative member of the group; the experiences of the different cohorts and the changing understandings of discipleship; the lifestyle of the major *ashram* or place of training; and, finally a survey of current work patterns, attitudes to celibacy, and spiritual practices.

Chapter Nine shows the structured and disciplined life led by full *sannyasin* disciples of Swami Satyananda, and their methods of readjusting to the Australian society after lengthy residences in India. Chapter Ten describes householder *sannyasins*, the most recent of the three groups, who follow an ethic dedicated to the sacralisation of their present work and family patterns. Chapter Eleven is concerned with neo-*sannyasins*, who, on the other hand, accept an unstructured lifestyle, in which a major emphasis is

placed on Rajneesh as an object of emotional focus and on psychological therapeutic techniques as the major means for self-awareness. The Rajneesh community also places little stress on discipline
or poverty, prefering spontaneity and beauty. Neo-*sannyasins*
have lower levels of education than Satyananda's disciples, less
commitment to rewarding work, and spend little time practising
meditation. In view of the decision to drop the wearing of the
external signs of renunciation in 1987, it must be questioned
whether neo-*sannyasa* now has anything in common with other
renunciate movements, either positively or in contradiction to
them. Ironically, it is noted that with the increasing loss of interest
in the Indian *ashram* by overseas visitors, the *ashram* is tending to
become a memorial to Rajneesh; the tradition has absorbed his
challenge and given him the status of a great teacher.

The Postscript suggests that both movements have been unable
to survive the moral shortcomings of their top leadership in the
middle of the last decade and are now dying. What promised to
be innovative transformations of an ancient spirituality, in accordance with contemporary needs and ways of thought, have come
to nothing.

This study is an extension of work done on Canadian renunciates
in 1988. The challenge to turn my interest to Australian renunciates
first came from Swamis Karuna Devi and Bhav-chaitanya,
organisers of the 1989 Yoga and Meditation Festival, Melbourne.

The research was conducted during 1989-1990 and presented to
the University of New England, Armidale, New South Wales,
towards the degree of Master of Education in Multicultural Studies
in March 1991. Dr. A. K. Eckermann was a patient and gracious
supervisor. I am also grateful for the interest, hospitality and
insights of Dr. G. Gunther, my associate supervisor.

Encouragement and support was given by many *sannyasins*.
Particular mention must be made of Swamis Ajnananda, Jivan
Christopher, Deva Daricha, Devanatha, Karmamurti, Muktananda,
Muktibodhananda, Naradananda, Sambodh Roman, Shan-
kardevananda and Tapasmurti, and Ma Anand Kalpana, Prem
Maneesha, Rajni and Shivam Rachana, who facilitated this work in
many ways. Ma Anand Ruchita has suffered 'the complexities and
paradoxès yet to be resolved in the heads of many sixties people',
and knows how much the seeing eye is part of what is seen.

Mrs. Coleen Clavdivs first typed an earlier version of the chapter on Osho. Mrs. Satwant Kaur typed the entire manuscript with care and good humour. Blessings on her son, Sandip, who was born during this time. Ms. Catherine Welch helped with the proof-reading; to her too I offer my sincere thanks.

The responsibility for this work is my own, as must be the karma associated with it.

Division of Asian Languages,   HARRY AVELING
La Trobe University,
Bundoora Vlc 3083,
Australia

THE LAUGHING SWAMIS

A story . . . There were three *swamis*. We used to call them the Laughing Swamis. They did nothing but laugh, all day and night. Wherever they went they laughed and laughed all the time, everywhere. They laughed through the villages, they laughed with the children, they were known everywhere as the Laughing Swamis. Finally the day came when one of them died, and the people of the locality wanted to know what the other *swamis* would do. After all, when someone dies there must be mourning. But when they came, they found both of them laughing heartily. Eventually, they prepared a bamboo stretcher, and put the dead *swami* on it, and took him to consign him to the flames as Hindus do. They were laughing, and everyone was laughing. There were no suppressed drums, there were no church cars, they were all laughing and laughing, and they brought flowers and laughter, and flowers and laughter. Finally, they put him on the flames. The Hindus first put logs of wood, and with the wood, if they can manage, sandalwood, and they bathe the body in Ganges water, give him a scented bath, and so many other things, and eventually put him naked on the fire. But this *swami* had made a will before he died. He said, "When I die I should not be given a bath. I should not be put on the flames naked. Still dressed in the clothes in which I die, without any ceremony, I must be consigned to the fire." So they had to accept what he willed. He was put onto the fire, and when it was burning, suddenly, putt, putt, putt, putt, the fire spat out everywhere. He had hidden fireworks and crackers, in his clothes. Before he died this man thought that even when his body was at the most lamented moment of the fire ceremony, people should not be sorry, they should not shed any tears, they should not say, "Poor man, he is gone, we will miss him." Instead, he must create something to make them burst into laughter. So he got a lot of crackers and put them everywhere inside his clothes; and when he was put on the fire the crackers started exploding and everyone laughed heartily.

This is the story of a swami who laughed when he was alive, and made others laugh when he died, and I think Australians are representative of this. I have been to almost all the countries of the world, and I can definitely tell you that nobody can laugh like you do. Those swamis are dead, and they must have been reincarnated as Australians. So, these Laughing Swamis, these laughing Australians, these relaxed beings, full of honey, full of apples, full of juice, now it is high time that they must be exported out of Australia to those countries where there is a scarcity of happiness, where the people are starving for it—the emotionally underdeveloped nations. Not India, but those nations which are psychically, emotionally and spiritually underdeveloped. . . .

Swami Satyananda Saraswati 1979 : 85-86[1]

---

1   The same story, without reference to Australians, is also found in the introduction to Rajneesh 1978b.

LIST OF TABLES

PART ONE

INTRODUCTION

CHAPTER ONE

MULTIPLE VOICES: ON METHODOLOGY

By 1985, perhaps as many as two thousand Australians claimed to follow the sacred Indian path of *sannyasa* (world-renunciation).

The figure is imprecise because few specific records were kept by any organisation. It included disciples of Swami Satyananda Saraswati (b. 1923) of Munger, Bihar State, who were to be found in India and in various *ashram*s across Australia, New Zealand, Fiji and America. Satyananda may have had up to two hundred Australian 'full-time *sannyasin*' disciples, and perhaps a further five hundred 'householder *sannyasins*', who lived 'in the world' but were also entitled to use the same distinguishing marks of a 'spiritual name', the honorific title "*swami*" (master), orange robes (*dhoti*) and prayer beads (*mala*).

There were also well over a thousand disciples of 'Osho', best known as Bhagwan Shree Rajneesh (1931-1990), who also used these marks and were commonly referred to as 'the Orange People'. The Rajneeshees (as they were then officially called) had an obvious presence in many large Australian cities because of their bright red clothing, and their lavish Centres, restaurants and discotheques. Attention also focused on them because of the eagerness of Rajneesh, and his foremost disciple Ma Anand Sheela, to court public outrage through their luxurious style of living (Rajneesh's ninety-nine Rolls-Royces were notorious) and their critical comments to the media about the Western bourgeois lifestyle and its heroes (American President Ronald Reagan, Pope John Paul II, Mother Teresa, among others).

Most of the *sannyasin* disciples of Swami Satyananda lived in
semi-enclosed *ashrams* and dedicated themselves completely to
the practice and teaching of yoga; the householder *sannyasins*
lived scattered throughout the community and followed more
conventional occupations. Some Rajneeshees lived in "neo-
sannyasa communes"; others were employed as doctors, law-
yers, builders, psychologists, computer programmers, commercial artists, teachers, masseurs, astrologers, healers (Wright 1989:
24). 'Full-time sannyasins' considered their status higher than
that of the householder *sannyasins*; there was no difference in
status between Rajneeshees in communes and the wider society
(most of whom would have preferred to be in Oregon with
Bhagwan).

These were not the only *sannyasins* in Australia. The Australian
'temples' of the Hare Krishna movement (ISKCON, International
Society for Krishna Consciousness) received visits perhaps twice
a year from two or three of their *sannyasins*, who engaged in
regular programmes of preaching, initiation of members into
various religious statuses, conducted marriages, and gave advice
to those they had previously initiated and to the members of
temples under their charge. Members of the Hare Krishna movement, despite their wearing orange robes, were not *sannyasins*
although the public often confused the various movements. The
Ananda Marga received visits from its *avadhutas* (monks), some
of whom settled here for extensive periods and engaged in rather
less obvious teaching because of the public mistrust of the movement following alleged terrorist activities (particularly the 'Hilton
bombing' of February 1978). None of the ISKCON *sannyasins* had
been born in Australia or identified with Australian culture.
There were probably only half a dozen Australian born Ananda
Marga *avadhutas*. Other movements also received visits from
their founders, such as Baba Muktananda, Swami Satchidananda,
and Guru Maharaj, all Indians, and from senior disciples, usually
American, but like ISKCON and Ananda Marga were slow in
producing their own members of the renounced orders. There
were a few other renunciates, mainly in Sydney, Melbourne and
Perth, who had been initiated by lesser-known teachers in India,
teaching on a local scale. It is unlikely that there were more than
half a dozen of these virtuosos. Almost all *sannyasins* to be found
in Australia, therefore, followed either Satyananda or Rajneesh.

This book is concerned with the adaptation of the Indian *sannyasin* (renunciate) lifestyle to the context of Australian Society. It seeks to explore how Australian disciples of Swami Satyananda and Osho interpreted their call to live as '*sannyasins*'. In particular, the study:

(i) presents some of the historical and cultural factors behind the contemporary interpretation of renunciation;

(ii) seeks to discover what led disciples to adopt this vocation and what it means to them; and

(iii) aims to describe how the lifestyle of a '*swami*' was worked out in everyday terms, both in *ashram* settings in India and locally, and within the wider Australian society.

Research as Discourse

One of the predominant metaphors in anthropological research is that of seeing. Facts are things to be observed by the participant observer who stands attentively within but to one side of the society which is to be studied, collecting data (Clifford and Marcus 1986 : 11). In time the data are written up, so as to provide a "transparency of representation and immediacy of experience" (Clifford and Marcus 1986 : 2).

Post-modern ethnography, strongly influenced by the theories of linguistics and subsequent developments in structuralism and semiotics, prefers a different metaphor, that of listening, or the decoding of 'discourses'. Following Foucault (1972 : 122), discourse may be defined as a complex linguistic practice, governed by analyzable rules and transformations. Discourse organises concepts in particular ways, around specific topics, describing them in specific ways which are internally coherent, rigorous and stable (Foucault 1972 : 64). Discourse formations may be distinguished from non-discursive domains, such as institutions, political events, economic practices and processes (Foucault 1972 : 162), while recognising that non-discursive domains themselves can only be described through language.

For some writers, decoding discourses is a process of hearing what is said, for others it is a process of reading what is done. In either case, anthropology is no longer considered a process of recording and describing objective facts, but more one of creating, interpreting and writing 'texts'. As Marcus (1986 : 264) suggests, 'Textualization is at the heart of the ethnographical enterprise'. A text is not a book to be put on the shelf in the library but a 'methodological field' for research based on language, which requires to be caught up into discourse to be meaningful (Barthes 1986 : 57).

In writing, the ethnographer 'decodes and recodes', that is, translates the language of the social reality of other persons, "telling the grounds of collective order and diversity, inclusion and exclusion." (Clifford and Marcus 1986 : 2).

The process of writing is one of shaping language in accordance with certain literary conventions, some belonging only to ethnography, others shared in common with other literary genres (e.g. the story of the arrival of the anthropologist and the travel narrative). Clifford (1986 : 98) describes ethnography as "a performance emplotted by powerful stories." Tyler (1986 : 125) takes the literary image further in stating:

> A post-modern ethnography is a cooperatively evolved text consisting of fragments of discourse intended to evoke in the minds of both reader and writer an emergent fantasy of a possible world of commonsense reality, and thus to provide an aesthetic integration that will have a therapeutic effect. It is, in a word, poetry. . .

'Poetry' (presumably) in the literal classical sense of 'something made', rather than an act of pure imagination.

Such an account can never be neutral: the anthropologist stands in a certain position of power and relationship to the society studied as do informants, as do the readers of the eventual text written. The position of each is different.

Our study will call upon a number of different types of texts to create the new text now before us. In Part Two we shall use classical Indian religious texts, which prescribe particular patterns of behaviour for specialist religious practitioners. These texts were created by ascetics, who were also philosophers and wordsmiths. In Part Three we will make use of lectures by Satyananda and Rajneesh, which build on previous discourse: Satyananda on various traditional teachings on renunciation, Rajneesh on the poems of Kabir. Both indicate that the commentaries of their present authors have significantly shaped the old discourses in new and even contradictory directions to the old discourse. Finally, in Part Four we will make use of personal responses by *sannyasin* disciples themselves, "integrating the macro into the micro, combining accounts of impersonal systems into representations of local life as cultural forms both autonomous and constituted by the larger order" (Marcus 1986: 170).

The process will, thus, be one of dialogue. One of the voices is that of the author himself, who writes on the basis of long-term participant observation. He was initiated into *sannyasa* in 1977 by Bhagwan Shree Rajneesh (as Swami Anand Haridas), while lecturing in Perth, Western Australia. After the departure of Rajneesh for America, the author left that movement in 1982. In December 1983, he was initiated into *karma sannyasa* by Swami Satyananda (as Swami Sureshwar Saraswati), at the Mangrove Mountain Ashram near Gosford, New South Wales, having spent eight months at Satyananda Ashram, Perth, during 1980. He received the title 'Yoga Acharya', Master of Yoga, in 1988 from Swami Vishnu Devananda, an Indian-born disciple of Swami Sivananda of Rishikesh.

The purpose of this study is descriptive and interpretive. Although it concludes that the Australian disciples'understanding of *sannyasa* differs in a number of significant areas from traditional Indian practices, the study neither seeks to criticise nor praise these differences. Rather, it hopes to explain the differences in terms of the teachings of the two founders and the values characteristic of Australian culture and counter-cultures.

Problems of Dialogue

Clifford and Marcus (1986:15) insist that "dialogical processes proliferate in represented discursive space." Our dialogue will involve not two but multiple voices.

In Part Four, the process of dialogue will be most evident but also most uncertain. There are a number of reasons for this.

Firstly, the relationship between Master and disciple is an individual dyadic bond. It is not meaningful to deal with whole communities: contact with individuals was essential. However, the incomplete records of the movements, combined with uncertain turnover rates and shifting populations, meant that it was impossible to carry out systematic random surveys of members. (A Canadian study between 1975 and 1980 indicated a drop-out rate of 75.8 per cent for all participants in New Religious move-

ments: Lawton 1988 : 89). There can be no guarantee that the
individual respondents are truly 'representative' of their movements. The author's experience leads him to believe that the
sample is, in fact, reliable.

Secondly, the movements have changed a great deal over the
past decade. In 1985, there were large numbers of disciples and
they were readily visible in public. Each system had an extensive
system of ashrams and well advertised meetings. Today both
movements are in considerable decline. The Rajneesh movement
has never fully recovered from the debacle of the collapse of
Rajneeshpuram, Oregon, in 1985, and the consequent bitterness
and mistrust this created among sannyasins and within the society. In 1986 the Australian sannyasa magazine, The Mesto Muse,
described the condition of the centres in Australia in this way:
Adelaide had a "Clayton's Centre—the centre you have when
you're not having a centre". Perth was down to "twenty people
in the commune and an outstanding debt of $ 23,000", although
two hundred and forty people had come to a meeting ('the first
without turmoil') to discuss the possibility of Bhagwan coming to
Australia. In Byron Bay, there were one hundred and fifty to two
hundred sannyasins 'in and around the hills', although 'not much
hanging-out goes on now'. Melbourne had 'a low profile', with
'an undisclosed number of sannyasins wandering about the streets'.
Sydney had 'nearly seven hundred names' on the communal
mailing list, but the Commune itself was down to fifty-nine
people after being over one hundred in November 1984. In North
Queensland there were two groups of sannyasins living around
Cairns: six to ten persons on a farm near; Mareeba and fifteen
'adults and kids' at Hot Springs, about a hundred miles to the
west of the city (Mesto Muse No. 3 1986: 4). By 1989, the Sydney
centre had closed down. The Perth centre was preparing to move
to smaller, and cheaper, quarters. The Melbourne centre, re-
formed in 1987, consciously described itself as not to 'be found in
a building, or an organisation, or under the management of
individuals', but rather as 'the expression of Osho Rajneesh's
message through the sharing of his meditations and words'. This
was done 'periodically' (and in rented halls) (Yes! Osho Nirmol
Newsletter, Issue 22, 3 April 1990). In 1990, the Sydney sannyasins
were meeting once a week in an auditorium of the State Library
to view 'darshan videos'.

The Satyananda movement, too, was seriously damaged by the eventual imprisonment in mid-1989 of the Director of Satyananda Ashram, Australia, for a series of financial misdemeanours and child sexual abuse. Almost all of the twenty-six yoga *ashrams* were closed, most *sannyasins* left the movement, and those *swamis* who had returned from Munger and remained outside the Australian system now set about creating an alternative system of Yoga Therapy centres. The Mangrove Mountain *ashram* was smaller in terms of numbers of residents and temporarily closed to most attention from the outside world.

Finally, the decline of both movements was further intensified in 1990 by the recent adoption of the status of wandering mendicant by Swami Satyananda and the death of Osho.

Decline, public disapproval, and self doubt have affected both the movements in a way which was unthinkable in 1985. The image of the movements is less obvious even to insiders now, throwing members back on their own understandings which they often expect others to mistrust.

The request to survey residents of Mangrove Mountain was refused because of "reservations in relations to questions of a personal and political nature" (letter to the author, 28 September, 1989). More extensively, the *sannyasin* who had hopes of reviving the Adelaide Rajneesh centre wrote:

> I passed around your survey. Reactions I received were "Why so much personal information?", "I don't like it", "I don't like the picture of Bhagwan", "Who is this guy?". As a fellow student I sympathize but am hardly surprised as
>
> (i) sannyasins are a unique bunch
> (ii) sannyasins are concerned about getting to Poona.
>
> I have filled in, only as I feel, your questionnaire. My main concern, since I happen to believe your interests are genuine, is that no matter how confidential, this information may, by some *long shot*, fall into the hands of the Indian government. Even though it sounds silly writing it.

(Questionnaire on Sannyasa, undated)

Thirdly, it is a common experience in such research as has been

done on *sannyasins*, both Indian and European, that renunciates
are always reluctant to humour outside observers (Tripathi 1978:
7, Agehananda 1970: 146, Aveling 1989: 35, Mullan, 1983).

Questionnaire on Sannyasa

Because of the dispersed and uncertain nature of the two
movements, it was decided to gather information through the use
of questionnaires, distributed during 1989 and 1990 through the
snowball method of seeking the assistance of sympathetic individuals who could vouch for the author's genuine interest in the
topic. The questionnaire (See Appendix) had been developed
from earlier research on *sannyasins* (Tripathi 1978 : 2-3 and Mullan
1983 : 167-170). It had been pre-tested in the author's research on
the *sannyasin* disciples of Swami Vishnu Devananda in 1988. The
questionnaire carried different cover-sheets of explanation for
the two movements , each emphasising the author's involvement
in and sympathy for that particular movement.

Replies were received from twenty Full Sannyasin disciples of
Swami Satyananda, all operating outside the Australian *ashram*
system; from twenty-two Karma Sannyasins; and twenty-five
Rajneesh *sannyasins*. No replies were received to the questionnaire from disciples of Osho in Adelaide (apart from the one
already indicated) or Byron Bay. No address was available for the
centres in Cairns or Sydney. It is likely that both movements now
have a total membership of three hundred to five hundred, by
comparison with the figure of approximately two thousand in
1985. If this is so, the responses represent between a tenth to a
fifth of all members. This would seem to be an acceptable figure
for research purposes.

Questionnaires have various goals. Kidder and Judd (1986 :
237) note that:

> In questionnaire based research, the goal may be to learn
> what the respondents know (facts); what they think, expect,
> feel, or prefer (beliefs and attitudes); or what they have done
> (behaviours).

The questionnaire on *Sannyasa* focuses on behaviours and
beliefs and attitudes in order to answer the questions pertinent to
this book: Who joins? What does *Sannyasa* mean to them? How

is the commitment lived out in everyday life?

Our first concern is what people have done before taking *sannyasa*. In order to determine 'who joined?', questions one to eight seek to discover the categorical variables of *sannyasins* (gender, age, place of origin, religious background, level of education, marital status), and the extent of their previous involvement with 'alternative' social movements in the areas of radical politics, feminism, humanistic psychology and yoga. The categorical variables were also intended to test whether certain background factors might dispose individuals to membership of these groups, by comparison with earlier research findings on similar groups. Questions on involvement with spiritual, social and political movements were intended to test the significance (if any) of a critical stance towards the mainstream of Australian society. Are the movements only attractive to those who have already left conventional society, as is often asserted?

Our second concern is with the taking of initiation and the life of the *sannyasin*. Questions 9, 11-12,15-17 ask for details of initiation into *sannyasa*, long-term and immediate factors leading to initiation, and issues of adjustment. Question 10 seeks to determine the current spiritual practices of the respondents; Question 18 asks about contact with other *sannyasins*; and Question 19 pertains to daily working activities. These questions are all relevant to how the lifestyle of *sannyasin* renunciate is worked out in everyday terms.

Three questions deal directly with beliefs and attitudes about *sannyasa*. Question 13 asks "What does *sannyasa* mean to you?"; Question 14 asks about the 'benefits of *sannyasa*'; while Question 20 asks for an assessment of personal change during the respondent's time as a *sannyasin*. Kidder and Judd (1980 : 239) indicate that there are many problems to do with questions related to attitudes: the respondents may not have an attitude; attitudes are complex and multidimensional; answers are often dependent on the wording of the question, the sequence of the question, and on interviewer effects. The questions were inserted close to other questions dealing with the taking of *sannyasa*, and those dealing with the summation of experience respectively, in order to anchor them in the respondent's personal development.

Through these questions on behaviours, beliefs and attitudes, it was hoped to deal with both the practice and theories related

to the definition of *sannyasa* in Australia. Some eight questionnaires were administered in the form of interviews and it was
obvious that far more information could be gathered in this way
than through the impersonal administration of a questionnaire in
which the respondent could choose to provide minimal or trivial
information. Again because of the dispersed nature of the *sannyasin*
communities, and constraints on the researcher's own time (and
finances), it was not practical to make extensive use of this method.

Sannyasa is not a Text

The dialogue is partial and incomplete. Talal Asad (1986 :155)
suggests that:

> society is not a text that communicates itself to the skilled
> reader. And the ultimate meaning of what (the speaker)
> says does not reside in society—society is the cultural
> condition in which speakers act and are acted upon.

The same is true of *sannyasa*. *Sannyasa* in Australia is not a
single unchanging text, waiting to communicate itself to skilled
readers of questionnaires in a single, unmistakable manner. Some
seventy-five multiple voices speak, act and are acted upon by
endless ideas and experiences of *sannyasa* and Australian society.
The researcher asks to be included in the discourse, and sometimes is, sometimes not. The reader may hear some of what the
author thinks he has heard, and perhaps some things that he too
has missed.

PART TWO

THE TRADITION OF
RENUNCIATION

CHAPTER TWO

THE CLASSICAL INDIAN TRADITION OF RENUNCIATION

Hindu monasticism, at least in the traditional understanding, is a way of Life. It is the very Life at the end of life, the goal of the journey, the life-stage beyond all life-stages, only improperly called the fourth one. If Christian monasticism is a vocation (you have to follow), Hindu monasticism is an answer (you give). The *sannyasin* does not renounce the world, or whatever, in order to achieve something. Because he has seen, experienced, lived the real, he discards all the rest . . . There is nothing he has to do, because all has already been done. He is at the Center, peaceful, quiet and serene. No sacrifice, no vow, no anything is required or remains to be done. The texts are quite explicit.

(Pannikar 1982 : 18-19)

In order to understand how the classical Indian tradition of religious renunciation, *sannyasa*, has been reinterpreted by Swami Satyananda Saraswati and Bhagwan Shree Rajneesh, it is necessary that we first know something about the original institution itself. In that light we will be better able to appreciate the changes proposed to that lifestyle which have allowed non-Indians and

non-Hindus to present themselves as Hindu holy men. We shall
also be able to appreciate how close the Australians came to the
original definition of *sannyasa*, how they differed, and some of the
reasons for these similarities and differences.

Life Stages

There has been a widespread acceptance in much writing
about Hindu society that each individual will pass through four
distinct stages in his life's journey. These stages are first prescribed in the ancient legal digest, the *Manu Dharma Sastra* or
"Law of Manu" (Buhler 1969).

The first of these stages was that of the celibate student, the
brahmacharya (II.70ff.). During this time, the student lived in semi-
seclusion with a teacher, gaining the necessary spiritual and
secular knowledge required for adult life. The second stage was
that of the householder, *grihastha* (III.1ff.). This time was devoted
to marriage, the raising of a family, and the pursuit of a career.
This done, husband and wife together entered the stage of retirement, *vanaprastha* (VI.1ff.), living in seclusion in a quiet place (the
term literally means 'forest dweller') and giving themselves up to
spiritual practices.

The fourth stage was that of the *sannyasin*. This term is derived
from the words *sam* and *nyasa*, meaning respectively 'perfect' and
'setting aside', 'abandoning', 'surrender' : hence, 'perfect surrender or renunciation' (Satyananda 1976 : 1). The first three stages
were theoretically open to both men and women; in the fourth
stage, the man was expected to leave his wife to be cared for by
their children and then set out alone in the full-time pursuit of
religious knowledge and experience (VI. 39ff.). As T.M.P.
Mahadevan, Professor of Philosophy at the University of Madras,
has written:

> The sannyasin spends his days in contemplation, ponders
> over the mysteries of life, and wanders far and wide as the
> spiritual sentinel of the human race. His striving is for
> perfection, and his experience of it when he attains it, is a
> great blessing to the world. If he scorns worldliness, it is
> because he desires to place the world above scorn. He is the
> free man of the spirit, who has broken through the narrow
> confines of clan and country. Praise and blame, success and

failure, make no difference to him. He has no private ambitions and no personal desires. He has nothing to accomplish for himself either in this world or the next. When he has achieved the supreme human goal, what need has he for the trinkets of the world? He beckons all—though only a few listen to the call—to share in the infinite happiness which has become his.

(Mahadevan 1967 : 165-166)

In practice, it seems likely that only a small percentage of Indians have ever followed these four stages, which are implicitly recognised as most appropriate for males of the highest castes, and that even fewer ever ended their days in the private search for bliss and perfect liberation. The reality of *sannyasa* is both a good deal more complex and more human, than the above account would suggest.

The Vedas: Renunciation as Ecstasy

The role of ascetic is one of the oldest known in Indian society (Miller and Wertz 1976:1) and many terms beside '*sannyasa*' have been used to describe it. Evidence from the Indus Valley civilisations of Northwest India and Pakistan suggest the existence of an indigenous complex of asceticism, celibacy and the practice of yoga, from about 3000 B.C., that is, prior to the introduction of Aryan culture into the main subcontinent (Ghosal 1962 : 10).

The first written texts, the hymns known as the *Vedas*, derive from the Aryan culture, and are variously dated anywhere between 6000 and 2500 B.C. In these works we find references to at least two kinds of ascetics, *yatis* and *munis*.

Evidence on the *yatis* is sparse. They are associated with the war god Indra (*Rig Veda*, VIII. 3.9), with 'the creation of all existing things' (VIII.6.18), and with 'manly strength'. Ghurye (1964 : 14) notes a number of early myths which characterise the *yatis* as beings 'of evil or low speech and worshippers of the male organ.' Such myths in the Aryan literature may tend to suggest that the *yatis* were of indigenous or Dravidian origin. Ghurye disputes this, arguing that the word '*yati*' is Sanskrit, which means: 'to control' (in this case, sexual power). He suggests that they were

a community not wholly un-Vedic in culture, but which had
developed a few special traits which did not meet with the
approval of the orthodox community.

(Ghurye 1964 : 14)

On the other hand, the evidence on the 'silent sages' the *munis*,
is very full. Pannikar (1982: 31-32) translates the relevant verses
in the tenth cycle of the *Rig Veda* (136:1-2) as follows:

> Within him is fire, within him is drink,
>   within him both Earth and heaven.
>
> He is the Sun which views the whole world,
>   he is indeed Light itself-
>   the long-haired ascetic.
>
> Girded with the wind, they have donned the ochre
>   mud for a garment. So soon as the Gods
>   have entered within them, they follow the
>   wings of the wind, these silent ascetics.
>
> Intoxicated, they say, by our austerities,
>   we have taken the winds for our steeds.
>
> You ordinary mortals here below
>   see nothing except our bodies.
>
> He flies through midair, the silent ascetic,
>   beholding the form of all things.
>
> To every God he has made himself
>   a friend and a collaborator.
>
> Hidden by the wind, companion of its blowing
>   pushed along by the Gods,
>   he is at home in both seas, the east
>   and the west—the silent ascetic.
>
> He follows the track of all spirits,
>   of nymphs and the deer of the forest.
>
> Understanding their thoughts, bubbling with
>   ecstasies, their appealing friend is he
>   the long-haired ascetic.

> The wind has prepared and mixed him a drink;
>   it is pressed by Kunamnana.
>
> Together with Rudra, he has drunk from the cup
>   of poison—the long-haired ascetic.

The image of the ascetic presented here is one which has persisted to this very day. The sage still dresses in orange robes or smears himself with mud. He wears his hair in an unconventional style (either long, as here, or clean shaven). He lives outside of regular society, usually in the forest, and is constantly on the move. His disregard for ordinary mortals is supposed to be matched by his love for, and knowledge of, supernatural deities, spirits and strange beings. He engages in silent spiritual practices, including sometimes the use of intoxicants. He suffers ecstasy, out of the body experience, in which he feels as though he is flying through the air. He knows 'the form of all things' and even the language of the animals. The tradition is fully formed from the beginning.

The Major Upanishads: Renunciation as Knowledge

The hymns of the *Vedas* were directed to particular, well-defined deities, and were recited as part of sacrificial services, in which the worshipper offered something to the god in return for what the deity might do for him. The hope for return might be as concrete as wealth, sons and long life, or as abstract as the forgiveness of sin and the re-establishment of a state of righteousness. Three layers of commentary gradually accumulated around each of the four Vedic books. Two of these were technical ritual exegeses. The last involved a series of abstract philosophical discourses, very different in spirit from the hymns. The discourses are known as 'upanishads', which etymologically meant 'sitting' (*sad*) 'nearby' (*upa*) 'devotedly' (*ni*); that is, they were teachings one gained from close proximity to the teacher (Tiwari 1977 : 22n.1). When each of the four layers of texts became associated with one of the life stages, the *upanishads* were deemed to be the proper province of the *sannyasins*, and the term is also sometimes interpreted as 'mystic doctrines' (so, for example, Hume 1968 : 131).

In fact, the most commonly described teaching situation in the major *upanishads* involves not a renounced individual but a forest-dwelling sage and his wife, together with the student of sacred knowledge (*brahmachari*). The *Mundaka Upanishad* describes the ideal teacher as one 'who is learned in the scriptures and established on Brahman' (that is, the indwelling divine presence), 'whose thought is tranquillized [and] who has reached peace' (Hume 1968 : 369).

The student was expected to approach the teacher with sacrificial fuel in hand and plead: "Teach me, Sir" (*Chandogya Upanishad*, 7.1.1. Hume 1968 : 250)—or, in full, "Sir, declare Brahman [to me]" (*Taittiriya Upanishad*, 3.1, Hume 1968 : 290).

The teacher had the right of accepting or rejecting the student's application. In the *Chandogya Upanishad*, Haridrumata Gautama accepted Satyakama as a student, when the latter candidly admitted that his mother was a serving maid and herself uncertain who the boy's father was. Obviously, the teacher decided, such honesty betokened a *brahmin* father! (4.4, Hume 1968 : 218).

Beside his learning, the student would have been expected to contribute to the upkeep of the residential group, teacher and other pupils, through regular participation in household duties, as well as to attend the regular worship required of the caste.

The list of what an expert teacher might impart is formidable. Between the age of twelve and twenty-four Svetaketu Arunya studied 'all the Vedas' (*Chandogya Upanishad*, 6.1.2, Hume 1968 : 240). The student Narada claimed to have learned more. 'Sir,' he tells Sanatkumara,

> I know the Rig-Veda, the Yajur-Veda, the Atharva-Veda as the fourth, Legend and ancient Lore (*itihasa-purana*) as the fifth, the Veda of the Vedas [i.e. Grammar], Propitiation of the Manes, Mathematics, Augury (*daiva*), Chronology, Logic, Polity, the Science of the Gods (*deva-vidya*), the Science of Sacred Knowledge (*brahma-vidya*), Demonology (*bhuta-vidya*), the Science of Rulership (*ksatra-vidya*), Astrology (*naksatra-vidya*), the Science of Snake-Charming, and the Fine Arts (*sarpa-deva-jana-vidya*) . . . Such a one am I, Sir, knowing the sacred sayings (*mantravid*), . . .
>
> (*Chandogya Upanishad*, 7.1.2-3, Hume 1968 : 250-251)

Beyond this knowledge, which the *Chandogya Upanishad* dismissed as 'mere knowledge', 'speech', lay the real knowledge which was spiritual and personal. Tiwari (1977:10) summarises the central teaching of the *upanishads* as being that

> *Brahman*, One's innermost Self, is the Ultimate Reality with which the individual Self is essentially identical. The cosmos is located within this identity as being neither different nor indifferent but indescribable (*anirvacaniya*) from it. Any perception of difference or plurality in the Reality is attributed to *avidya* (ignorance) which can be eliminated by *Jnana* (knowledge, insight) which goes hand in hand with *Sannyasa* (Renunciation).

Svetaketu learned this truth from his father through a series of vivid demonstrations. One of these is as follows:
"Bring hither a fig from there."
"Here it is, Sir."
"Divide it."
"It is divided, Sir."
"What do you see there?"
"These rather (*iva*) fine seeds, Sir."
"Of these, please (*anga*) divide one."
"It is divided, Sir."
"What do you see there?"
"Nothing at all, Sir."

Then he said to him:

> "Verily, my dear, that finest essence which you do not perceive verily, my dear, from that finest essence this great Nyagrodha (sacred fig) tree thus arises"

> "Believe me, my dear", said he, "that which is the finest essence—the whole world has that as its soul. That is Reality. That is *Atman* (Soul). That art thou, Svetaketu."

> (6.12, Hume 1968 : 248)

'Brahman' is 'Atman', God and the Soul are one and the same, and "That thou art." It was this same knowledge which Yajnavalkya gave to his wife Maitreyi before leaving the householder state:

> Not for the love of the husband is the husband dear, but for the love of the *Atman* (Soul) a husband is dear (*Brihad-*

Aranyaka Upanishad 2.4.5, Hume 1968 : 98).

Similarly, wife, sons, wealth, priesthood (*brahma*), warriorhood (*ksatra*), the worlds, the god, the being (*bhuta*), everything . . . all are dear 'for the love of the Soul'. So:

> Lo, verily, it is the Soul (*Atman*) that should be seen, that should be hearkened to, that should be thought on, that should be pondered on. O Maitreyi, . . . with the thinking of, and with the understanding of the Soul, this world—all is known.

> (2.4.5, Hume 1968 : 100)

For:

> This Soul (*Atman*) is honey for all things, and all things are honey for this Soul. This shining, immortal Person who is this Soul, and, with reference to oneself, this shining, immortal Person who exists as the Soul he is just this Soul, this immortal, this Brahma, this All.

> Verily, this Soul is the overlord of all things, the king of all things. As the spokes are held together in the hub and felly of a wheel, just so in this Soul all things, all gods, all worlds, all breathing, all these selves are held together.

> (2.5.14-15, Hume 1968 : 103-104)

This positive teaching of identification received its inverse or negative formulation later in the same text, when the same instruction was given but with the different conclusion:

> The Soul (*Atman*) is not this, it is not that (*neti, neti*). It is unseizable, for it cannot be seized, indestructible, for it cannot be destroyed, unattached, for it does not attach itself; is unbound, does not tremble, is not injured.

> Lo, whereby would one understand the understander?

> (4.5.15, Hume 1968 : 147)

Even the knowledge of the identity of *Brahman* and *Atman* was considered mere speech if not joined to the practice of spiritual disciplines. The *Maitri Upanishad* linked austerity (*tapas*) and meditation (*cinta*) to knowledge (*vidya*) as the major means for attaining *Brahman* (4.4, Hume 1968:421). The *Prasna Upanishad* encouraged austerity (*tapas*), chastity (*brahmacharya*) and faith (*sraddha*) (1.2, Hume 1968: 378). *Chandogya Upanishad* listed a fivefold vow of "austerity, alms-giving, uprightness, harmlessness (and) truthfulness" as the basis of spiritual life (3.17.4, Hume 1968:213). For *Kena Upanishad*, austerity (*tapas*), restraint (*dama*) and work (*karman*) were the foundations of mystical doctrine (38, Hume 1968:340).

Various meditation practices were taught to the student, such as the control of breath, interiority through physical restraint (*yoga*), and chanting of the sacred syllable 'Om', all with the aim of steadying the mind and the emotions so as to allow contemplation.

Breath was considered the body's prime link with the outside world and a major source of physical energy. *Chandogya* described the different breaths (in, out, restrained, expelled) as "doorkeepers of the heavenly world" (3.13.6, Hume 1968 : 209). *Kaushitaki* described 'the breathing spirit' as *Brahman*, and the mind (*manas*) as its messenger, the eye its watchman, the ear its announcer and speech its handmaid (2.1, Hume 1968 : 308); control of the breath, therefore, was a means of controlling all the senses.

Yoga, too, was a way of "holding back the senses" (*Katha Upanishad*) 6.11, Hume, 1968: 360). In a passage reminiscent of the *Bhagavad Gita* (6.10ff.), the *Svetasvatara Upanishad* described the rules and results of yoga:

> Holding his body steady with the head, chest and neck erect,
> And causing the senses with the mind to enter the heart,
> A wise man with the boat of Brahman should cross over
> All the fear-bringing streams.
> Having represented his breathings here in the body, and having his movements checked,
> One should breathe through his nostrils with diminished breath,
> Like the chariot yoked with various horses, His mind the wise man should restrain undistractedly.
> In a clean, level spot, free from pebbles, fire, and gravel,
> By the sound of water and other propinquities

Favourable to thought, not offensive to the eye,
In a hidden retreat, protected from the wind, one should
    practise yoga . . .

                                    (2.8-13, Hume 1968 : 398)

After listing physical health, strength, and the ability to face
sickness, old age and death, as among the benefits of the practice
of yoga, the text continued:

Even as a mirror stained by dust
Shines brilliantly when it has been cleansed,
So the embodied one, on seeing the nature of the Soul
    (Atman),
Becomes unitary, his end attained, from sorrow freed.
When with the nature of the self, as with a lamp,
A practiser of Yoga beholds here the nature of Brahman,
Unborn, steadfast, from every nature free—
By knowing God (deva) one is released from all fetters!

                                    (2.8-15, Hume 1968 : 399)

More concisely, *Maitri Upanishad* listed the "six-fold yoga" as:

. . . restraint of the breath (*pranayama*), withdrawal of the
senses (*pratyahara*), meditation (*dhyana*), concentration
(*dharana*), contemplation (*tarka*) and absorption (*samadhi*).
                                    (6.18, Hume 1968 : 435).

The *Mandukya Upanishad* was a meditation on the mantra *Om*
(*Aum*). It described the syllable as "the whole world . . . the past,
the present and the future, and whatever else transcends three-
fold time". The stages of chanting the sound were supposed to
recapitulate the four states of human existence—(*a*) wakefulness;
(*u*) the dreaming state; (*m*) the state of bliss that is sleep beyond
all dreams; and the state which is simply known as 'the fourth
state', beyond all others—without inner or outer cognition, senses,
awareness, personal characteristics, "tranquil, benign, without a
second", which is represented by the silence following the chant
(Hume 1968 : 391-393). The centring effect of chanting the sacred
syllable was presented by *Maitri* in this vivid metaphor:

The body is a bow. The arrow is *Om*. The mind is its point.
Darkness is its mark. Having pierced through the darkness,

one goes to what is not enveloped in darkness. Then having pierced through what is thus enveloped, one sees Him who sparkles like a wheel of fire, of the colour of the sun, mightful, the Brahman that is beyond darkness, that shines in yonder sun, also in the moon, in fire, in lightning. Now, assuredly, when one has seen Him, one goes to immortality.

(6.24, Hume 1968 : 438)

Equipped with knowledge and spiritual disciplines, the student was expected to take these qualities into his life as a householder. He was required to continue to study the *Vedas*, to produce sons and pupils of his own, to 'concentrate all his senses on the Soul (*Atman*)', and to live in a non-violent way. In this way, he would live a full and long life, " reach the Brahman world", and not be subject to rebirth (through the effects of *karma*) in this realm (*Chandogya Upanishad* 8.15, Hume 1968 : 274). The *Upanishads* tell of brief acts of intense self-mortification aimed at forcing the gods to grant some boon, but they have little sympathy for such acts (e.g. *Brihad Aranyaka Upanishad* 1.2.2ff, Hume 1968: 74: *Prasna Upanishad* 1.4, Hume 1968: 378). Rather, the *Upanishads* encouraged a life-long asceticism, in which 'study and teaching' encompass all forms of spiritual knowledge and virtue (*Taittiriya Upanishad* 1.9, Hume 1968:280).

Only occasionally was there even reference to a man setting out from the householder state, as Yajnavalkya does, to embark upon the life of the 'wandering religious mendicant' (*paravrajaka*). The *Maitri* insisted:

Pursuit of one's regular duty, in one's own stage of the religious life—that, verily , is the rule! Other rules are like a bunch of grass. With this, one tends upwards; otherwise, downwards. (4.3, Hume 1968 : 421).

The most positive references to moving outside ordinary society are to be found in the *Mundaka Upanishad*:

They who practise austerity (*tapas*) and faith
        (*sraddha*) in the forest,
The peaceful (*santa*) knowers who live on alms
Depart passionless (*vi-raga*) through the door
        of the sun,

To where is that immortal Person (*Purusha*),
    e'en the imperishable Spirit (*Atman*).
                              (1.2.11, Hume 1968 : 369)
and in the *Maitri Upanishad:*

Having bidden peace to all creatures, and having gone to
the forest, then having put aside objects of sense, from out
of one's own body one should perceive Him,
Who has all forms, the golden one, all-knowing,
The final goal, the only light, heat-giving,
The thousand-rayed, the hundredfold revolving,
Yon sun rises as the life of creatures.
                              (6.8, Hume 1969 : 429)

Just as the *Upanishads* maintained a general sense that sacrificial worship is an inferior activity unless informed by the Self
(*Brihad Aranyaka Upanishad* 1.4.17, Hume 1968: 85), so did they
hold that silent asceticism (*mauna*) and "betaking oneself to the
hermit life in the forest" was best fulfilled in "the chaste life of a
student of sacred knowledge" (*Chandogya Upanishad* 8.4.3, Hume
1968 : 266). *Maitri* insisted that the person who knows the *Atman*
and illusory nature of transitory sense-reality "is an ascetic
(*sannyasin*) and a devotee (*yogin*)" and an offerer of ritual sacrifice
(6.10, Hume 1968 : 432). It was possible to renounce the world
while still living in or near the world; total renunciation was a
valuable, but not a crucial option for the authors of the major
Upanishads. It was enough to be at most a forest-dweller, with
wife and dedicated students.

The Sannyasa Upanishads: Renunciation as World-Abandonment

The number of *Upanishads* has traditionally been set at the
sacred number of 108. Of these, the thirteen major *Upanishads*
discussed above may be dated between 700 and 550 B.C., prior to
the rise of Buddhism (Dutt 1962 : 37). With Buddhism, and its
close predecessor Jainism, a new type of asceticism emerged in
India. Buddhism encouraged a strict asceticism under a code of
written rules. It emphasised membership of an impersonal, demo-
cratically elected body, the *Sangha*, rather than the link of one
individual with one individual teacher (*guru*) who had, at some
point of time, initiated the renunciate into spiritual life. Further,

Buddhism encouraged its monks to assemble together during the rainy season, and in this way gave impetus to the development of monasteries where communities might live together. In the course of time, as Pande (1978 : 46) states, these monasteries became:

> noble monuments of art and architecture, places of pilgrimage and centres of education and learning. Beginning as the isolation of the monk from society, the movement ultimately placed him in the midst of a new society!

It seems likely that the definite and unified form of Buddhist asceticism also forced some Hindu renunciates to consider more closely the nature and purpose of their own way of life. Of the 108 *Upanishads*, seventeen deal with the "characteristics, qualifications, life, and other particulars concerning those who have renounced the world." (Ramanathan 1978 : viii). These seventeen *Upanishads* are known as the *sannyasa upanishads*. They appear to have been written at a variety of places and times, perhaps from 500 B.C. to 1000 A.D., and are reasonably consistent with each other. Most are framed (like the post-Vedic scriptural traditions) as dialogues between a spiritually advanced individual and a pupil, who are usually divine, e.g. Samkriti and Dattatreya (*Avadhuta Upanishad*), Aruna and Prajapati (*Arunyupanishad*), Narada and Narayana (*Paramahamsopanishad*).

In the *Avadhuta Upanishad* it was said: "Not by rituals, not by begetting children, not by wealth, but by renunciation (*tyaga*) alone a few attained immortality" (6, Ramanathan 1978 : 3). In the *Katharudropanishad*, the last part of this statement was rephrased to read: "only by knowing *Brahman*, a man attains *Brahman*" (13, Ramanathan 1978 : 16). As in the major *Upanishads*, the purpose of human existence was considered to be liberation from the cycle of birth and rebirth, and the suffering involved in that process, through union with the Divine. In the *sannyasa upanishads*, renunciation is a necessary step in the whole process of realisation.

Not everyone was entitled to take to renunciation. The *Narada-Parivrajakopanishad* and the *Samnyasopanishad* considered the following persons unworthy: a eunuch, an immoral person, a deformed person, a woman, the deaf, a child, a heretic, an emperor, a religious student, various Vaishnava and Saivite sectaries, a hired teacher, a man without a prepuce, and one who does not maintain the sacred fire in his house (Ramanathan 1978 : 45-46, 212). Those of the second caste were encouraged instead to seek liberation through death on the battlefield, fasting, drowning, self-immolation, or walking to the point of exhaustion (*Jabalopanishad* 5.2, Ramanathan 1978 : 34).

The qualifications for those *brahmins* entitled to *sannyasa* were that they should have undergone the forty purificatory rites (*samskaras*) at previous appropriate points in their life, "have detachment from all worldly things, have acquired purity of mind, have burned out desires, envy, intolerance and egotism, and be equipped with the four disciplines of spiritual life", namely, the ability to discriminate between permanent and transitory things, non-attachment to the 'fruits' of action, possession of a peaceful mind and self-control, and the desire for liberation from worldly life (*Samnyasopanishad*, 2.1, Ramanathan 1978 : 211).

The normal time for renunciation was after twelve years of study as a celibate student, twenty-five years as a householder, and twenty-five years as a forest dweller (*Narada*, 1.2, Ramanthan 1978:42). This would have made the renunciate very old indeed, and there were provisions for a person close to death to renounce at once, as well as curses for those who so resolved but subsequently recovered their health and ignored their vow (*Samnyasopanishad*, 2.2, 2.74, Ramanathan 1978 : 212, 223). The *Jabalopanishad*, and some other texts, allowed entry into renunciation from any of the life-stages, stating that: "a person may renounce worldly life on that very day on which distaste for it", regardless of his condition (4.1, Ramanathan 1978 : 31).

The process of renunciation is summarised in *Arunya* as:

> renounce your sons, brothers, relatives, the tuft (of hair worn at the back of the head), the sacred thread (worn only by the brahmins), the sacrifices, the rules, the study of the Vedas, the worlds . . . and varily the whole universe. Retain only the staff and the loin-cloth for covering the body. Give up all else.
>
> (1, Ramanathan 1978 : 9)

Narada listed eight ceremonies which were to be held prior to departure for the forest. The ceremonies involved various offerings to the gods, sages, and spirits of the departed, including the renunciate's own spirit. These ceremonies were to be performed in presence of other *brahmins*. They could be held over eight days, or on one day (4, Ramanathan 1978 : 70). Some other texts appear to have rejected this, and emphasised instead a single sacrifice in which Agni, the fire-god, was the presiding deity (e.g. *Jabala*, 4, Ramanathan 1978 : 32). Following the other rituals, the head was shaven, the sacred thread broken, and the three worlds renounced (*Narada* 4, Ramanathan 1978 : 73). Only the *Satyayaniyopanishad* allowed Vaishnava sectaries to retain the tuft and the thread (11, Ramanathan 1978 : 201). In all other cases, these signs were considered to have been internalised, the thread becoming true knowledge (*Parabrahmopanishad* 14-20, Ramanathan 1978 : 151), the tuft being gnosis (*jnana*) (*Brahmopanishad*, 12, Ramanathan 1978 : 169). The renunciate then assumed the orange cloth and a staff; sometimes other items such as a bowl and purifying cloths; and then left. The *Katharudropanishad* adds the touching words "While parting from the son, he should not shed tears" (2, Ramanathan 1978 :14).

Bhiksukopanishad stated that "mendicant monks desiring liberation are of four kinds" (1, Ramanathan 1978 : 172).

The first kind was that of *Kuticaka*, hut-dwelling, and lasted a year. During this time, the novice lived with his teacher and received food ('eight mouthfuls') from the one consistent source. He was entitled to the use of a loin-cloth, a patched shawl, a three-fold staff, and wore a perpendicular sign of white sandal on his forehead.

During the second year, he became a *Bahudaka* renunciate and began to travel about, visiting in particular the holy bathing-places (*tirtha*). His accoutrements were similar to those of the *Kuticaka*, and he now begged his food randomly from house to house 'like a bee'. The mark on his forehead consisted of three horizontal lines of sacred ash.

There were greater limits on the residence of the *Hamsa* ascetic, the third stage: "one night in a village, five nights in a town and seven nights or more in a holy place." His hair was commonly matted, he wore the loin-cloth and a piece of cloth over the mouth, the mark on his forehead was either the horizontal mark of ash or the vertical stroke of sandal. He subsisted on five mouthfuls of food, gathered at random from different houses,

using his hand as an alms bowl. His mantra was 'Soham',
(Parabrahmopanishad, 5, Ramanathan 1978 : 149), or in full:

Om Soham hamsah, parama hamsah, paramatma Chinmayoham,
Satchidananda Swaroopoham Soham Brahma Om", meaning "I am
that Brahman, the Absolute Brahman, the all-pervading Atman,
I am pure Consciousness; I am of the nature of Existence, Knowledge and Bliss; I am that Brahman, Om," (Sivananda 1963 ; 157)

The fourth stage, that of the Paramahamsa ascetic, would
appear to have been the major renunciate category. The head was
shaven, use was made of the loin-cloth and shawl. There is some
difference in the texts as to whether the Paramahamsa carried a
single staff but otherwise he had no possessions at all and no
distinguishing emblems, apart from his body being smeared with
ash. He also had no 'religious or secular duties', being firmly
established in 'the non-duality of the self' (Turiyatitavadhutopa-
nishad, Ramanathan 1978: 38). To the worldly person, his behaviour
was like that of a mad man (Yajnavalkyopanishad, 6, Ramanathan
1978:193).

Narada insisted that there are not four but six kinds of renunciation, placing two further grades beyond that of the Paramahamsa ascetic (5.11, Ramanathan 1978 : 78). In both the grades the
ascetic was unclad. (It is also possible to read these states as
alternative styles of Paramahamsahood, determined by the choice
of clothing or otherwise.) The Turiyatita ascetic subsisted on fruit
fed into his mouth or on rice taken from three houses, treating his
body as if it were 'a corpse' (Samnyasopanishad, 2.28, Ramanathan
1978 : 217). The Avadhuta took food as it came from almost anyone, like a python (Narada, 5.21, Ramanathan 1978 : 82), and
lived totally absorbed in Brahman. The Avadhuta Upanishad insists
that the avadhuta had no need to study even the scriptures, having
known the reality, and no need to meditate, for 'having no illusion, what meditation can there be for me?' (18-19, Ramanathan
1978 : 5).

Bhagavad Gita : Renunciation as Yoga

The Upanishads, even the most blatantly sectarian of them,
form part of the 'revealed scriptures'. They are considered to be
Vedanta, both the 'end' and the 'goal' of the Vedas, and the
philosophy they teach commonly bears this name. Beyond the
Vedas lays an endless range of further scientific and sacred litera-

ture. Much of the sacred literature consisted of myths, legends and philosophies devoted to either of the gods Shiva or Vishnu and their cults. The two epics, the *Mahabharata* and the *Ramayana* dating from early in the common era, also formed part of this literature. A much smaller part was comprised of '*tantra*' texts, none of which were put into written form much earlier than the thirteenth century, which deal with the psycho-physical processes of *yoga*. In the development of thinking about *sannyasa*, the most important non-Vedic text is the *Bhagavad Gita*.

The *Bhagavad Gita* is a single section of the *Mahabharata*. It consists of the teaching given by Lord Krishna to his nephew Arjuna prior to the outbreak of a war between two factions of the same extended family. Krishna being an incarnation of Vishnu, the text properly belongs with Vaishnava literature. Since the Hindu Renaissance of the nineteenth century, the book has often been represented as central to the whole of Hinduism, partly because of the strongly devotional attitude it takes towards Krishna, but also because of the richness of its philosophy. One philosophical strand is *Vedanta*. The other is a type known as *Samkhya*.

Unlike Vedanta, *Samkhya* was based on an absolute distinction between Spirit (*Purusha*) and Matter (*Prakrti*). As Zaehner (1973:140) suggests, Spirit is "immutable, unchanging, beyond space, time, and causation", while Matter exists "in a perpetual state of flux, without beginning or end." According to the myth, at a certain point in time masculine Spirit beguiled by beautiful Matter entered into her and that began the process of the evolution of the universe and of individual consciousness. The first evolute was *buddhi*, or higher, integrative consciousness. This was followed by *ahamkara*, the ego (*aham* means 'I am') or the sense of the individual self. From ego derived the mind, *manas*, as a means for gathering information, and the five senses, as well as the five 'motor' organs of speech, handling, walking, evacuation and reproduction. There are also five 'subtle' elements, which are the objects of the senses, and five 'gross' elements (space or ether, air, fire, water and earth). The whole process is constantly kept in action through the endless instability of the three 'strands' (*guna*) of existence: *sattva* (light, truth, goodness), *rajas* (energy) and *tamas* (sloth, inertia, darkness).

'Samkhya' means 'to count, to enumerate'. To the twenty-five

principles enumerated above, Yoga Philosophy added one more:
Ishvara, or God. As the classical text the *Yoga Sutras* taught, God
is a special kind of *purusha*, or spiritual monad, being "untouched
by care, works (*karma*), the ripening of works, or hope. In him the
seed of omniscience is perfect. He is the *guru* even of the ancients,
since he is not limited by time" (I.24-26, quoted in Zaehner
1973 : 141). It is the performance of works, for better or worse,
and their consequent production of merit or demerit, which
keeps the individual *purusha* trapped in matter, and forced to
suffer the pains of human existence one life after the other. To
gain liberation, one must somehow deal with action and its
consequences.

The *Bhagavad Gita* teaches Samkhya both as 'wisdom' (*jnana*),
and as a method of contemplation. But it also teaches *Yoga* as the
practical path to salvation. Verse 3.3 states:

> In this world there are two roads of perfection . . . Jnana
> Yoga, the path of wisdom of the Samkhyas, and Karma
> Yoga, the path of action of the Yogis.
>
> (trans. Mascaro 1970 : 60)

(Zaehner (1973 : 161), paraphrases the same words, *jnana-yogena
Sankhyanam, karma-yogena yoginam*, as: for men of theory the
spiritual exercise of wisdom, for men of action the spiritual
exercise through works).

Yoga is, therefore, not simply a variant of Samkhya. "As
everybody knows", to use Zaehner's words, it is also

> a technique for achieving spiritual 'liberation': it uses matter,
> that is, the body, to enable the spiritual monad to divest
> itself of matter once and for all.
>
> (Zaehner 1973 : 141)

Yoga is about a particular type of action, undertaken to overcome the effects of all actions. Samkhya on the other hand, is
about the stopping of works, so that the process of devolution of
matter back into spirit may take place.

The consequence was that those who practised yoga, *Yogis*,
formed a different type of community from those who practised
Samkhya (just as 'active' communities in the Roman Catholic

Church are different from 'contemplative' communities, even though both follow the same theological tenets). In the *Gita*, the man who has left 'the sacrificial fire' behind him, and who 'does not work', is the renunciate, or the *sannyasin* (6.1, Zaehner 1973 : 219). The choice before Arjuna, as Zaehner rightly points out in his commentary of Chapter Six, and verse 1 in particular, without however seeing the full implication of his own words, is this:

> Which *one* of the the two alternatives is he to follow: is he to become a professional *sannyasin,* an ascetic who has wholly put the world behind him, or is he to 'get going'. . .

In other words, is he to become an 'inactive' *sannyasin*, or a 'man of action', a *yogi*? (Zaehner 1973 : 200-201).

It is clear that the author of the *Gita* saw both *yogis* and *sannyasins* as superior to other types of ascetics, whom he describes in 17.4-6 as 'men of darkness', worshippers of 'ghosts and spirits of the night', 'men selfish and false who moved by their lusts and passions, perform terrible austerities not ordained by sacred books: fools who torture the powers of life in their body and (the God) who dwells in them" (trans. Mascaro 1970 : 118). It is rather less obvious that the author also wished to establish the *yogi* as the highest type of renunciate. As 6.46 states, "the Yogi goes beyond those who follow only the path of the austere, or of wisdom, or of sacrifice." (trans. Mascaro 1970 : 78, modified by the word 'sacrifice' following Zaehner 1973 : 241).

Yoga is superior to meditation because it is impossible not to work, says Krishna in Chapter Three. God works to sustain the universe (3.22-24). The forces of Nature, the *gunas*, are constantly active (3.27). Great men of the past achieved perfection through action and have left us their example (3.20-21). Even those who think they are performing no actions are still bound by the normal physiological processes (3.5, 5.9).

The trick is to work in a particular way, so that work becomes an end in itself and not a source of further action. In this, attitude is everything. Pure work is performed "free from anxious desire and fanciful thought"(4.19). The worker "has no vain hopes, he is the master of his soul, he surrenders all he has, only his body works: he is free from sin" (4.21). Further, "he is glad with whatever God gives him", for "he has risen above the two

contraries here below" (pleasure and pain); "he is without jealousy, and in success or in failure he is one: his works bind him
not"(4.22). Thus: "He has attained liberation; he is free from all
bonds, his mind has found peace in wisdom, and his work is a
holy sacrifice. The work of such a man is pure" (4.23). Later
chapters, following the strain of Krishna devotion less in evidence earlier in the text, suggest a religious foundation for the
attitude: "Do works for Me, make Me your highest goal, be loyal-
in-love to Me, cut off all other attachments, have no hatred for
any being at all: for all who do thus shall come to Me" (11.55,
trans. Zaehner 1973 : 320).

Yoga, then is a "skill in performing works" (2.50), and, in terms
which sound more negative than they ought,"sameness and indifference" (2.48, Zaehner 1973 : 146). True renunciation is "the
renunciation of selfish works" not "the renunciation of action"
(18.2-3). The true renunciate is "he who craves not nor hates"
(5.3), and it is extremely difficult to be a renunciate without first
practising the "Yoga of work"(5.6).

As Feuerstein (1974 : 137-138) notes:

> With Krishna, renunciation assumes an entirely new
> significance. It is not cutting oneself off from the world, but
> disinterestedness as an *inner* attitude of disapassionate
> samemindedness. In other words, he brings the mind as the
> main spring of all external deeds into full focus. We have to
> shake off not the actions as such, but their underlying
> egocentric motive forces. Stringent control of the mind
> prevents sin to enter our deeds. It is the thoughts which
> defile us, not their physical expression in the form of acts.

And further:

> . . . the life of the recluse must be the exception rather than
> the rule. Man ought not negate God's 'lower' nature, the
> manifested world. Those who oppose life's movements are
> said to be sinful and live in vain (III.16). Instead of forsaking
> the world established by God, we are called upon to fulfil
> its purpose by becoming instruments of the Divine Will. We
> are asked to promote the welfare of the world (*loka-samgraha*)
> by maintaining the order innate in the universe. The wheel

of becoming only grinds those who pursue selfish ends. It cannot affect the man who has conquered himself by the Self and whose deeds have become sacrifice.

The concept of 'karma-yoga', Yoga of action and karma-sannyasa-yoga, Yoga of renunciation in action (which are the traditional colophons to Chapters Three and Five of the Gita: Feuerstein, 1974:129) are important points in the further development of Indian thought about renunciation. They are also central to the understanding of both Osho and Satyananda on the nature of transcendence in the modern world.

In order to complete our survey of the classical Indian tradition of renunciation, we now turn to a short survey of institutional developments and to recent studies of particular communities committed to traditional Hindu lifestyles.

CHAPTER THREE

CLASSICAL INDIAN
RENUNCIATE LIFESTYLES

The French sociologist Louis Dumont (1970: 37) has argued that
"the secret of Hinduism may be found in the dialogue between
the renouncer and the man in the world." Because ordinary
Hindu society is based on caste, it is hierarchical. All relationships among human beings, human beings and the gods, and the
gods themselves, are based upon comparative statuses, to such
an extent that "an individual divinity in isolation is as usual as an
individual human being" (Dumont 1970 : 38).

The most important social value is conformity, or obedience
to one's *dharma*, that is: to the duties proper to one's status in life
and the community. As the *Bhagavad Gita* insists:

> do thy duty even in it be humble, rather than another's, even
> if it be great. To die in one's duty is life; to live in another's
> is death.

(3.5, Mascaro 1970 : 63).

The renouncer, however, turns his back on society and suddenly becomes an individual with a personality so strong that all
his efforts seem directed to extinguishing or transcending this
distinctiveness (Dumont 1970 : 45). It is the renouncer, as an
individual thinker, who has been the major creator of values and
the major agent of change in Indian religion and speculation
(Dumont 1970 : 46). Most of what is considered "Indian thought"
belongs to him (Dumont, 1970 : 12).

Despite this apparent opposition of renouncer and man in the world, the relationship between the two ideal types is really complementary. Dumont (1972 : 231) explains:

> At the end of the movement ... the renouncer is in fact absorbed, whether he invents a religion of love open to all, whether he becomes the spiritual head of worldly people, rich or poor, or whether he remains a Brahman while becoming a sanyasi, as with Ramanuja.

As he states elsewhere,

> The two kinds of thought, the two ideal types I set out to distinguish, mingle at the mercy of various milieux and temperaments, and some men who are in spirit sannyasis live in the world (Dumont 1970 : 59).

Sannyasa does not necessarily mean "a stepping out into solitude or a lapse into a social vacuum" (Dutt 1962 : 44), so much as the establishment of a new relationship with society. Like any social institution, renunciation has its own rules and history.

There are remarkably few studies of those rules and that history. This chapter aims to provide a brief overview of the development of institutional renunciation and of the few available studies of classical lifestyles.

History of Renunciation

For the believer, the history of any religious institution begins with the gods. Satyananda (1979 : 3-6) presents the Lord Shiva as the archetypal *sannyasin*, drawing attention to His mastery of yoga, His depiction as a wandering ascetic dressed in a tiger skin and bearing a trident for His staff, and the many legends indicative of His perfect freedom. After Shiva comes Dattareya, another wandering figure, smeared with ashes and with wild uncut hair, the author of many treatises on renunciation and the founder of many *sannyasa* sects (Satyananda 1979 : 6).

In more human times, Ghurye (1964 : 39) draws our attention to "the plethora of ascetic orders" which existed at the beginning of the Christian era. There were *sramanas*, followers of a naked teacher, who may have been Jains. There were ascetics dwelling at sacred rivers, *tirthikas*; ascetics with long matted hair, *dirghajatas*;

as well as life-long *brahmacharis, naisthika brahmacharis*. There were *panchagnitapas*, who sat between four fires, facing the sun as the fifth. Others lay on beds of thorns, ashes or grass. There were bizarre performers of strange yogic exercises. These references are drawn from the Buddhist literature, particularly the travel diaries of visiting Chinese scholars, which may account for some of their strangeness and lack on sympathy. The Greeks accompanying Alexander, on the other hand, found "Naked Ones", living in the open air and "practising endurance", ideals surely close to their own culture. These men were sometimes accompanied by women "bound in continence". Strabo noted that the people had great respect for these ascetics (Ghurye 1964 : 40).

The principal sects at the beginning of the Common Era seem to have been the *kapaladharins*, and the more numerous *pasupatins* who were spread across the whole of the North of India. The *pasupatins* worshipped Shiva, in his form as Lord of the Animals. They practised self-mortification, smeared the body with ash after worship, and begged their food. They practised yoga, either for physical and mental self-control, or as the less sympathetic Vaishnava Madhava suggested, for the miraculous powers it could give them (Ghurye 1964 : 115).

The *kapaladharins* also worshipped Shiva, in the form of Kapalin, one who holds a skull. One of the few theological descriptions of Kapalin belief comes from the Vaishnava teacher Ramanuja in the eleventh century A.D. He describes the six means of attaining desires in this world and the next: eating food from a skull, besmearing the body with funeral ashes, eating such ashes, bearing a club, keeping a pot of wine, and worshipping god "as seated on the female organ" (Ghurye 1964 : 121). Male *kapalins* were accompanied by female ascetics, Ghurye notes without explaining further, because "they were a necessary adjunct to sectarian practice" (Ghurye 1970 : 141). The alleged preference for wine and women formed the basis of a number of Sanskrit farces from the fourth to the eleventh century A.D. directed against *kapaladharin* ascetics. (These are described in Ghurye 1964 : 116-128).

A major reform of institutional patterns of asceticism was carried out in the ninth century by Shankaracharya (788-820 A.D.). Comparatively speaking, a fair bit is known about Shankara. He was born in a *brahmin* family from the Kerala region and left home at an early age to become a wandering ascetic. Shankara had a powerful intellect and wrote many major philosophical and devotional works, including commentaries on the *Upanishads*, *Bhagavad Gita* and the *Brahma Sutra*. He was a tireless opponent of Buddhism and of the "immoral" sects. Shankara founded four monastic centres, one in each of the corners of the Indian sub-continent, to be the centre of ten religious lineages, each with its distinctive name. (These lines are called *dasanami*, "the ten names".) The names were (and are) added to the names of *sannyasins* to indicate the centre of initiation or attachment, and more commonly, the name of the initiating preceptor. (Details of Shankara's life may be found in Lorenson 1976, and Ghurye 1964 : 54, 82). Within these various *dasanami* groups, there also developed the militant warrior orders known as *Nagas* and the yogic *Kanphata* groups (see Ghurye 1964 : 110-140 for details).

Shankara's propounding of Advaitic philosophy aroused a strong reaction among the Vaishnavas of the South of India.He was opposed by four great *acharyas* (teachers)—Ramanuja (late tenth century), Nimbarka (d. 1162), Madhava (middle of the thirteenth century), and Vallabha (1479-1531). Each of these teachers developed a distinctive philosophy, based on the worship of Vishnu, and a separate religious order. For the first time, therefore, Vaishnavism too developed its own monastic organisation (see Ghurye 1964 : 150-76 for details). These ascetics inhabit "almost a different world" from the Shaiva ascetics, and have traditionally been known as *vairagis* rather than *sannyasins* (Ghurye 1964 : 150). Other reformist *vairagis*—such as Kabir (d. 1518) and Dadu (1544-1603)—founded their own lineages, rejecting the use of images in worship and admitting non-Hindus to their membership (see Ghurye 1964 : 188-209).

What was arguably a third major reform of Indian patterns of renunciation took place in the late nineteenth century and is still working itself out, not without a good deal of resistance. Soon after the death of the Bengali religious genius Ramakrishna Paramahamsa in 1886, his major disciple Vivekananda established a monastic order known as the Shri Ramakrishna Mission. The order had two aims : firstly, to organise a band of monks leading a life of renunciation, and secondly, to send out appropriately trained monks to serve humanity in every possible way, "looking upon all, irrespective of sex, age, caste, creed, nationality and colour, as veritable manifestations of the Divine" (Ghurye

1964 : 233). The idea of monks serving society was itself new. But in 1895 Vivekananda went further. After attending the World Parliament of Religion in Chicago, he initiated two European *sannyasins*. The first was Leon Landsberg, a Russian Jew, whom he named Swami Kripananda. The other was a woman, Madame Marie Louise, who became Swami Abhayananda (see Ghurye 1964 : 234, French 1974 : 61).

One of the very few outside the Mission to follow Vivekananda's examples in both these regards was Swami Sivananda of Rishikesh (1887-1963). After his own initiation into the "Saraswati" line of *dasanami sannyasins* in 1924, Sivananda continued to provide medical services to other renunciates and the general public. He gave *sannyasa* liberally, initiating people by the hundreds. As Ananthanarayan (1976 : 139-140) states:

> In India's religious history, no other saint ever turned so many into monks. Swamiji gave Sannyasa to men; he gave Sannyasa to women. He gave the ochre robe to old men with a few years left to life; he gave it to teenagers about to start their adult life. He gave Sannyasa to Indians and he gave Sannyasa to foreigners. He gave Sannyasa in person and he gave Sannyasa by post. To some who still had worldly responsibilities to discharge, he gave mental Sannyasa. Sivananda asked them to colour their mind. He told them to live in the world, but be not of it.

Some of his Indian disciples who later established lineages in the West consisting of both male and female *sannyasins* include Swami Satyananda, Swami Vishnu Devananda (whose community is discussed later in this chapter) and Swami Satchidananda (who helped open the Woodstock Music Festival in 1969).

Sociological Studies of Traditional Renunciation

In the Foreword to his book *Indian Sadhus*, Professor G.S. Ghurye (1964 : viii) somewhat bemusedly noted that

> Within my individual knowledge there are four American scholars, anthropologists or students of comparative religion, either going over the length or breadth of India in search of ascetics and their institutions or piling up the available knowledge in the libraries of U.S.A. into monographs.

Four is perhaps not a large number of scholars for a topic as vast as "ascetics and their institutions", yet the number of published works even today scarcely stretches beyond that. In this section, I shall present the findings of Miller and Wertz (1976) on Bhubaneswar, and of Tripathi (1978) on Uttar Pradesh. This will be followed by my own study of the disciples of Swami Vishnu Devananda (1989). Finally, reference will be made to four studies of the Hare Krishna movement: one done in Australia—O'Brien (1971); two in America—Daner (1974) and Rochford (1985); and one in England—Knott (1986). Although not predominantly a *sannyasin* group, the Hare Krishna are mainly European ascetics attempting to lead a traditional Indian religious lifestyle that respects both caste and life-stages.

Bhubaneswar

The book *Hindu Monastic Life* is a study of "the practice of Hindu monasticism at Bhubaneswar, Orissa, a medium-sized pilgrimage center, as it existed in 1964" (Miller and Wertz 1976 : 1)

The authors provide the following important definition of the qualities expected of a renunciate by both Hindu tradition and the contemporary laity:

> 'charismatic qualities', rather loosely described as holiness or saintliness, that the layman can worship or revere; knowledge of Hindu religious thought and the teachings of more recent religious leaders; devotional knowledge of ritual performance (*puja*) or of religious songs (*kirtana*); a distinctive life style, accompanied by austerities or by ordering one's entire life around a schedule of devotions and recitations of the name of his chosen deity; the observance of vows of celibacy, poverty, vegetarianism, and abstinence from intoxicating beverages.

> (Miller and Wertz 1976 : 2-3)

In their research Miller and Wertz secured personal information on thirty-two ascetics in Bhubaneswar. The data provided on fifteen *sannyasins* and *brahmacharins* show that they were mainly *brahmins*. Five had attended Sanskrit schools, the other ten had attended public schools. Their previous occupations had included lives as Sanskrit students and teachers, Ayurvedic medical practitioners, a priest, one landowner and a few merchants. Most had come from traditional occupations connected with religion. The average age was fifty-five: average length of residence at Bhubaneswar was sixteen years. On the other hand, the fifteen *Vairagin* informants derived from all socio-religious groups, including one *Shudra*. One had attended Sanskrit school, the other fourteen had attended public school. By occupation, they had been merchants, artisans, civil servants, draftsmen, and two tenant farmers. Most were from secular occupations and less schooled in tradition. The average age was forty-three; the average length of residence was seven years, although five had arrived in 1963-1964 (Miller and Wertz 1976 : 76).

Psychosocial factors motivating entrance into monastic life varied according to age. Little can be said about earliest childhood, although the researchers were struck by the frequency of experience of death in the family, noting however that this is a frequent experience for most segments of the population. Almost all were middle children, having commonly two to five other siblings. Some had been raised by loving parents in a harmonious environment; others by relatives after their parents died and were considered a burden (Miller and Wertz 1976 : 78).

Seven had proceeded directly from Sanskrit or public school to the monastery, at ages between twelve to twenty-two, without facing the adolescent crises of marriage and occupational choice. Two others, while giving "religious" explanations for their behaviour, had entered monasteries primarily because they feared sexual experience and marital responsibility. Nine persons, aged seventeen to thirty, had entered out of fear of continuing in a secular occupation, six having tried or failed at various occupations and then given up. One, now the head ascetic at a heavily endowed monastery, had entered to escape the poverty of his youth, where he was one of eleven hungry siblings. One was the son of a goldsmith with defective eyesight, unable to carry on the family trade (Miller and Wertz 1976 : 79-81).

Four of the five individuals who entered while in their thirties had failed either in marriage or earning a living or both (Miller and Wertz 1976 : 81).

Fourteen ascetics claimed to have entered orders on account of conversions occurring at a wide variety of ages, from fifteen to fifty-two. Most of these were not sudden, positive visions of the deity, but a growing sense of weariness with the world and a desire for the eternal (Miller and Wertz 1976 : 83-84).

Finally, seven informants had entered following retirement, at ages between forty-seven to seventy-three. Miller and Wertz consider these "some of the most competent men" among all the renunciates (Miller and Wertz 1976 : 84).

Miller and Wertz note that Indian asceticism allows its practitioners great freedom in the choice of the form of the deity to be worshipped, the setting of one's own daily schedule, and the regulation of private morality. It therefore appeals to "many strong personalities with different eccentricities and different styles of life" (Miller and Wertz 1976 : 195). Some of this variety was undoubtedly constrained by residence within a monastery, and their sample biographies include few individuals devoted to solitary nomadic mendicancy. The satisfactions derived from commitment to religious life in Bhubaneswar were many. Some ascetics valued escape from "a hungry childhood, a quarrelsome family, or economic failure with the attendant ability to support wife and family" (Miller and Wertz 1976 : 195).

Some enjoyed the leisure and support provided by the wealthier monasteries. Others were solitary by nature, sometimes being gifted with outstanding musical talents appropriate for devotional worship. A few had inherited their present positions and were hazy of their calling (Miller and Wertz 1976 : 88). The volume presents detailed biographies of a major teacher, an outstanding preacher, a father and son who spend most of their time engaged in devotional chanting, a troubadour, and a solitary ascetic. They also deal with the "atypical" life histories of "an easy-going funloving ascetic who enjoyed smoking *ganja* and gossiping", an ambitious wandering ascetic, and a grizzled old man, living a fringe existence between the monastery during the day and his wife and property at night (Miller and Wertz 1976: 21-74). Despite this variety, the authors have no doubt that the religious quest was a compelling and sincere motive for "many" of their informants' lives. Six ascetics, almost a fifth of the thirty-two interviewed, claimed "decisive visions of the deity", which entitled them to *moksha* (total release from future rebirths and suffering) at the time of death. This, they consider, is a 'surprisingly high' figure (Miller and Wertz 1976 : 88-92).

Uttar Pradesh

Bansi Dhar Tripathi's study of *sadhus* was undertaken in the state of Uttar Pradesh and completed in 1967. (*Sadhu* is the most general term for an Indian holy man. Walker's encyclopedic survey of Hinduism, *The Hindu World* (1968), lists fifty-three different titles under the heading 'Hierophants', not including the common affectionate term of address "Baba".) Tripathi's study was done with the aim of exploring "the institution of Sadhuism as it functions in the rapidly changing society of today" (Tripathi 1978 : xi). In this study, five hundred *sadhus* from one hundred religious centres were interviewed, following an exhaustive interview schedule. The *sadhus* constituting the sample were selected from sixty-six sects and sub-sects of Vaishnava, Shaiva and other orders (*sampradayas*), using a ratio of 60 : 38 : 2. The researcher worked as a participant observer, being initiated first as a Shaiva ascetic (taking the name Swami Vidyananda Saraswati), and then as a Vaishnava ascetic in the Nimbarka line (as Vraja Gopal Das).

Tripathi (1978 : 82) found that 70.6 per cent of his sample came from small joint families. Half were unmarried in their pre-ascetic life (49.4 per cent), 29.6 per cent had renounced the world after the death of their wife (Tripathi 1978 : 82-83). Members of the three "twice-born" castes, mainly *Brahmins*, comprised 73.2 per cent of the populations; *Shudras* formed 38.66 per cent of the Vaishnava ascetics, but only 6.84 per cent of the Shaivas (Tripathi 1978 : 84-85). Levels of education were higher for the Shaiva ascetics than for the Vaishnavas, 15.8 per cent claiming various levels of education compared with only 9.8 per cent, but overall the illiteracy rate was 70 per cent, a reflection of patterns in the wider community (Tripathi 1978 : 86). Prior to initiation, 53 per cent of the *sadhus* had been engaged in some profession, mainly farming (40.2 per cent). Of the previously unemployed, 17 per cent of the whole sample had renounced directly after school, 14.4 per cent were retired persons, while 10.8 per cent were physically or otherwise handicapped (Tripathi 1978 : 88-92). The majority of *sadhus* were from low or lower middle income groups (46.0 per cent, 27.8 per cent respectively), suggesting to Tripathi (1978 : 93) that "the majority of Sadhus look upon the institution of Sadhuism more as a convenient means of livelihood than a missionary order."

In attempting to determine the factors which attracted *sadhus* to take to renunciation, Tripathi found that 24 per cent sought a convenient and respectable livelihood, 20.8 per cent wished to be of social service (17 per cent belonged to Shaiva lines), 6 per cent wished to enhance their social status. Only 5.4 per cent stated any desire to lead "a spiritual life" (3.2 per cent Shaiva : 2.2 per cent Vaishnava). The immediate factors pushing people into renunciation were mainly socio-familial factors 41.6 per cent (18.4 Shaiva : 22.6 Vaishnava), economic 14 per cent (3.4 : 10.2), and mixed extra-spiritual factors 21.8 per cent (7.4 Shaiva : 14.4 Vaishnava). Again spiritual factors were comparatively insignificant, 5.4 per cent (3.2 Shaiva : 2.2 Vaishnava) (Tripathi 1978 : 93-97).

Economically, 20.6 per cent of *sadhus* derived their income from offerings by devotees and disciples. A further 20 per cent resorted to begging, while 19 per cent relied on the results of their social services. Only 1.6 per cent relied on employment in their *ashram*. The income so derived was commonly less than Rs. 100 a month. Ascetics who used dubious means to gain an income, either force or attention-gaining practices such as extreme self-torture and magic, 7.8 per cent of the sample, were commonly well-off, as were those heads of monasteries who had the use of landed property, 4.8 per cent (Tripathi 1978: 98-107). Only 4.6 per cent of the sample had an income over Rs. 500.

The majority of Shaiva ascetics had been initiated between the ages of thirty and fifty-nine (94.5 per cent). Vaishnava ascetics had either been initiated between the ages of one and twenty-nine (53 per cent), or sixty to sixty-nine (22.66 per cent). Almost all (92.2 per cent) still maintained some links with their families, 76 per cent offering assistance in cash or kind, 52 per cent to continue formal sexual relations with their wives. This was no doubt assisted by the fact that fully 90.6 per cent observed nomadism at different regional levels. The major techniques used by the *sadhus* to realise their aims and objectives included worship (23.2 per cent), begging (20 per cent), social service (18.4 per cent), and meditation (6 per cent), followed by penance (5.8 per cent), trickery (5.2 per cent), hatha yoga (5 per cent), palmistry (4.4 per cent), tantra (3.2 per cent), pseudo-yogic feats (1.2 per cent), and miscellaneous (7.6 per cent) (Tripathi 1978: 110-52).

Finally, Tripathi also surveyed the beliefs and attitudes of the renunciates. Of the Vaishnavas, 61.33 per cent worshipped some form of Vishnu and His consort, while 32.33 per cent worshipped God without form. All the Shaivites worshipped Shiva. The overwhelming majority of *sadhus* believed in transmigration of the soul and rebirth, fate, karma and, to a lesser degree, grace. They supported the caste system and untouchability, and their various social ramifications. They had little faith in free will and were positively opposed on the whole to modern science. Most were pessimistic about the future of their institution (Tripathi 1978: 153- 205).

Western Renunciates: The Sannyasin Disciples of
Swami Vishnu Devananda

Although the renunciation of world involvement in favour of religious experience is undoubtedly a universal phenomenon, it is clear that the patterns of asceticism discussed so far are deeply rooted in the beliefs and social structure of Indian society. The questions which lie before us in much of the rest of this work are these: What happens when a cultural institution like *sannyasa* is taken up in a non-Indian environment, and in particular by Europeans? What sort of people will be attracted to it? Why? How will they adapt the institution to fit in with their own cultural patterns? Our concern in the rest of this chapter is with ascetic groups who have tried to adjust the institution as little as possible, the mainly European *sannyasin* disciples of Swami Devananda, and members of the Hare Krishna movement.

Swami Vishnu was born in Kerala in 1927 to a prosperous farming family. He first served in the army, then moved to the *ashram* of Swami Sivananda at Rishikesh, being initiated by him into the statuses of *brahmachari* and *sannyasin*. In 1957, he set out for the West, finally settling in Quebec State two years later. His *Complete Illustrated Book of Yoga* (Vishnu Devananda 1960) was for many years the major work available to the public on this topic.

Over the years, Swami Vishnu has initiated more than over a hundred people into *sannyasa*, most of whom have subsequently left his *ashram* system. In 1988, while residing at the Quebec *ashram*, the author made a study of thirteen of the currently serving fifteen *swamis* (Aveling 1989). The questionnaire was distributed with the approval of Swami Vishnu. Ten replies were received. Swami Vishnu himself also answered the questionnaire, both in writing and orally at an evening worship service (*satsang*).

The respondents ranged in age from twenty-five to forty-three years, with a mean of 36.5 years. Two had been born in New York city, two in Germany, two in South Africa, and one each in Canada, Italy, New Zealand and Vietnam. All indicated a religious background as a child: Protestant (three), Catholic (two), Jewish (four) and Buddhist (one). Nine of the ten had studied for a university degree, three at the Master's level. Seven had never married. Six had never been involved in politics; the others had been active but, for various reasons, disillusioned. The women expressed a cautious interest in feminism; only one of the five men respondents showed any interest. Almost all (eight) disclaimed any interest in the growth movement. Most had followed extremely successful careers before coming to the movement.

One of the major concerns of Swami Vishnu's work is the teaching of yoga. The average age for starting yoga practice was 20.6 (range seventeen to twenty-eight). Various reasons were given for starting, but overall none of the answers referred to the influence of any other person, and none dealt with health or beauty. Instead, there was an emphasis on the need for intellectual understanding of the self and life.

The average age of initiation into *sannyasa* was twenty-nine (range twenty-two to thirty-two). At least six of the respondents had been previously initiated as *brahmacharis* at an average age of 23.2 (nineteen to thirty), serving in this novice stage for an average of 4.1 years. The factors leading to the decision to renounce were variations on the single theme of world-weariness. Descriptions of the actual step leading to the taking of initiation tended to emphasise the major role of Swami Vishnu in reaching a decision, and be otherwise vague as to time, place and circumstances.

Renunciates interpreted the meaning of *sannyasa* as freedom, devotion to a particular lifestyle, love, service, helping humanity, and a tie with Swamiji. Few found the adjustment to the new status difficult. All acknowledged the difficulty of celibacy and the importance of yogic practices in sublimating physiological desire.

For reasons of time, the study did not investigate the personal daily life patterns of the renunciates other than by careful observation. The normal routine of the *ashram* involved meditation at 6 a.m., followed by an hour of devotional chanting and discourse; two hours, from 8-10 a.m., were given over to the practice of yoga. The first meal was taken at 11 a.m. The middle of the day was used for teaching and work around the *ashram*. A further two hours of yoga took place from 4 to 6 p.m., followed by a second meal, and evening meditation, chanting and discourse. *Sannyasins* were constantly involved in teaching, administration, editing and other duties. It seemed they were free to fit in with the normal routine or not; most did not, usually dining separately. Private practices of yoga and meditation were, of course, expected. Work, as in the teachings of the *Gita*, was seen to have its own merit, and may, on occasion, have been used to excuse participation in public and private spiritual activities. No questions were asked in the questionnaire about belief, as it was assumed that the answers would tend to follow the standard Vedantic framework taught by Vishnu Devananda.

It seems clear that Swami Vishnu had attempted to establish in Quebec the same way of life he had known at Swami Sivananda's *ashram*, and had been reasonably successful in this. His relationship with his disciples was decidedly that of mentor: teacher, sponsor, host, guide, exemplar and counsellor. Economically, the *ashram* relied on a host of Yoga and meditation weekends, Yoga Intensives, Yoga vacations, Teacher Training Courses, festivals and symposiums. Apart from these externals, few compromises appear to have been made with the traditional lifestyle, including the demand for celibacy. To some degree, the rewards were the opposite of those the initiates had sought: solitude gave way to a high public profile for the individual, freedom was submerged in service to a demanding organisation, community was frequently broken as one moved from centre to centre, intimacy was forbidden. For those who stayed, the positive personal changes— "from hard to soft", "from seclusiveness to openness", "more love", "more energy", "more courageous", "more understanding"—made it worthwhile. The struggle was not so much to destroy individual personality but the selfish ego. Western renunciates were as much affected by this issue as were the Indians noted by Dumont at the beginning of this chapter.

Hare Krishna (ISKCON)

The study of Vishnu Devananda's disciples was based on a small group of ten people. In order to broaden our focus, we now turn to a much larger group, the Hare Krishna Movement, or to use its full title the International Society for Krishna Consciousness (ISKCON), founded in New York in 1966 by A.C. Bhaktivedanta Swami Prabhupada (1896-1977).

Peter Levi, former Professor of Poetry at Oxford University and a Jesuit for almost thirty years, has noted that

> monks dramatize themselves and their vocation, communally or to one another, but also to the people around them. Their lives are ritualized.
>
> (Levi 1988 : 203)

Over the past three decades, few religious groups have been as successful at dramatising themselves in public as ISKCON. Kim Knott captures the image well:

> Here they are, the Oxford Street chanting party, the men in orange robes, their heads shaved but for a topknot or ponytail of hair, the women in bright saris, in blue, green, pink, white or yellow. Smiling, chanting and swaying, they move through the crowd. Some are playing instruments, perhaps finger cymbals or small drums. Some are handing out leaflets about their nearby vegetarian restaurant and temple. They are both familiar and at odds. We all know who they are—it is in the words they are singing—they are the 'Hare Krishnas'.
>
> (Knott 1986 : 10)

They are, in the words of Australian poet Hal Colebatch, part of "Disneyland of the soul" (Kelly 1990 : 12), once glimpsed never forgotten.

The distinctiveness of the "devotees" derives from their scrupulous adherence to the image of Indian culture and spirituality taught by Prabhupada himself. They follow the teachings of Lord Chaitanya, a fifteenth century Bengal mystic, who is regarded by them as a manifestation of Krishna and His beloved Radha combined. The *mantra* they chant 1728 times a day (sixteen rounds on a set of one hundred and eight beads) is the *mantra* Chaitanya wished to see proclaimed "in every town and village". They rise each day at 3.30 a.m. to participate in a worship service which is identical with that conducted by fellow Vaishnavas in India.

Their worship is followed by the study of the sacred texts: the *Bhagavad Gita*, the *Bhagavata Purana* (on the life of Krishna), and a life of Caitanya, the *Sri-Caitanya Caritamrita*. After a year's training, new members are initiated "into the Holy Name", and become either *brahmachari*s or *brahmacharini*s (the male and female terms respectively) or *grihastha*s, householders. *Brahmachari* men wear the orange *dhoti*, married men wear white. The women wear *sari*s; those who are married wear the red dot on their forehead and red powder along the part of the hair. After several years, they are entitled to the *brahmin* initiation, which enables them to conduct the religious services in the temple. In time, some men may become *sannyasin*s travelling and preaching the message of Krishna Consciousness. Their wives, now considered widows, will wear white and be highly venerated; their children will continue to attend the *gurukul*, or special Sanskrit school.

Rochford (1985) provides the most detailed categorical analysis of such demographic variables of the devotees as age, social class, religion, race and family backgrounds. His data are based on a non-random survey of two hundred and fourteen adult devotees in six ISKCON communities, approximately 10 per cent of the entire membership in the United States (Rochford 1985 : 7). He found that over half joined before the age of twenty-one, and 80 per cent before the age of twenty-six (1985 : 47). O'Brien (1983: 139) similarly reports that the youngest respondent to her survey of the Melbourne (Australia) temple in 1972 was sixteen, the oldest was twenty-six; the mean age was twenty-two. Rochford records that 80 per cent of American adherents are Anglo-Americans; only half of the remaining non-whites were born outside of the United States. O'Brien (1983 : 139) implicitly confirms this for the Australian membership through her reference to the one devotee of "mixed Polish and English ancestry". Knott is rather vague on these matters, but states that at "the British ceremony" of initiation into the movement in 1984, "young Indians, West Indians, and Africans were initiated along with young Anglo-Saxons" (1986 : 46).

Only 13 per cent of Rochford's population had not completed high school. Sixty-five per cent of the High school graduates had attended college for at least a year before dropping out, 16 per cent had graduated, and 6 per cent held graduate degrees. Half of the devotees surveyed had joined ISKCON within the first year of leaving school (Rochford 1985 : 49). O'Brien (1983 : 139) too notes that the majority of her Australian respondents were educated to a level at or above the national average : two were university graduates, seven had begun a degree or diploma course but not completed it, one had successfully finished high school, and three women had not. She was aware that another two devotees were graduates and three had left university prior to completing their courses.

The devotees came from financially stable and relatively prosperous middle and upper-middle class families (Rochford 1985 : 51; also O'Brien 1983 : 139, although a little more uncertain). Most had been members of one of the established churches (Protestant 35 per cent; Catholic, 33 per cent; Unspecified Christian, 6 per cent) or synagogues (Jewish, 15 per cent) during their childhood. About 40 per cent were still practising some religion, not necessarily the faith they were raised in, when they joined ISKCON (Rochford 1985 : 52-57). O'Brien (1983 : 141) notes "a questioning and eventual rejection of family and dominant institutional (including orthodox religious) beliefs" as typical of the first stage of coming to membership of her Australian sample but is otherwise unspecific about previous religious beliefs. A strong teenage interest in religion is also a feature of Daner's (1975) biographies of those Americans who become successful devotees.

Why were devotees attracted to ISKCON? Rochford (1985 : 44) suggests four possible levels of analysis. The first, categorical-demographic analysis (as above), provides important background data on members, but fails to explain why

> the vast majority of white middle-class youth of America with family backgrounds much the same as those of the devotees, have failed to join ISKCON, or even to have expressed an interest in doing so.
>
> (Rochford 1985 : 56)

The second level consists of macro-structural and social psychological analysis. Gussner and Berkowitz (1988 : 137) claim that joining New Religious Movements is encouraged by a combination of processes related to social and personal disintegration, personal neediness, and community belongingness, which they summarise as the "DNB thesis". O'Brien (1983) uses the turbulence and change experienced by youth in the late 1960s and

early 1970s, despite the apparent maturation of industrial capital-
ism, as the reason for "one group of disaffected people" adopting
a religious response to "the difficulties they encountered with the
dominant institutional order" (O'Brien 1983 : 135).

The same argument is used in Daner (1974). Her first chapter
(1974 : 6-14) is entitled "Hippies into Happies" and consists of
three logically related sections: "Manifestation of a problem:
Alienation", "The Underlying problem: Identity", "A Possible
Solution: The ISKCON Temple". Within the literature on New
Religious movements, DNB is the most common overall answer
to the problem of recruitment.

The third approach comes from asking members themselves
why they joined. Knott focuses on this, which is consistent with
her aim of attempting

> to bridge the divide between the Hare Krishna movement
> and those outside it . . . to present the movement and its
> philosophy largely from the viewpoint of those inside it
> (1986 : 17).

Rochford (1985 : 68-79) suggests the following as major reasons
given by devotees themselves for joining: the movement's philosophy (39 per cent), the warmth and friendliness of devotees (16
per cent), attraction to Srila Prabhupada (12 per cent), the desire
for a better lifestyle (8 per cent). But he also warns against taking
such explanations as hard data, arguing that the ideology of any
movement may serve as a screen for the individual to reconstruct
past experience and find a trajectory which will lead to his/her
present position (Rochford 1985 : 73).

The fourth approach deals with micro structural or interac-
tional processes between a recruit and adherents of a movement.
This approach sees movement participation as being strongly
influenced by three factors: contacts with the movement; structural availability (that is, a lack of alternative commitments and
obligations that might limit an individual's ability to participate);
and the alignment of recruits' cognitive orientations with the
movement's ideology (Rochford 1985 : 45). Rochford argues that
men and women were recruited into ISKCON through different
influence structures: 51 per cent of the men after initiating contact
with devotees in public places, 60 per cent of the women through
social network linkages with members or sympathisers (Rochford
1985 : 125). He argues that their status as young, unattached,

newly out of school, and unemployed or barely employed, gave
them the subsequent freedom they needed to join (Rochford 1985:
76-83). This is confirmed for Australia by O'Brien (1983 : 141-142)
and for England by Knott (1986 : 45).

Conclusion

We have now traced the history, philosophy and social dimensions of *sannyasa*. It is clear that the word has a number of
meanings. In the broad sense, it refers to anyone who has entered
the last of the four life-stages by renouncing the world, his family
and possessions. By so doing, the renouncer enters a social state
which is apart from society proper (Dumont 1970 : 43), but still
in a complementary relationship with it. In the narrow sense, the
term is applied in particular to Shaiva ascetics, and most specifically to the members of the ten *dasanami* orders. Vaishnavite
sectarians are more commonly known as *Vairagis*.

Externally, the status of renunciate is marked by the insignia
of his order (clothing, hairstyle, sect marks, a staff, pot. etc.); by
the charismatic quality of "holiness" (*sadhu* means one who is
"accomplished", "virtuous"); knowledge of ancient Sanskrit texts
and the teachings of more recent religious leaders; some skill in
ritual performance or devotional leadership; and the leading of a
distinctive lifestyle based on asceticism and religious devotion,
such austerity normally including physical self-control, celibacy,
poverty, vegetarianism and an avoidance of intoxicants. Internally, as the *Bhagavad Gita* suggests, *sannyasa* is an attitude of
detachment and tranquillity, in which not action but the "fruits"
of one's actions are renounced.

Sociological studies of *sadhu*s in India indicate that ascetics
tend to derive from small joint families of the *brahmin* caste,
particularly those engaged in farming. Vaishnava ascetics are
either very young when initiated (one to twenty-nine years) or
very old (sixty to sixty-nine), while Shaiva ascetics are usually
initiated between the ages of thirty to fifty-nine. A majority of
*sadhu*s are illiterate. They most commonly depend on begging or
the gifts of supporters for their livelihood. Tripathi found that the
desire to lead a spiritual life was, in fact, a small factor in leading
the *sadhu*s he surveyed into religious life. Much more important
was the opportunity to lead a convenient and respectable way of
life.

Although *sannyasa* is rooted in Indian beliefs and social practices, there have been many attempts since the time of Swami Vivekananda of the Sri Ramakrishna Mission to make this way of life available to Europeans as well as Indians, and to women. A study of the *sannyasin* disciples of Swami Vishnu Devananda, shows his followers to be young, well educated European men and women, who had been raised with a religious background. Most had never married, some were divorced. They explained their attraction to the movement in terms of its philosophy of the desire to escape from the confusion and meaninglessness of the world, and the mentor-like role of Swami Vishnu. Their behaviour attempted to conform to the external characteristics of renunciation outlined above. All granted the difficulty of their present lifestyle, including the practice of celibacy, but justified it through the personal freedom and positive change it promoted in their lives.

Through reference to studies of the members of the International Society for Krishna Consciousness, we are able to see that the characteristics of the *sannyasin* disciples of Swami Vishnu are shared by members of this neo-Hindu movement in America, Australia and England. Both groups draw on young, well educated, middle-class persons, deriving from religious backgrounds and seeking meaning in their lives. The Krishna devotees, many of whom are *brahmacharis* but not *sannyasins*, also aim to conform to an Indian ascetic lifestyle, including the practice of sexual self-control, in the name of religious values. More obviously than do Vishnu Devananda's disciples, the devotees show the processes related to "personal and social disintegration, personal neediness and communal belongingness" (DNB), which have brought them to their present status. (The *sannyasins'* rhetoric of world weariness and desire for renunciation exclude these factors as acceptable modes of self-explanation. It also excludes reference to the influences of others, apart from Swami Vishnu, in the decision to join and then to commit oneself to a total ascetic lifestyle.)

With all these factors in mind, we may now turn to Swami Satyananda and Osho, and their efforts to bridge and even remake, Indian and Western cultures.

PART THREE

THE REDEFINITION OF RENUNCIATION

CHAPTER FOUR

SATYANANDA AND INNER RENUNCIATION

The word *guru*, often translated into English as "teacher", strictly speaking refers to the man or woman who gives *diksha*, authentic initiation into a sect of renouncers (Lanoy 1971: 347). Swami Sivananda's *guru* was Swami Viswananda Sarswati. Swami Vishnu Devananda's *guru* was Swami Sivananda. Once he has turned his back on society, the renouncer's most decisive human relationship becomes that with his Master. The relationship may be short in terms of physical presence: after initiating Sivananda, Viswananda left for Varanasi the next day, sending his disciple only the briefest of instructions on the life he was to lead. It may be a long relationship: Swami Vishnu was with Sivananda for over ten years. But it is the preceptor who is the gateway to the potential renouncer's "dream" of what it means for him to be fully himself (Levinson 1978 : 91).

Where the relationship is ongoing, the *guru* plays two roles. One is indeed that of instructor, supplying "correct answers to the riddles of life because he has transcended the law of opposites" (Lanoy 1971 : 249). Formal teaching does not play a large part in the life of most *ashrams*. The second and more important role of the *guru* is closer to that of "a competent therapist" (Lanoy 1971: 349). The disciple has come to him because living in the world is no longer a tenable option. The disciple surrenders to the *guru* in order to lose his own ego and gain a new sense of wholeness. The first stage of the relationship is dependence and transference, the second independent maturity, the third the pupil's discovery of "the *guru* within", the One (Lanoy 1971:352). The process is not without its risks but under the conditions of caste society, where hierarchical interdependence and ritualistic interpersonal relationships introduce an element of formal and emotional constraint into every relationship, it is the one place where an "authentic meeting . . . can still occur between two human beings stripped of their masks" (Lanoy 1971 : 347).

There are no formal organisations known as the "Osho movement" and "Satyananda movement". Indian religions are not structured the way churches and denominations are, with formalised beliefs and a clear hierarchy and pattern of administration. Instead we find a whole number of people, Indian and European, who may believe many things but share one thing in common: their commitment to a relationship as disciple with a particular *guru*, Satyananda or Osho. Social structures may exist around the teacher: the major one is the common residence or *ashram*. Not all disciples live in these residences or desire to. It is the link with the teacher which is crucial. In the next two chapters, therefore, we must first study the lives of these Masters, and their understanding and redefinition of renunciation.

Swami Satyananda

Swami Satyananda Saraswati (as he was later to be known) was born in Almora, a small town at the foothills of the Himalayas, in 1923. At the age of nineteen he left home and after wandering in search of a *guru* for some time came to reside in the *ashram* of Swami Sivananda in Rishikesh. He was initiated directly into *Paramahamsa sannyasa* in 1947, as was Sivananda's frequent practice (See Sivananda 1963: 157-159). For nine years Satyananda remained with Sivananda, receiving little formal instruction but constantly working from dawn until late at night. In 1956 Sivananda sent his disciple "away, into the wide world, to do what I could, to see and understand" (Cited in *Yogakanti* 1989 : 9).

Basing himself at Munger, Bihar, Satyananda took to *paravrajaka* life, and wandered extensively through India, Afghanistan, Burma, Nepal and Sri Lanka. Part of the time from 1960 to 1963 was spent in seclusion. In late 1962, devotees created the International Yoga Fellowship Movement in Rajnandgaon, but the fellowship struggled because of Satyananda's reluctance to stay in the one place and direct the work (Yogakanti 1989 : 23). In the following year, the Bihar School of Yoga (B.S.Y.) was founded at Munger. The aim of the school was "to prepare a few swamis with proper training for the propagation of yogic culture" (Yogakanti 1989:23). The first formal training course for one hundred and eight *sannyasins* was instituted in 1970, but does not appear to have ever been very structured.

Some training was also to be offered to householders. For the first few years, fifteen day residential yoga courses were held twice a month (Yogakanti 1989 : 8). In 1967, the first nine-month Teacher Training Course was held (Yogakanti 1989 : 21). At the invitation of overseas students who had attended the course, Satyananda began to travel internationally. From April to October 1968, he visited Malaysia, Singapore, Australia, Japan, USA, Canada, England, France, Holland, Sweden and Italy "offering yoga to the west" (Yogakanti 1989 : 27-29). The Bihar School of Yoga soon became the centre of a chain of *ashrams* and yoga schools offering Satyananda's teachings. By the mid-seventies, there were fifty-four "major yoga ashrams (not yoga centres)" which conducted yoga classes "under the guidance of Satyananda Paramahamsa and on behalf of Bihar School of Yoga, Sivanandashram, Monghyr, Bihar, India" (Satyananda 1976 : 99).

Eight of these *ashrams* were in Australia. Sixteen of the *ashrams* were under the direction of initiated *sannyasins*, including three of those in Australia (Satyananda 1976 : 99).

Satyananda again visited Australia in 1969, presiding over an international Yoga Convention held at Richmond (N.S.W.) which was organised by Roma Blair (Swami Nirmalananda). He then returned in 1973, and each year from 1976 to 1980. In 1977 he presided over the annual *Guru Purnima* celebrations held at the Mangrove Mountain *ashram*, near Gosford. *Guru Purnima* is celebrated in India on the night of the full moon in July and honours the *guru*: it was the first time Satyananda had celebrated the day outside India and his absence would have been keenly felt there. Satyananda last visited Australia in 1983 (Yogakanti 1989).

While in Australia in 1983 Swami Satyananda quietly announced his resignation from the Presidency of the Bihar School of Yoga. He became permanent Founder President instead and appointed Swami Niranjanananda (born in 1960 and initiated into *sannyasa* at the age of ten) as his successor. On the 8th August 1988, Swami Satyananda left the B.S.Y. and Munger, to resume the free life of

the *Paramahamsa* ascetic (Niranjan 1989), "moving dispassion-
ately, without working for any organisation, sect or system"
(Satyananda 1986:1).

Sannyasa Tantra

Sannyasa Tantra is a modern text on the way of life of the
sannyasin. Although undated, it was probably first published in
the late 1960s. The work is attributed to Swami Satyananda, and
accepted by his disciples as such. In fact, the book was actually
"edited by Swami Nischalananda" and a small note inside the
book acknowledges "writing, editing, composing, printing and
binding" were all "done by the swamis of the Bihar School of
Yoga". The extensive literary quotations, including many from
the Bible and from Chinese sages, one even from the poetry of
D.H. Lawrence, certainly suggest the work of other hands. The
cover was drawn by Swami Chinmayananda, who became one of
Rajneesh's earliest disciples. In accordance with the common
perception, we shall refer to the understanding of *sannyasa* found
in this book as Satyananda's own.

The introduction to *Sannyasa Tantra* states that its aim is "to
explain the traditions of sannyasa, its purpose, implications and
to indicate the role sannyasa can play in the world." Significantly,
it then states: "We will also describe the system of sannyasa that
we feel is most relevant in this modern day and age" (i, further
numbers in this section are to pages of the text).

Two steps are involved in this redefinition. The first is to shift
the meaning of *sannyasa* from its outer characteristics to an inner
attitude. Thus:

> It is really impossible to define a sannyasin by external
> actions because sannyasa is really an inner attitude. One
> person may be surrounded by wealth and another by
> poverty, but if there is an aspiration or an attitude of
> renunciation of surrender, then both can be defined as
> sannyasins. Of course in the text we will describe many
> external attributes of a sannyasin: robes, way of life, initiation
> and so forth. These are only the outer marks of a sannyasin:
> the important attributes are within. (ii)

The second move, logically related to the first, is to disconnect
the institution from its past context. Traditionally, the text grants,
the word *sannyasa* has been used to describe "a Hindu monk or

renunciate". Here, however, "we will use the word to mean any person of any religion or mystical sect, even of no sect or religion at all, who follows the general sannyasa way of life."

The decision to "separate the word from the confines of Hinduism so that it can be applied throughout the whole world" (ii), is justified by the claim that: "a sannyasin should really be beyond all religious and specific dogmas" (ii) and "aspire beyond the limitations of any system". (ii)

To be a *sannyasin* one need neither be a Hindu nor an Indian: "Sannyasa ideally transcends all boundaries and national sentiments. It is this inner attitude that is important." (ii)

Thus we are led to the final definition that: "a sannyasin is a person, regardless of age, race, country, belief or non-belief, who has the aspiration to understand himself or herself, and who adopts the sannyasa way of life." (iii)

The First Chapter of the *Sannyasa Tantra* is concerned with "Tradition". It begins by describing *sannyasa* as

> a means to overcome and remove conditioning of the mind, false beliefs, dogmas, concepts, etc., that prevent the mind functioning as a perfect instrument. It has been adopted by those people who wanted to free the mind of its bondage and thereby gain an insight into the deeper aspects of existence. (1)

As such, *sannyasa* probably existed from the dawn of time, but became increasingly important as large complex social groups arose, placing greater pressures on the individual, and encouraging ambition, neurosis and egoism (1). In time, society accepted *sannyasa* as "an ideal way of life for those people who sought wisdom" (2), and who could give "sensible, constructive counsel" to others (2). Although probably a universal way of life: "It is only in India and a few other countries that sannyasa has remained fully intact to the present day" (3). In the "age of Aquarius" it will, hopefully, be reinstated "as an acceptable way of life for those seeking wisdom" (3).

The life histories of the "Luminaries of sannyasa" show that "sannyasa knows no boundaries , is the essence of all religions, and has existed in various forms throughout history" (3). The "few perfected and well known sannyasins" (3) dealt with include Shiva (despite his being married, for "It is the inner attitude that is most important," 6), Dattatreya, Diogenes, Christ, Buddha, Lao Tsu, Guru Nanak, and Shankaracharya. As well, artists such as Leonardo da Vinci, Michelangelo, William Blake, scientists such as Einstein, and politicians such as Jagadish Chandra Bose and Mahatma Gandi, "were able to express themselves more powerfully in the world because they had the attitude of sannyasa, whether knowingly or not" (13).

The chapter then finally deals with the life-stages of ancient India, the ancient categories of *sannyasa*, and classes of renunciates (*sannyasins*) in the major world religions (13-25).

The Second Chapter, "The Heart and Structure", is the longest. Basically, it can be divided into three sections.

The first section suggests some of the qualities of expanded awareness which mark the life of the *sannyasin*: "letting things happen" (27), "inner freedom" (28), "living in the present" (29), "talking a chance of life" (30), "the taste and test of experience" and, for some, "devotion" as a spontaneous feeling (31).

The second section deals with the nature of renunciation. The addiction to the world of objects (rather than the objects themselves) "tends to dull one's perception and understanding of oneself and life itself" (32). Detachment from this addiction leads to wisdom and gives life a new meaning (33). Detachment is an attitude which should be practised towards personal interests (family, business, fame, name, respect and so forth) (35), and outer events and inner psychological processes (36). Attachment causes suffering and frustration (38); detachment leads to the overcoming of desire (41), an attitude of playfulness (42), greater joy (43), and the reduction of egoism (44).

Sannyasa is not for everyone (53). For some, however, it is part of their life path, as determined by *prarabda karma* (past life experiences) (54). It should be adopted when one feels "an overwhelming sense of dissatisfaction with worldly life", and "a degree of detachment". For true initiation into *sannyasa*, the *guru* is essential (54).

The third section of Second Chapter therefore deals with initiation, as a symbolic process of death and resurrection (57); the wearing of special robes, as a way of maintaining tradition, as well as of stirring the consciousness of the renunciate and those he meets (59-62); and the culmination of the life of the sage in self-realisation (64-67).

The Third Chapter, "Sannyasa in the Modern World", rejects the old way of "ascetism and rejection of participation in the world" in favour of "participation . . . with an attitude of detachment", "*karma yoga combined with awareness*" (68, emphasis in the original text). It is an active lifestyle (69-71). For some this will mean living in "a spiritual community", an *ashram* (72). Others, with spiritual aspirations but more naturally inclined towards marriage, children, etc., should try to live the life of 'a householder sannyasin', "to be a sannyasin while being a householder." Initiation is recommended for householder *sannyasins* but the wearing of robes is unnecessary—"You should try to be an 'inner sannyasin' without robes" (74). Children may also adopt *sannyasa* (73-74). "Inner sannyasa" is also an appropriate attitude for those people inclined towards the arts, technology and science (75). Perhaps not surprisingly, the *Bhagavad Gita* is recommended as "the scripture par excellence" for the dynamic or active *sannyasa* way of life (76-80).

The last chapter, "Odds and Ends", covers only a few pages. It quickly dismisses any objections to *sannyasa* as an unnatural or a parasitic way of life (81-82). The rest (82-84) is devoted to "sannyasa in a nutshell", which is summarised as "*renounce and enjoy*":

> The sannyasin should transform every act into an act of perfection. He should be relentless, unflinching and unwavering. Every act, from eating, sleeping, working—everything . . . should be done with awareness. Every act should become an act of bliss. If he is a teacher, his teaching should become flawless; if he is a cook, his cooking should become perfect; if he is a painter, his painting should become perfect. Every act should be infused with wisdom (83).

In this way, the *sannyasin* may play a role in society without any identification with that role, leading to the further paradoxes of "spontaneously controlled actionless acts, thoughtless thoughts and egoless ego" (84).

Karma Sannyasa

Sannyasa Tantra is a radical, and apparently comprehensive, redefinition of an ancient institution for the "New Age". In his second book on *sannyasa*, called *Karma Sannyasa* (*The Noble Path for Householders*) (1984), Swami Satyananda apparently drew back from some of the more extreme implications of the first volume, most particularly those which related renunciation as a full-time vocation to the life of the householder.

Karma Sannyasa now presented "full sannyasa" as being only for the very few (1984: 109, further page references are to this work). Total *sannyasa* requires a complete abandonment of worldly life (233), in favour of absolute self-dedication to spiritual growth (296). It is "a different type of life", free of "scriptures, canons, institutions and organisations" (113), lived in full submission to the *guru* (150). As such, it involves "a special way of living which was codified in the vedic tradition, regarding eating, sleeping, walking, friendships, attachments, detachments, attending to births, deaths and marriages" (277).

> The 'real' *sannyasin* is: "a veritable moving God upon the face of the earth . . . wherever he moves, that becomes a holy place; whatever he utters becomes the scriptures, and whomsoever he touches or talks to, that person becomes blessed" (303).

Satyananda notes several times that such a lifestyle may become an extreme. Many renunciates in his opinion seek "an exclusive way of life . . . living in seclusion, hating life, detesting everything" and living "more or less the life of an addict." Because they have "no philosophy or system for balancing the passions," such people lack dynamism and are unable to adjust to "the frivolities of life." Such a path is incomplete (167, see also 269). In contrast to the "orthodox style" of renunciation, he argues for the "tantric style" which seeks to "integrate" and "correlate" the two poles of energy which are found throughout the universe and within the human body. Within Indian mythology, these forces are represented by the major god Shiva and his female counterpart Shakti. Within the body, these forces function as consciousness (*chitta*) and energy (*prana*), and as the psychic channels *ida* and *pingala* (168). So there is really no question "whether a man can live with a woman and still be a sannyasin" (168). One obviously can.

Unfortunately, Satyananda does not pursue his discussion of this alternative style with relation to the "full sannyasin". Rather his major concern in this book is with the ways in which a householder may also be a renunciate although not a full renunciate.

The first way is "temporary sannyasa". For at least fifteen days, the householder should go to an *ashram* and live the life alone:

> Shave your head completely, put on geru, sleep on the floor, eat only once a day, practice complete brahmacharya in thought, word and deed, and live like a poorna sannyasin (full renunciate), no smoking, no transistor radio, no newspaper, no politics, no business, no market; just one thing—your sadhana. . . (278).

Sadhana is a spiritual practice: it may be the recitation of a *mantra*, writing a *mantra* many times, reading scriptures, *asanas* (yoga postures), or, if the guru doesn't advise anything, "just work in his kitchen or garden" (278-79). Then one should return enriched to normal life and "play the role of a perfect householder and a part-time sannyasin" (279, 295).

Swami Sivananda found it necessary to defend the courage of those who had renounced "the pleasure of the three worlds" for only a few days (Ananthanarayan, 1976 : 139-40). In the eyes of orthodox Indian society such persons are "fallen *sannyasins*" unworthy of their initiation, and subject to contempt, along with all their family (Tripathi 1978 : 117). Perhaps for this reason, Satyananda does not dwell at length on this alternative.

The second way of partial renunciation, which would seem to be a later development, is that of *karma sannyasa*. In the *Bhagavad Gita*, the term refers to the renunciation of the "fruits" of one's actions. Satyananda shifts it to mean *sannyasa* for those persons who still have *karma* to complete in their lives, and translates the term as "householder *sannyasa*".

The householder *sannyasin* is initiated by a *guru*, and given a spiritual name, an orange robe, *geru* and a set of beads (*mala*) for meditation, in the same way as the full *sannyasin*. Outwardly, should he or she choose, there may be no subsequent difference in name or dress between the *karma* and the full *sannyasin*. Householder *sannyasa* is, however, "a preparation for full sannyasa" and not the real thing (303). The householder still lives in the world, has his (or her) ordinary family, work and social commitments to attend to, and is "an aspirant" rather than a perfect *sannyasin* (299).

As a stage of preparation, *karma sannyasa* would appear to be closer to the third *vanaprastha* stage of life. This is, indeed, the strategy adopted throughout most of the book to resolve the contradiction of traditional statuses of householder and renunciate (see especially page 112). The *karma sannyasin* lives with his (or her) family, attends to important and necessary obligations, guiding family affairs, but is "not bothered by other obligations and complications". Being dedicated to the spiritual life, the householder is, at the same time, "free" (298).

Karma sannyasa is, from one perception mainly a "philosophy" of life. So we find statements such as these: "With initiation into karma sannyasa, a new meaning, a new philosophy comes into your life" (232); "If you are a person with a wise philosophy, then you will face destiny with wisdom" (256) and "If you cannot get out of (householder life), the alternative is to live in it with a different awareness and a different philosophy. That is called karma sannyasa" (275).

The principles of the philosophy tend not to be set, but shift from one chapter, one talk, to the next. At the basis of *karma sannyasa*, however is not a set of principles but "the art of living a detached life" (275), of being in the world but not easily upset by the changes and uncertainties taking place around one. Life is to be accepted and experienced in all its fullness, nothing is rejected, nothing (and no one) despised (270). The ordinary householder lives a life of guilt and repentence (168), emphasising the body and its senses (269). The householder *sannyasin* is :

> trying to integrate both the internal and external elements of life, because, according to the laws of nature, neither is empirical wordly experience untrue, nor is the transcendental experience difficult to attain. As a householder, whatever experiences you are going through, whatever experiences you have already undergone, and whatever experiences you will be going through, are all part of your spiritual life, and are not detrimental to it. This is what a karma sannyasin has to understand (270).

Thus the vital difference between the ordinary householder and the householder *sannyasin* is more than philosophical. What ultimately distinguishes the *karma sannyasin* from the common householder is the bond with the *guru* which the initiation into *karma sannyasa* provides. "In the spiritual life or for karma sannyasa", Satyananda states "the guru-disciple relationship is not only most important, it is the only important thing" (116).

Initiation provides an inner link, a transmission of spiritual energy and awareness from one who is evolved, the embodiment of spiritual knowledge and truth, to one who is aspiring towards inner self-transformation (115-16, 182-83, 291). The aspirant receives not only a new spiritual identity (145, 164), but also a new destiny (279), and a new means of personal integration (270). The focus on the *guru* rather than on the individual self, the petty ego, is a way of transcending personal limitations in favour of a greater participation in a wider consciousness (114).

Conclusion

The two books *Sannyasa Tantra* and *Karma Sannyasa*, provided important redefinitions of a traditional Indian social and spiritual institution, in such a way as to allow non-Indian and non-Hindu access to the external characteristics and the inner spirit of that way of life. For many of Satyananda's *sannyasins*, *Sannyasa Tantra* served to define what that lifestyle might be at its best. *Karma Sannyasa* was a more general and a later work, appearing after the majority of *karma sannyasins* had been initiated during the period 1973 to 1984, and probably served more to confirm a general impression of a way of life rather than to provide specific details of how to live. To the traditional Indian mind, the idea of "householder *sannyasa*" would seem to be an impossible hybrid. The book *Karma Sannyasa* served to mute this contradiction by realigning householder spirituality with the *vanaprastha* state. Sociologically, it also had the effect of defining the relationship between those initiated into different types of *sannyasa* by Swami Satyananda, so that a clear superiority was given to an inner circle of "full sannyasins".

There is a simplicity and practical directness in the writings of Satyananda Paramahamsa devoted to renunciation. His concern is to redefine, rather than reject, the institution. As far as possible, he sought to do this in terms provided by traditional Hindu discourses (modernised by some "New Age" thinking).

We now turn to a much more radical analysis of religious life and institutions, that of Osho, which is at once more intellectual and more poetic, and ultimately, totally opposed to the parameters of the traditional thought.

CHAPTER FIVE

OSHO AND NEO-SANNYASA

Satyananda sought to maintain an emphasis on the inner nature of *sannyasa* together with the most obvious external features of the traditional lifestyle. Bhagwan Shree Rajneesh (later known only as Osho) was far more radical. He worked within the tradition, skilfully drew out its parallels with much of contemporary Western psychological and philosophical thought, but also sought deliberately to destroy the external form of the tradition by bringing out its radical inner essence. In so doing, he provoked outrage and hostility, both in India and abroad, on an extraordinarily wide scale. This chapter attempts to bring out the complexity and paradoxical characteristics of which were typical of Osho's thought on religion and renunciation.

Rajneesh
Chandra Mohan Jain was born on 11 December 1931 in Kuchwada, a small farming village in Madhya Pradesh. He was the eldest son of a cloth merchant who belonged to a small Jain sect known as Taran Panth, after its founder Taran Swami, a sixteenth-century Digambara monk who preached against idolworship in favour of devotion to a formless God and a deep personal spirituality (see Joshi 1982 : 198-90). "Rajneesh" (as he was dubbed by his grandparents) seems to have been a difficult child, frequently challenging the authority of religious and bureaucratic figures around him, but at the same time he was also indulged with good deal of physical and intellectual freedom.

Rajneesh claimed to have gained enlightenment on March 21, 1953, at the age of twenty-one. As he tells the story in *The Sound of Running Water* (cited in Joshi 1982 : 55):

> One night I got so lost in meditation that I did not know
> when my body fell down from the tree (where I was
> meditating). I looked about in askance when I saw my body
> lying on the ground. I was surprised at this happening. How
> it happened that I was sitting on the tree and my body was
> lying on the ground I could not understand at all. It was a
> very queer experience. A bright line, a glittering silver cord
> from the navel of my body was joined on to me up above
> where I was perched on the tree. It was beyond my capacity
> to understand or foresee what would happen next, and I
> worried how I would return to my body. How long that
> trance lasted I do not know but that unique experience was
> not known to me before.
>
> That day for the first time, I saw my own body from the
> outside, and since that day the mere physical existence of
> my body finished forever. And from that day death also
> ceased to exist, because that one day I experienced that the
> body and spirit are two different things, quite separate from
> each other. That was the most important moment: my
> realization of the spirit that is within every human body.

Within the next six months, a series of experiences in meditation led him to "ultimate transcendence—to VOIDNESS" (Rajneesh
1975 : 10-11).

Rajneesh maintained his enlightenment as a secret until 1974.
In the *Discipline of Transcendence* (1978c : 301-10), he describes in
more conventional terms how on that night in 1953:

> The moment I entered the garden everything became
> luminous, it was all over the place the benediction, the
> blessedness. I could see the trees for the first time—their
> green, their life, their very sap running. The whole garden
> was asleep, the trees were asleep. But I could see the whole
> garden alive, even the small leaves were so beautiful.
>
> I looked around. One tree was tremendously luminous—
> the maulshree tree. It attracted me, it pulled me towards
> itself. I had not chosen it, God himself had chosen it. I went
> to the tree, I sat under the tree. As I sat there things started
> settling. The whole universe became benediction.

It was difficult to say how long I was in that state. When I went back home it was about four o'clock in the morning, so I must have been there by clock time at least three hours—but it was infinity. It had nothing to do with clock time. It was timeless.

Those three hours became the whole eternity, endless eternity. There was no time, there was no passage of time; it was the virgin reality—uncorrupted, untouchable, unmeasurable.

And that day something happened that has continued—not as a continuity—but it has still continued as an undercurrent. Not as a permanency—each moment it has been happening again and again. It has been a miracle each moment.

Rajneesh graduated from the D. N. Jain College with a B.A. in Philosophy in 1955, and was an All-India debating champion in the same year. He continued at Saugar University and earned his M.A. in Philosophy with distinction in 1957. Subsequently he was appointed Lecturer at Raipur Sanskrit College that same year, and joined the faculty of the Mahakoshal Arts College of the University of Jabalpur in 1958, teaching there until 1966 (see Joshi 1982: 76-77, 185-86). While at Jabalpur, he began speaking in public on religious topics. In June 1964 he led his first ten-day Meditation Camp at Muchala Mahavir in the hills of Rajasthan (Joshi 1982:81). On each of the four mornings he gave an address; in the evening he answered questions. Those present were asked to practise two meditations he had devised: in the morning a sitting meditation concentrating on the navel, and in the evening a prone relaxation. [The earliest talks are contained in *The Perfect Way* (Rajneesh 1984)].

After resigning from the University in 1966, Rajneesh began to travel around India, preaching and publicly challenging conventional religious and political thought. He was supported by a group of Indian businessmen,who were probably mainly Jains. In 1968 he settled in Bombay. At this time he used the title *Acharya* (Teacher), a term claimed by graduates in some traditional Indian academic disciplines, including Sanskrit and Philosophy, but also by religious teachers including Jain monks. His first books were published by Motilal Banarsidass, a prominent Jain firm; his

supporters may have been a combination of Jains and some
wealthy Bombay theosophists; his first initiated sannyasin, Ma
Yoga Laxmi, certainly was a Jain.

In a meditation camp at Nargol, Gujarat, in 1970, Rajneesh
introduced what was to become the major meditation practice of
his movement, Dynamic Meditation. This is a noisy, physically
demanding series of exercises, often undertaken, even in public,
in a state of near nudity.

In September of that year, he initiated his first six disciples
including Chinmayananda at a camp held at Manali. There would,
he announced, henceforth be three categories of disciple or
sannyasin, significantly using the Hindu term and not the Jain.
The first category would take *sannyasa* for a few months, follow
some kind of spiritual discipline at a secluded place, then return
to their old lives. (They would be "temporary Sannyasins" possibly an indication of the influence of Satyananda's practice on
him.) The second category would

> continue in their occupations as before, but they will now be
> actors and not doers, and they will also be witnesses to life
> and to living. (Rajneesh 1985 : 619)

Members of this category were to bear the title *Sadhu* and to
wear white. [Gordon (1987 : 50) suggests that within a few years
there were "hundreds or thousands or 'white Sannyasins' (Indians who did not wear the mala or colours)."] The third category
were expected to

> go so deep into the bliss and ecstasy of sannyasa that the
> question of their return to their old world will not arise.
> They will bear no responsibilities as will make it necessary
> for them to be tied to their families: nobody will depend on
> them and no one will be hurt by their withdrawal from
> society. The last category of sannyasins will live in meditation
> and carry the message of meditation to those who are thirsty
> for it.
>
>   (Rajneesh 1985 : 619)

They were to wear orange robes, and to be known either as *Swami*
(Master) or *Ma* (Mother) (Rajneesh 1985 : 619-20).

By this time the movement around him had been formalised

under the name *Jeevan Jagriti Kendra* (Life Awakening Centres), with I. N. Shah as its Secretary. The Kendra, first founded in 1965, aimed to conduct Rajneesh's tours and meditation camps, to publish his lectures and the quarterly magazine *Jyoti Shikha* (Divine Flame), as well as the monthly bulletin *Yukranda* (Religious Youth). The major language of the movement was Hindi, with some use of English.

In Bombay, Rajneesh's disciples soon came to include more Europeans. The book *I am The Gate* is based on questions and answers from between April and June 1971, and carries an Introduction by Ma Anand Pratima,"World President of Neo-Sannyasa International, New York, USA" (1975 : 9-12). After 1973 Rajneesh dropped the title *Acharya* and began to call himself *Bhagwan*. The latter title can mean "a person who has merged with God", and has so been used by many outstanding Indian teachers. It can also mean "God". When asked several years later why he called himself God, Rajneesh replied: "Because I am. . ."

He then continued:

> And because you are. And because only God is. The choice is not between whether to be a God or not to be a God, the choice is whether to recognise it or not. You can choose not to answer the call, but you cannot choose not to be (Joshi 1982, 111).

In March 1974, Rajneesh left Bombay and moved to the hill town of Poona in the Maharashtra State. The Rajneesh Foundation was established in 1975, under the leadership of Ma Yoga Laxmi, who was credited not only with the first wearing of orange robes but also the design of the one hundred and eight bead necklace (*mala*) with Rajneesh's picture on it which all his disciples wore. The Jeevan Jagriti Kendra was wound down; its members were asked to wear orange all the time and call themselves *swami* or *ma* while continuing to lead their normal daily lives. In ordinary Indian society, this was asking a good deal, and the movement soon became predominantly European in its membership.

In Poona, Rajneesh spent most of his time in the privacy of his own quarters, appearing only in the morning to drive the several hundred yards to his discourse presentation, and in the evening to meet small groups in *darshan* (audience with a holy person), in which he conferred *sannyasa*, welcomed disciples who had come to the *ashram*, farewelled those who were leaving, and answered questions on the problems arising in his disciples' personal lives.

The morning discourses lasted some ninety minutes. They were delivered one month in English, the next in Hindi. (The Hindi discourses were always given to much smaller audiences, as the English speaking population around the *ashram* tended to move to Goa.) On one day Rajneesh would deal with a few verses from a particular religious scripture; on the next he would answer questions, which were sometimes related to the scripture but more often not. Between 1974 and 1980, the English discourses covered Patanjali's *Yoga Sutras;* the *Isa, Atma Pooja, Akahya,* and *Mandukya upanishads;* the *Dhammapada, Diamond* and *Heart Sutras,* together with some tantric Buddhist texts; various Zen stories and writings; the *Tao Te Ching* and anecdotes about Chuang Tzu and Lieh Tzu; Sufi tales (but never the *Koran);* Kabir and the wandering Bengali mystic poets known as Bauls; the Sermon on the Mount; the gnostic *Gospel of Thomas;* Jewish Hasid stories; Heraclitus, Pythagorus and Dionyius the Aeropagite; Mabel Collin's *Light on the Path;* and even the *Desiderata.* In Hindi, Rajneesh spoke at length on the *Bhagavad Gita;* Mahavir; and on various Hindi devotional (*bhakti*) mystics. In form the discourses invariably consisted of a long preamble, followed by commentary on the selected verses. They were delivered spontaneously, on the basis of a few notes Rajneesh had on a clipboard which he held in front of him as he sat comfortably on a lounge chair, and were punctuated from time to time by the jokes he laboriously read. After 1979, the number of jokes rose rapidly and many appeared to have been drawn from *Playboy* or similar sources.

Evening *Darshan* was always conducted in English once the few Indian disciples present had been dealt with in Hindi and dismissed. The quality of interaction between Rajneesh and his disciples also declined visibly during 1979. Written records of both his discourses and *darshan*s were published. Joshi (1982 : 199) counts one hundred and twenty-eight volumes of English discourses, one hundred and forty-four of Hindi discourses, and sixty-four *darshan* "diaries".

Unexpectedly, Rajneesh suddenly stopped speaking in public

in March 1981 and it was announced he had "entered into silence", the final phase of his work. The administration of the *ashram* and its affairs were entrusted to Ma Laxmi and a senior English therapist Swami Anand Teertha. Rajneesh then secretly left the *ashram* which was apparently to be wound down. In June after much speculation, he reappeared in America, where it was said he had gone for medical treatment. Rajneesh eventually settled on a 64.229 acre ranch in Central Oregon and this now became the centre of his movement. Disciples in Poona were left to relocate to America or return home as best they could.

In America, leadership of the movement was placed firmly in the hands of Ma Anand Sheela, who consolidated "Rajneeshism" for the first time into a tight and highly authoritarian political structure. A few thousand disciples worked long hours to transform the run-down farm into a utopian ecological community (Larkin *et at* 1987). Four times a year many thousands more *sannyasins* flew in from around the world for the major festivals, the most important of which was Master's Day, as *Guru Purnima* was retitled. In 1984 Rajneesh was refused permanent residence in America, partly because he was not teaching, partly because of various immigration and taxation charges likely to be brought against him before long. In October 1984 he therefore began speaking to small groups again. After July 1985, the audiences were further increased.

On 14 September 1985, Sheela suddenly left the ranch, followed the next day by ten other senior officials. Rajneesh himself left the Ranch on October 27 with three female disciples and was arrested the next morning when his chartered jet landed in Charlotte, North Carolina. He was tried in a court of law on the 14th November 1985 on some thirty-four charges particularly related to immigration offences, and entered an "Alfred plea" of guilty to two of the charges. After paying a fine of $ 400,000, and being ordered to leave America within the next five days, he departed immediately together with a different group of very rich disciples. After returning to India, where there were likely to be further investigations into the financial affairs of the earlier *ashram*, Rajneesh left for Nepal, then in January 1986 began travelling around the world. When he returned to India in July 1986, he had been deported from or denied entry to some twenty-one countries (Appleton, 1987). The *ashram* was re-established in Poona.

Rajneesh passed away on the 19th January 1990. *The Illustrated Weekly of India* (February 11-17, 1990) suggested that he may have been poisoned by his disciples. His disciples insisted he was still suffering from radiation poisoning received while he was held in American prisons. At the time of his death he was known simply by the Japanese buddhist title "Osho", (Beloved Master), which he had assumed in February 1989 after announcing on New Year's Eve that he had become the vehicle for the coming Buddha. (A claim he almost as quickly dismissed as a joke.)

The Path of Love

No one book by Rajneesh is considered the essence of his teachings of which *sannyasa* is an integral part. Rather, those teachings appear again and again throughout his different works, now as commentary on these verses, then as commentary on those verses from quite different religious traditions. In order to examine his teachings in some depth, an analysis will be made of one work, selected more or less at random, *The Path of Love: Discourses on Songs of Kabir* (1978). The book records eleven talks given at the Shree Rajneesh Ashram in Poona, between 21-31 December 1976, on eleven poems by the medieval mystic Kabir.

Kabir may have been born in 1398 and died as late as 1518 as tradition holds. ("Anything is possible", says his American poet translator, Robert Bly 1972: end note). The latest research by Vaudeville (1974 : 36-39) tentatively suggests the dates of 1398-1448). Kabir was the son of a Muslim weaver in Benares, and a follower of the liberal Vaishnava teacher Ramananda, who worshipped God without form. He was a religious reformer and opponent of caste. Today his sect is followed by nearly a million north Indians. Rajneesh's comments are based on translations in *One Hundred Poems of Kabir* (1915) by Rabindranath Tagore and Evelyn Underhill. At the time of the translations Kabir was considered by Bengali intellectuals to be "a great mystic", "the herald of Universal Religion", "a champion of the unity of mankind" and "a bold social reformer" (Vaudeville, 1974:19). Rajneesh himself says of Kabir in *Books I have Loved*:

> Nothing like *The Songs of Kabir* exists in the whole world. Kabir is incredibly beautiful . . . Kabir, I love you as I have never any other man.
>
> (Rajneesh 1985 : 55)

In what follows, our treatment of Rajneesh's discourses on Kabir will be presented thematically.

God

In *The Path of Love*, Osho presents a theology of immanent vitalism. God is, on the one hand, beyond all time and experience (93, 96). On the other hand, nothing is "outside of God" for God has no "outside". A rock may be only matter, it has no soul or mind; man has both—this is his agony and his ecstasy (59); but God is "pure consciousness", He only has His interiority (124).

God is formless, yet reveals Himself in a myriad of forms:

> The creator is not separate from His creation. He is involved in it, He is in it, He *is* it. Creator is creation . . . God is a dynamic creativity (209).

In endless ways, the creator is revealed through the world as it is:

> Each flower is an invitation, an appointment with God. Each song of the bird, and each cloud floating in the sky, is something like a message, a coded message. You have to decode it, you have to look deep into it, you have to be silent and listen to the message (22).

Creation is not finished, as in the traditional Christian understanding: rather, it is an ongoing process. The world is a dance, not a "painting" (210). It is also, in the classical Hindu term, a *leela*, a game, God's sport. He divides Himself into many forms and enters into everything:

> Somewhere He is the man and somewhere He is the woman, and they sing songs of life and dance dances of love. Somewhere he is the master and somewhere the disciple— the same polarity. Somewhere He is matter and somewhere He is mind; and somewhere He is sound and somewhere he is soundlessness; and somewhere He has become life and somewhere He has become death . . . but the same polarity (133-34).

This is not duality. If:

> the whole existence is a hollow bamboo—God flowing

through it, being expressed in millions of ways (232),

then an interdependence is created:

the formless needs form to be expressed through, God needs you as much as you need Him (232).

Imagine, Rajneesh suggests,

God without existence ... it will be just emptiness, a wasteland. Think of God without trees and without rivers and without oceans: think of God without man and bird and animals: think of God without sun and moon and stars ... and it will be just a wasteland, a desert (233).

The whole depends on the parts; the parts on the whole (233).
It is a play. God plays the role of wife, son, husband, even enemy, "to make life a little more exhilarating", richer, more creative and dynamic (184). But this is the secret of human existence:

Nothing is needed. We *are* in the play, God is the other partner, and this whole love affair has continued for ever and ever. We have just forgotten: we have forgotten the obvious (20).

God is humanity's centre and true nature.

Human Existence
Man is not separate from nature and cannot be (31). Life is "a process" (159, 321); it is dynamic, like a river, sometimes flowing north, sometimes south, sometimes to both sides, until, one day "it reaches the ocean." (159)
Because perfection is a static state, it cannot be part of life. "Perfection means there is no possibility to grow"; it means death, "everything is finished, the full point has been reached" (321).
Each individual is unique (217), and must discover his or her own identity (80-81), "create his own path while walking on it" (32). All other animals are satisfied as they are; the human being is "discontent in his very soul", constantly restless and in search of his own being (59). "Man is a promise," Osho insists:

he can be, but is not yet—so there is hope and there is fear, there is possibility and there is apprehension. It may happen and it may not, so man is never in certainty (60).

The search arises because of man's dual nature:

Man is tremendous because he bridges matter and mind, he bridges the world and God. With one hand he holds matter, with the other he holds God. He is the bridge. Look at the beauty of your humanity, the glory ... and that is your anguish too—because man is always being pulled apart, torn apart. On one side matter pulls him, on the other the call of God: on one side material possessions, on the other side love, prayer, meditation: on one side ambition, money, respect, on the other side silence, beauty, good (124).

In the Third Discourse, Rajneesh cites Nietzsche's use of the bridge metaphor, recalling that

man is a rope stretched between two eternities: the eternity of nature and the eternity of God (59).

It is impossible to rest on the bridge, one must go on; our very being is the quest for truth, to "come home", recognise, know and encounter ourselves (115). Human birth is not enough; as Jesus said, a spiritual rebirth is also necessary (203).

Mind and Illusion

Man's alienation from himself is caused by the "mind". Here Rajneesh's Vedantism (and his similarity to Krishnamurti) becomes very explicit. Insofar as the mind is cognitive, it depends on the senses. Insofar as it is rational, it relies on memory, logical categories and language. Memory derives from the past, not the present. Categories constrict by forcing shifting reality into small frames. Language fixes experience and is the final villain: "The whole problem has arisen out of naming things" (126). Naming creates distinctions and oppositions (male/female, young/old, like us/enemies, etc.). It creates false security: we think we know, and we do not; the world becomes "second-hand" (148), not the world God creates, but the world we have created from a dead past.

Even most suffering—anger, hatred, ambition, greed, jealousy, and so on—is "bogus", "meaningless", "irrelevant" (116). Suffering arises from our illusions as to who we think we are, while "that which you think yourself to be right now is not your real nature. It is a deception that you have managed. It is a hallucination, it is an auto-hypnosis" (118). The world of "poverty, violence and greed" is "your projection" and "vibrates with your ugliness" (206).

The Search for Truth

Rajneesh suggests that there are four stages in the search for truth which is the ultimate purpose of human existence. He structures these stages around the levels of existence described in the *Mandukya Upanishad* (see page 24 above), another indication of his underlying Vedantism.

The first stage is that of the jungle or deep sleep (*sushupti*). The jungle is a place of sloth, with no paths; it is the lowest state of consciousness, or almost complete unconsciousness. In it, man is subject to whims and desires, instincts, impulses, obsessions and insanities (68). The person who lives here is not an individual, but a crowd with "many selves" and "no soul" (63). The person in the jungle lives in complete ignorance. He is no more interested in answers than he is in questions: "any stupid answer will do" (63). Borrowed answers are sufficient to provide the knowledge and security he needs.

At this stage, a certain type of religion is attractive: a religion based on the claim of others to know about God. It is a fixed and dogmatic religion, emphasising knowledge and not personal experience. It will be against life, because life is "dangerous" (66). Ascetic and punitive, burdened by a sense of guilt, it will try to tether the individual to living at the minimum, escaping this world in favour of another, constantly moral, heavily ritualistic and reliant on ancient scriptures. Such a religion is pathological, a neurotic expression of guilt and self-loathing.

The second stage is that of the forest, of dreaming (*swapna*). This is the land of:

> the starry-eyed, the hippie, the so-called religious searcher, the drug-addict—trying to find any way, any means, shortcuts, to somehow get out of the forest (70).

The dreamer may be a fool but at least he has begun to search. The problem is that there are too many paths. In the jungle belief is settled, orthodox, the priest has all the answers. In the forest, the fool exercises his own individuality, but is confused because he has moved to the other extreme: all the answers are available but he has no criterion on which to base a decision. He lives in the sub-conscious.

There may even be a certain reasonableness in the seeker's confusion. Past religious certainty was the result of the isolation of different religious traditions from each other. This is no longer possible. Confusion is, therefore, inevitable:

> Even for an idiotic Christian, it is very difficult to continue to believe in one life, because millions of Hindus, Jains, Sikhs—half the world is not a small matter—half the world says there is rebirth, reincarnation. Now it is impossible not to listen to this other half, and they also have their reasonings (315).

But this is still the confusion of a plurality of other people's answers; the dreamer is still asleep.

The third stage, the garden, is that of awakening (*jagriti*). Here the searcher is not interested in books, guides or teachers; the quest is personal and insistent. It involves unlearning, rather than more learning. Being arduous, it is for the few (115, 145):

> That hurts, because you would like religion to be for everybody. But I cannot help it. If music cannot be for everybody, and painting cannot be for everybody, and dancing cannot be for everybody, then—excuse me, I cannot help it—religion too cannot be for everybody (103).

In accordance with tradition, the third stage takes place in the presence of a Master, the *guru*. Not a metaphysician; for the metaphysician "talks without knowing" (231). Not a mystic, for the mystic knows but keeps quiet (231). Or, if he speaks, his experience, which was without words, is translated by his mind (a mind formed by society) and retranslated by the mind of the listener, which is "a thousand miles away" from the original experience (175). The Master is both: he "knows as much as can be known, and yet is articulate enough to express, to communicate" (231).

The communication consists of the destruction of all answers in favour of the one question: "Who Am I?". Only an individual can answer this question:

> When your answer is left there, and there is no answer from the outside, you start falling into yourself.

Thus:

> The question penetrates you like an arrow to the very source of your being—and *there* is the answer. And that answer is not verbal. It is not a theory that you can come across. It is a realisation. You explode. You simply know. It is not knowledge, you know. It is experience. It is existential (76).

Enlightenment comes in that moment in whcih the mind "disappears". Droppping out of language, the searcher drops out of religion and everything that is man-made (127), and touches his or her own centre. Paradoxically, the Master, who seems to exist outside of the disciple, is then found to be "within you: your centre". For the outer Master serves only to point the searcher to the inner Master, whom Kabir calls "the Guest", He who comes uninvited and unannounced, God. (The outer Master exists because "man needs a few fictions to live" (158), nothing more.)

Rajneesh claims that with this experience, the nature of religion is completely transformed. Saviours are symbols of what is possible for the individual. They are not still existing literal figures whose experience can substitute for that of the believer:

> Krishna, Buddha, Christ—these are not the names of certain persons. They denote a certain state, the same state. Christ means the one who has realised himself, and through that realisation has realised the whole: one who has come home, who can say "I am God". The same is the meaning of Buddha, or Jaina, or Krishna (117).

The written words of scriptures count for nothing. The source of all scriptures is in the soul:

> Now you need not go to the *Koran*. You can go to your inner interval and again the messenger will come and say 'Recite'.

(This is the opening word of the *Koran* and the beginning of the revelation to Muhammad.)

Whenever there is an interval, God's messengers are around you. When there is tremendous silence, God is within you. You are fulfilled (129).

Prayer becomes listening, not speaking and demanding (176). Meditation and prayer do not "make God flow towards you", they simply record that "God is flowing towards you" (108), God being willing (like a lover) to take the initiative in these matters (90).

Finally, the attitude to self and society changes. Rajneesh dismisses social morality as false, hypocritical and violent. Spirituality is a gift (325), which expresses itself as one allows oneself to:

laugh, love, be alive, dance, sing, become a hollow bamboo, and let His song flow through you (252).

True religion is inner harmony, "to let go into yourself" (217). Men have been fighting and killing in the name of abstractions throughout the ages; it is time to love specific human beings, trees, rocks:

love the immediate. Enjoy this moment, don't prepare for tomorrow. Today is beautiful: delight in it, let it be a celebration (249).

Osho admits that he teaches what might be considered selfishness. But he insists: Know who you are. Love yourself so that you can love others. Live in the moment, "delightfully, celebrating". In this way "become a Buddha, awakened. That's all you can do" (53).

By so doing, the searcher has reached the fourth stage, that of being "at home", known in the *Upanishads* as *turiya*, the fourth, about which nothing can be said. Here all duality disappears. The experience is nameless and already present. Even the journey itself is an illusion.

Renunciation

Because Rajneesh's approach to religion is so different, it is evident that his understanding of *sannyasa* is likely to be very different from the traditional, orthodox understanding. Certainly he used some of the external features of the role: the titles, the

new name, orange robes, and the one hundred and eight beads.
Disciples were encouraged to meditate for an hour every day. But
these features were "just a device to help you—to help you
toward freedom, to bring you toward total action" (Rajneesh
1975 : 43). They were a sign of personal commitment to change
and growth, a reminder to the individual and to those around
and not the essence of a traditional institution.

In fact, no beliefs and no rules were to be given to his *sannyasins*.
That was logically impossible. Such would be external imposi-
tions, false answers to someone else's questions:

> You are totally free. I throw you into an openness. That is
> what is meant by initiation. It is not narrowing you down.
> It is giving you an open sky. It is just pushing you to fly in
> an open sky. Of course, there are no routes and no road
> maps. There cannot be. And there cannot be any road in the
> sky. So you have to fly alone, you have to depend on
> yourself alone. Your existence will be the sole company—
> the only company (Rajneesh 1975 : 44).

Sannyasa means complete freedom:

> taking life as a dream; rejecting all claims of being somebody;
> being insecure; living moment to moment; being total; being
> free; being courageous; giving all one's energies towards
> growing something; accepting the human being as he is—
> totally with no denial at all, even in the area of sexuality
> (Rajneesh 1975 : 39-50).

Rajneesh saw this as a totally new form of *sannyasa* "or totally
an ancient one which has been forgotten completely," (Rajneesh
1975 : 44). The old system had given way to social renunciation
and imitation, systems destructive of inner freedom (Rajneesh
1975 : 44). The new system was to be positive, basically spiritual,
demanding no superficial changes but the deeper, inner, spiritual
transformation of the mind (Rajneesh 1975 : 45). Inner desires
were to be transcended, accepted and surpassed, not denied
(Rajneesh 1975 : 46). Even sex would be transcended once the
inner flowering had taken place (Rajneesh 1973).

The challenge he presented to the old tradition is expressed in
answer to a question in *The Art of Dying* (Rajneesh 1978b). The

question is this:

> Why do you give us these religious titles? They seem absurd.
> Outside the ashram Indians seldom call me swami with a
> straight face (Rajneesh 1978b : 37).

The answer begins by explaining that although the word *swami*
means "lord", it is only given to the disciple to indicate his path.
"The path is that you become lord of yourself". The title is not
meant to make others "slaves to you", and one must not "hanker"
after this. In fact it is dangerous if others call one *swami*, because
then one may start feeling that "you are a holy man or something". This is nonsense. "I am not here to make you holy or
saintly or anything" (Rajneesh 1978b : 38). The religious titles are
absurd. They help the individual laugh at himself. To want to
become special is "irreligious" (Rajneesh 1978b : 38).

They also show that the sacred and the profane are not two
things: the profane is sacred, the ordinary is extraordinary, the
natural is supernatural. God is in the world:

> The old concept of a religious man is that he is anti-life. He
> condemns this life, this ordinary life—he calls it mundane,
> profane, illusion. He denounces it. I am so deeply in love
> with life that I cannot denounce it. I am here to enhance the
> feeling for it (Rajneesh 1978b : 38).

When worn by a doctor, an engineer, a labourer, in the market
of a factory, the robes will act to dissolve the differences in
society, rather than reinforcing them.

Rajneesh delighted in the challenge he was providing to the
old system in destroying the superiority of the traditional
sannyasins and their "holier than thou" attitude. He states:

> You cannot conceive of what is happening. When an orange-
> robed sannyasin walks with his girl friend on the street, you
> cannot conceive what is happening. It has never happened
> in India, not for ten thousand years. People cannot believe
> it—and you are expecting they should call you swami? It is
> enough that they are not killing you! You are destroying
> their whole tradition. A sannyasin was one who would
> never *look* at a woman. Touching was out of the question—
> and holding the hand, impossible! That was enough to

throw him into hell (Rajneesh 1978b : 39).

The new kind of *sannyasa*, "neo-sannyasa", is thus deliberately intended to destroy the difference between the marketplace and the monastery. It is a resacralisation of the patterns of ordinary life.

The answer concludes:

> That is what I would like you to become. Be ordinary, but bring a quality of awareness to your ordinary life. Bring God to your ordinary life, introduce God into your ordinary life. Sleep, eat, love, pray, meditate, but don't think you are making or doing something special. And then you will be special. A man who is ready to live an ordinary life is an extraordinary man. Because to be extraordinary, to desire to be extraordinary, is a very ordinary desire. To relax and to be ordinary is really extraordinary (Rajneesh 1978b : 42).

It was a brave paradoxical attempt by an intelligent and sensitive man to redeem what he believed to be the core of Indian teaching on renunciation and to turn it into an attitude of world affirmation. How far his Australian disciples understood and attempted to follow him is the subject matter of a later chapter.

PART FOUR

AUSTRALIAN RENUNCIATES

CHAPTER SIX

RELIGION AND ASIAN RELIGIONS IN AUSTRALIA

The Denominational Experience

From the beginning of white settlement, the Christian religion has held an embattled position in the Australian society. There were no religious motives behind the foundation of the colony, as there were in other European settlements in North and South America (Hogan 1987 : 9). Indeed, there was no church building, until 1793: this was erected at the personal expense of the one Anglican chaplain and was soon burned to the ground, not to be replaced for many years (Breward 1988 : 2). The majority of members of the First Fleet of 1788 were nominally Anglican. There was also a significant minority of Catholics (Hogan 1987 : 10) but the first permanent Catholic priests did not arrive until 1820 (Mol 1972 : 27).

In accordance with the pattern of recruiting immigrants from England and Wales, Scotland and Ireland, a pattern of varied denominational adherence soon developed. In England the Anglican Church was "by law established" under the 1559 *Second Act of Supremacy;* the Presbyterian Church became the "established" church in Scotland after the *Act of Union* of 1707 (Srivasta 1983 : 273). No church was "established" in Australia. Instead allowances were paid after 1825 to Anglican, Catholic and Presbyterian chaplains alike (Mol 1972 : 28). Not surprisingly, convicts and emancipists both rejected the compulsory religion and morality of the Protestant ruling class, and, in the bush, away from churches and parsons, no priority was placed on religion at all (Breward 1988 : 4).

During the second half of the nineteenth century, the states abolished financial aid to religion and denominational schools

(Mol 1972: 28). In 1901, Section 116 of the *Constitution* for the Commonwealth of Australia provided that:

> the Commonwealth shall not make any law for establishing any religion, or for prohibiting the free exercise of any religion, and no religious tests shall be required for any office or public trust under the Commonwealth.

These words closely follow the *Constitution of the United States*, Art. VI, sec. 3, and Amendment 1, and seem to have been added to the Australian Constitution as an afterthought (Quick and Garran 1901: 204). An attempt by the Commonwealth government to extend the freedoms guaranteed under this clause was decisively rejected at a national referendum in 1988.

Methodism, an English alternative to Anglicanism, became a major denomination by 1881 (Mol 1972 : 31). These four denominations—Anglican, Catholic, Presbyterian and Methodist (the latter two being largely combined in 1977 to form the Uniting Church of Australia)—have dominated the public religious identification of 80 per cent of the Australian population (Mol 1972 : 31) until very recently.

Religiousness in Australia

Religious identification is different from commitment, membership, involvement and belief (Bouma and Dixon 1987 : 3). In 1983, the Australian Values Study Survey sampled the values and attitudes of one thousand two hundred and twenty-eight Australians (six hundred and twenty women: six hundred and eight men) from all cities and across the country areas of the nation. The study included persons belonging to the major denominations, the smaller denominations, and those claiming no affiliation at all. On the basis of its findings, Bouma and Dixon (1987 : v), conclude that it cannot be said that Australia is essentially secular and irreligious when:

1. 57.9 per cent of Australians claim to be religious persons and only 4.5 per cent claim to be atheists.
2. 57.4 per cent of Australians rate the importance of God in their lives as six or more on a scale of one to ten. Only 13.7 per cent rated God as one (not at all important).
3. 85.6 per cent of Australians identify with some religious group.

4. Two-thirds of Australians pray, meditate or contemplate occasionally or more frequently.
5. 27.1 per cent of Australians claim to go to church once per month or more frequently.
6. Nearly half of those who claim to have no religion pray, meditate or contemplate occasionally or more frequently.

The denominations play a limited role in expressing religion in Australian society. They are divisive of social integrity (Mol 1972 : 28) and irrelevant to the major concerns of the state. Although most Australians (85.6 per cent) identify with them, few (27.1 per cent) use them to anchor concepts of God or spiritual practices. If Bouma and Dixon are correct, and Australians are essentially neither secular nor irreligious, how is religion expressed outside of the denominational Christian mainstream?

Two answers, at least, are possible.

The Australian Myth

The first relies on the existence of a widespread but seldom articulated communal "myth" to do with the Australian landscape and destiny. The outlines of the myth have been described in Millikan *The Sunburnt Soul* (1981) and Brady *A Crucible of Prophets* (1981).

At the core of an Australian experience is the land, the "vast and silent spiritual heart" of the desert (Millikan 1981 : 27), which has meant only frustration and disappointment for the white settler. Brady suggests that the savagery and irrationality of the environment so overwhelmed the first settlers that it rendered the traditional myths of human society and nature as "part of a benign, benevolent and orderly divine economy" completely untenable. This was a world in which God seemed powerless, the only true power being blind necessity—"physical necessity first of all, and then secondly historical necessity": this, she suggests, was the primary challenge facing the settlers and it remains true today. Millikan (1981 : 27) cites Manning Clark's Boyer lectures to argue that climate and environment:

> ... gradually made us ... fatalists, accepters, and sceptics about the fruits of human endeavour. The spirit of the place had contributed to an Australian understanding of failure— to our conviction that no matter how hard a man might try he

was bound to fail, that in Australia the spirit of the place
makes a man aware of his insignificance, of his impatience. . .

The character produced by such a harsh environment is isolated, inarticulate, unintellectual, and beaten (Millikan 1981 : 63).
In contemporary culture, he is glorified by his common touch and
egalitarian spirit (Millikan 1981 : 15), his self-reliance and scorn for
conventions of social rank, his impatience with abstract thought
and concern for the immediate in matters of sex, morality, personal
certainty and the existence of God. (See Millikan 1981 : 54), where
the examples of Paul Hogan, Norman Gunston and Ned Kelly are
cited as representative of the image). Brady speaks of "the great
refusal" to face the land which leads to an easy opting for security,
and attitudes of fear, boredom, repression, spiritual cowardice
and, potentially, great violence.

Both authors see the way out of this impasse in terms of a
renewed religious experience. Millikan describes himself as, "like
many born in the 1940s", being among the last participants in the
church's heyday, for whom the church was an accepted social
reality (1981 : 48). He looks for an Australian Jesus, with "an
Australian iconoclasm and laconic humour" (1981 : 111). Brady is
more mystical. One must accept the risk of "love in the full sense
of the word", accept emotional intensity without withdrawing,
recognise the body and the instinctual life, and commit oneself
fully to another (human and/or divine). If evil is "the consciousness of being at odds with some larger order of things" (1981 : 91),
then freedom derives from the recognition of one's limitations, on
the one hand, but also through being able to situate oneself within
"a mysterious, often painful but always worshipful cosmos"
(1981 : 112).

Brady and Millikan read the Australian myth from the texts of
literature and popular culture respectively. The French literary
sociologist Lucien Goldman (1975) has argued that writers and
philosophers are "privileged" in the degree of depth and clarity
which they are able to bring to bear to the articulation of particular
"world views" belonging to specific social groups. Not all Australians would be able to describe the full dimensions of the myth, or
accept the supernatural resolution offered, but it seems likely that
most individuals would recognise particular parts of it and be able
to provide their own symbols for the path out of wilderness.

Asian Religions

A second way of expressing an alternative religious conscious-ness outside the denominational mainstream has involved a turn-ing away from Christianity towards other great religious tradi-tions, especially Hinduism and Buddhism. These Asian traditions have long been represented in Australia by immigrant adherents (Croucher 1989 : 1-18, on Buddhism; Bilimoria 1989 : 15-22, on Hinduism). The major ideas of both the systems have been avail-able to the European enquirers in a modified form for over a century through the Theosophical Society, which has branches in every capital city (Roe 1986). Both Hinduism and Buddhism attained widespread popularity after the mid-sixties. Over the next decade Australia was visited by a wide range of *gurus* around whom committed followings grew, including Swami Ranganathananda (of the Ramakrishna-Vivekananda Mission), Maharishi Makesh Yogi (Transcendental Meditation), Baba Muktananda (Siddha Yoga), Guru Maharajji (Divine Light), Meher Baba, Sri Chinmoy, Swami Satchidananda, Swami Venkatesananda and Swami Satyananda. Breward (1988 : 79) notes the "marked increase in the variety of Australian religiosity" which dates from 1965, stating that:

> the desire to experience new kinds of community led a number of thoughtful and idealistic people to reject the patterns of vocation, family life and religion with which they had grown up.

These people were seldom fully-integrated member of conven-tional middle-class Australian society.

Switching to an Asian Religion

The interest in Asian religions was limited to a small number of persons. For example, Ananda Marga claimed a maximum of five hundred members in the late 1970s; the Hare Krishna movement had two hundred full-time members (Crowley 1986 : 254-55). Several reasons may be proposed for this.

The first is probably the strongly racist nature of the mainstream of Australian society (Dalton 1973), which has little interest in, and less respect for, Asian cultures.

Secondly, despite widespread indifference to belief of any kind, religious groups outside the major denominations have little

legitimacy in mainstream Australian society. Bouma and Dixon
(1987 : 53) found that 31.3 per cent of persons surveyed would not
like "members of minority religious sects or cults" as neighbours.
(Other positive dislike was directed towards heavy drinkers, 55.6
per cent; persons with a criminal record, 42.4 per cent; emotionally
unstable people, 38.8 per cent; homosexuals, 33.2 per cent; left-
wing extremists, 29.5 per cent; and right-wing extremists, 25.9 per
cent). A credibility poll released in the daily media on October 21,
1986, asking for a rating between one to ten for a selection of well
known politicians, actors, celebrities and media stars, found Paul
Hogan, Bill Cosby and Bob Geldoff rated most highly, while
Rajneesh scored a low 1.45, a little above Ferdinand Marcos at 1.22
and just below Queensland premiere Sir Joh Bjelke Peterson (*Mesto
Muse*, November, 1986: 10). This dislike is common in the popular
press. In mid 1988, for example, the May issue of *The Australian
Woman's Weekly* ran an article on " Combating the Cults that Prey
on our Children"; June *Cosmopolitan* coyly asked "Could you be
seduced by Sects Appeal ?", stating that the sects recruit from
"hypnotised, brainwashed or just naive people"; and the *Bulletin*,
9 August, detailed leadership problems in ISKCON under the
heading "Crisis among the chanters", in its Anthropology section.

Thirdly, switching to an Asian religion in Australia offers no
social advantages. Membership does not offer social prestige, the
possibility of intermarriage or of economic advancement. In Malaysia and Singapore, Chinese and Indian converts to Islam and
Christianity are like converts elsewhere, "young, unmarried, mobile, relatively friendless, educated and urban" (Tamney and
Hassan 1987 : 12). Lim Hin Fui (1983 : 39) has shown that 50 per
cent of the conversions in Malaysia to Islam which he studied could
be accounted for by the desire to marry a Muslim partner. Tamney
and Hassan (1987 : 12) agree with the importance of marriage as a
factor in conversion in Singapore. That this is not commonly a
significant factor in even conventional switching in Australia is
shown by Mol (1972 : 32-33), who suggests that intermarriage may
account for at best 5 per cent of all conversions to Anglicanism and
6 per cent to Catholicism. Amran Kasimin (1985 : 96) indicates that
access to the special economic privileges granted to Malays, who
are by definition Muslims, accounted for a large portion of Chinese
conversions to Islam during the late seventies (see also Lim Hin Fui
1983 : 39).

Conclusion

So why should even a small number of Australians consider the possibility of converting to an Asian religion and adopting an apparently deviant lifestyle?

In Australia, religion is considered a private matter; as Cock (1979 : 237) notes "we have been socialized to live essentially private lives in impersonal worlds." The reasons for religious switching, as well as the subsequent rewards, are private rather than social. There is a great deal of truth in the claim of Ackerman and Lee (1983 : 3) that:

> these new religions promote an individualistic mysticism that contributes to the integration of personal identity in a society characterised by highly impersonal patterns of interaction.

Tamney and Hassan (1987 : 11) may take us further. They argue that four conditions are necessary for experimenting with a "foreign" religion:

   (i)   exposure to the new phenomenon;
  (ii)   the opportunity to experiment with it;
 (iii)   experience of a problem for which the innovation is relevant; and
 (iv)   the accordance of legitimacy to the innovation.

It would seem that if an Asian religion offers a solution to a perceived personal problem—the need for personal integration and identity—and if the individual discovers the group, experiments with it and is above all prepared to concede it legitimacy, joining is a viable individual option. Further, when the person lives at the edge of conventional society, the approval of the wider community ceases to be a significant issue. Mullan's assessment of the "average Rajneeshnee" (1983 : 50-51) was that he or she was:

> 'middle-class', well-educated, professionally qualified, has been divorced at least once, has suffered a personal crisis, has been through mysticism, drugs, politics, feminism, and is 'thirtyish'—in short, the counter-culturalist brought up to date.

The next few chapters are devoted to describing the nature of the counter-culture in Australia and the relationship of the disciples to it. Here we may note that many of those attracted to Asian religions after the mid-sixties were marginal to the dominant values of the Australian society, either by force of circumstances or deliberate choice. The identity of the renunciate is one which is both complete and extremely powerful. In adopting this strong and stable, albeit very unconventional, persona, individuals were able to answer the questions which were dormant in conventional society but of major concern to those seeking meaning outside of it: "Who am I ? And how can I ensure that my life has its fullest worth?".

CHAPTER SEVEN

THE "COUNTER-CULTURE"

During the late sixties, a movement opposed to the major political, social and economic values of Australian society became widespread among many educated, middle-class people in their late teens and twenties. The movement had its origin in similar reactions to post World War II industrial society in America and Europe. In this chapter, we shall sketch the major outlines of the "counter-culture" as it existed in Australia from about 1965 to 1975. In the next chapter, we shall see how the values of the counter-culture related to the backgrounds of those drawn to the teachings of Swami Satyananda and Osho.

The End of an Era

On the 10th January 1966, Sir Robert Gordon Menzies resigned, having served as Prime Minister of Australia for over eighteen years. For twenty years Australians had experienced "almost uninterrupted prosperity with stable economic growth, price stability and minimal inflation" (Crowley 1986 : 8), based on a government policy of Full Employment. The policy depended on the continuing growth of the manufacturing industries, many supported by high tariffs; the acceptance of private foreign investment and management; and a favourable overseas balance of trade, heavy reliance on the export of wool, wheat, meat, sugar and dairy products. The foundation of the boom was the immigration programme: Australia's population grew from eight million in 1950 to thirteen million in 1970, including three million immigrants, nearly half from continental Europe (Crowley 1986 : 7-8, 29). Hallmarks of the dominant value-system were a cash income from paid employment or self-employment in a small business; the privatised nuclear family structure; the private ownership of property; urban residence; and definitions of success and identity in terms of material achievement (Muktananda, n.d. : 6). The nuclear family was the consuming unit. As Crowley (1986 : 11-12) writes:

> The husband had a secure job, a 35- or 40-hour, five-day working week, three weeks annual holidays, long service leave, house mortgage, car, motor-mower and possibly also a trailer boat or a caravan or a second "pre-owned" car. The wife had two or three children, a washing machine, refrigerator, vacuum cleaner, radiogram, TV set, Hills Hoist and a paraphernalia of other household goods—mostly being paid off on hire purchase—and, if possible, a part-time job during school hours, to help pay off the children's school clothes, weekend excursions to the beach or the country, annual holidays, the second car or extensions to the house. What they expected for themselves, parents also expected for their children.

The conscious cultural identity of the nation was less secure. John Douglas, in a paper prepared for the Jesuit Order's Asian Bureau Australia in 1972, stated:

> There is certainly an Australian way of life, but it is not a culture in the traditional anthropological sense, with religious values at the apex. It is derived from the anglosaxon Christian tradition in its post-industrialization form. Economic opportunity and social mobility are central keynotes, material and economic values are central; earning-power stratification is also a notable feature. The independent nuclear family with its quarter-acre block is something Australians treasure and strive for. Overall, there is a levelling process and belief that every man is as good as the next and only earning power differentiates them. Our culture is based on the consumer capitalist system of society, where the spiritual element is so unimportant in day-to-day living that the reflectiveness that helps define a cultural identity is not easily discernible ... We do not offer other people

> that come here a higher cultural choice, but a materialistic temptation.
>
> (Cited by Crowley 1986 : 32)

Following the Depression of the thirties, and the six years of World War II, in which Australia was at war because Britain was at war, the materialistic temptation was perhaps natural.

The War, however, not only pulled Australia out of the Depression, it also created a certain mindset which persisted through the fifties and into the sixties. The war taught the importance of discipline, the power of the chain of command, organization, "the subordination of man to country, and everyone doing her part cheerfully and obediently" (Pichaske 1989:1). The enemy lived overseas (particularly in Asia), had his own dangerous ideas (Communism, a Russian philosophy derived from Germany), and envied Australia's wide open spaces and prosperity. Arthur Caldwell supported his post-war immigration policy with the words: "We may only have the next twenty-five years in which to make the best possible use of our second chance to survive" (Crowley 1986 : 8). The military process was one of:

> hair cut, bodies standardized into drill field rows and blocks, eyes straight ahead, chin in, chest out, salute and return salute, all part of a finely tuned machine that goes when it's told to go, holds when told to hold, and fetches on command.
>
> (Pichaske 1989 : 1)

The consequence was a pervasive conservatism, social rigidity, and distrust of ideas (Pischaske 1989 : 3); or as John Gunther noticed in the last of his "Inside" books, "pragmatism, hedonism and philistinism" (Cited in Crowely 1986 : 32).

The Vietnam War

One of Menzies' last significant acts in Parliament was the introduction of compulsory military conscription in November 1964. In April 1965, an Australian battalion was sent to Vietnam, to combat the threat of Communism there and, potentially, to the whole of Southeast Asia, and thus, through the theory of toppling dominoes, to Australia itself. By 1972, some fifty thousand Australians had served in Vietnam and some five hundred died there (Crowley 1986 : 41).

In the beginning, the "Vietnam War" had widespread public support. The Labour Party announced in 1966 that if elected it would abolish compulsory conscription, and suffered one of its most decisive defeats ever. Nevertheless, "a large, vocal and very active minority" remained opposed to Australian involvement, and prepared to present its opposition to the public through whatever other means was available to it now that parliamentary channel was decisively closed (Crowley 1986 : 39). Their protests focused on:

> both the general wrongness of war and on specific issues too: even if war were right, the Vietnam War was wrong; even if the Vietnam War were right, Australian participation was wrong; even if Australian involvement were right, conscription was not. Even ignoring those issues, both American atrocities and Australian use of torture were horrifyingly wrong, even supposing they were not in aid of an ally (South Vietnam) which was a fascist dictatorship.
> (Fred Cole, Association for International Cooperation and Disarmament, cited in Smith and Crossley 1975 : 131).

Opposition to the war was expressed in various ways. There were teach-ins at the universities. There was covert sending of financial assistance to assist the "dissident" (or "patriotic") Vietnamese Forces. And most publicly, there were the street demonstrations which culminated in the Moritorium marches between 1969 and 1971. The march of May 1970 involved about seventy thousand demonstrators in Melbourne, twenty thousand in Sydney, and large crowds in other cities and towns (Crowley 1986 : 37. Cock 1979 : 17 suggests a figure of one hundred thousand for Melbourne). In the September 1970 March, violent scuffles broke out between police and protestors in both capitals, and the police made many arrests. Because the war was not censored, the public media were able to show these conflicts in the living rooms of the nation, and to report that members of the police force had removed their identification numbers in New South Wales or worn false numbers in Western Australia (Smith and Crossley 1975 : 131). Television presented the destruction of war, night after night, in a way never before possible (or permitted). The cry of the frustration felt by many young people is well recorded in

one of Craig McGregor's short stories, when the main character
says helplessly:

> Everyone's dying and everyone's getting hurt and I can't do
> anything about it. I can't make it stop and I can't help any
> of them. I can't even help myself (Cited in Lawton 1988 : 96).

Other Public Protest Movements

The techniques of public protest continued to be used after the
concern with Vietnam. These techniques, and the repeated violence they provoked from politicians and the police, were evident
in the opposition to the touring all-white South African Springbok Rugby Union team, in June to August 1971. In Melbourne one
hundred and fifty-one demonstrators were charged with violent
behaviour. The tour led, according to one journalist (Robert Mayne,
cited in Crowley 1986 : 43), to "uncounted disputes, arguments
and brawls in homes, clubs and hotels about the rights and
wrongs of it all" and was "even more divisive than Vietnam and
conscription." Organiser Meredith Burgmann commented:

> Vietnam did not concern them because it was up there but
> they were faced with this issue every Saturday down here—
> someone was messing around with the football. The hostility
> was incredible (Crowley 1986 : 43).

In the area of the conservation of the environment, public
protests over the commercial destruction of the rain-forests, the
beaches, and even older parts of the urban environment, were
backed by the Green Bans which the Builders' Labourers' Federa-
tion and other groups imposed on developments they disap-
proved of. Even the wheat farmers of Western Australia protested in the streets of Perth in 1974, pelting Prime Minister
Whitlam with eggs and drink-cans (Crowley 1986 : 108).

The end of the efficacy of street marches came in 1975, with the
failure of the Whitlam and Fraser governments to respond to
protests over the incorporation of East Timor into Indonesia. For
some, this failure was the final evidence that change was being
asked of the very people who created and supported the policies
they so abhorred (Smith and Crossley 1975 : 5). The same disillu-
sionment is expressed in the words of the editor of the *Australian*,
written after the Springbok tour in 1971:

the division of the Australian people, the mutual hatred of
citizens and police, the external appearance of official
attitudes of racism linked with the hankering for police-
state methods reminiscent of South Africa itself, will be
lasting legacies of the conduct of a few members of our
radical right... Unfortunately, the persons in positions of
authority to whom we must turn to relieve the social fabric
of this shocking damage are the people who have so far
calculated that they have a vested interest in provoking
turbulence.

(Crowley 1986 : 43)

The dismissal of the Whitlam government and the foundation
of the new Fraser government on the simple promise that "Life
isn't meant to be easy" concluded the involvement of many
concerned citizens in the public arena for at least another decade.

The New Consciousness

The wake of the Vietnam protest movement caught up many
other issues of a more private nature as well. Groups concerned
with the definition of new lifestyles, different from those which
were conventional in Australia, began to appear in "spontaneous,
unconscious and unintentional" ways during the late sixties, and
then to consolidate in the early seventies. The major issues taken
up by these groups included the role of women in society and the
nature of the family, communal living arrangements, and new
forms of consciousness, in some cases inspired by drugs and/or
Eastern philosophies. During the sixties, protest was directed
within the mainstream of society; in the seventies, personal issues
were increasingly taken up on the edge of, or even outside, the
major culture. As Pichaske (1989 : 155) notes:

It was the generation of the seventies that actually dropped
out: politically, socially, educationally (and musically).

The move to self-reliance and simplicity was not only ideological: it was also assisted by the slow movement into recession of
this decade, which was characterised by rising inflation, unem-
ployment (especially among the young), and widespread, if
"hidden", poverty. (For details see Crowley 1986.)

Feminism

At the heart of the Women's Movement was the analysis of power relationships between men and women. According to Anne Summers, the movement began when

> a dozen women, mostly educated middle class and left-wing, met to tentatively discuss sex roles, the family, sexuality and generally what it meant to be a women in a male dominated society. Within a year the movement was Australia wide...

(Crowley 1986 : 206)

Its concerns included the right of women to have control over their own bodies, abortion on demand, safe contraception, equal pay, free twenty-four hour child-care and equal education. The easiest issue was, perhaps, contraception: in 1970 it was estimated that Australian women led the world with the highest per capita consumption of the Pill, one newspaper suggesting in 1973 that the number of women using oral contraceptives was in excess of seven hundred and fifty thousand (Lawton 1988 : 67). Surgical sterilisation, especially for men, became widespread after its approval by the Australian Medical Association in 1971; more than a quarter of a million Australians were sterilised during the seventies (Crowley 1986 : 199). A survey of thirty thousand readers of the *Australian Women's Weekly* in 1980 showed that 38 per cent of women using contraception were on the Pill, 31 per cent were sterilised or with partners who had chosen vasectomy and 10 per cent used a form of I.U.D. (Crowley 1986 : 199). Public support for abortion grew steadily and by the end of the decade many doctors, as well as the management of the Australian Medical Association, had accepted that abortion no longer constituted a hazard to their profession. The Women's Movement was active in establishing discussion groups, collectives, women's houses, women's refuges, child-care centres, in running conferences and demonstrations, in establishing magazines and journals, in producing films and plays, and in objecting to sexist advertising. The movement may not have succeeded in reaching those Germaine Greer called, in an interview with the *Age* in 1980, "the poor or the ugly or the old ... the majority" (Crowley 1986 : 223), but it did lead to significant legislative reforms relating to discrimination and sexism in employment (Crowley 1986 : 223).

The Family

To a great extent, the nuclear family remained normative throughout the seventies. The 1981 census showed that 60 per cent of Australians lived in conventional two-parent families, a further 15 per cent consisted of couples with no children present, and 7 per cent were living as one parent families. There had, nevertheless, also been great changes. Divorces had increased by 100 per cent; marriages had declined by 22 per cent; more people were interested in starting partnership-marriages than family-marriages; and there were many more late marriages, late births of children, second marriages, *de facto* marriages, single parents, illegitimate births and abortions than previously (Crowley 1986 : 234). The average length of marriages fell from fourteen to ten years and the proportion of marriages ending within the first five years rose from eight to twenty per cent (Crowley 1986 : 234). Almost half of the married women had jobs by 1980 (Crowley 1986 : 225); single parent families, mainly those without fathers, were according to social workers, "the most destitute group in the community, apart from the aborigines" (Crowley 1986 : 235).

Shared Living

The movement towards alternative communal dwelling arrangements began about 1971; by 1974 there was a significant number of viable shared communities established which seemed likely to survive in the long term (Cock 1979). In these communities people "came together consciously " to eat, work and live together as a group with a relatively strong self-awareness. Cock (1979) describes a large range of current rural and urban counter-cultural communities, bourgeois communities ("more intentional and conservative", Cock 1979 : 3), and religious communities. At their worst, he suggests, some communities were subject to deficient diets, disgusting poverty, were apolitical, anti-social, and dismissive of individual dignity. They were down-trodden youthful skid rows, encouraging hard drugs, low drive, a disregard for others and oneself (Cock 1979 : 139). At their best, communes served to encourage the pursuit of autonomy, self-awareness, personal power and freedom from unwanted dependencies (Cock 1979 : 90). Unlike many other groups, religious communities had explicit aims and processes for accepting new members and resolving conflict (Cock 1979 : 234). J.D. Pringle has estimated that by 1980 Australia had about six hundred alternative communities and about one hundred thousand people had at some time or other been involved in them (Crowley 1986 : 257).

Personal Power and Self-Understanding

The personal values and attitudes of the alternative movements of the late sixties and the seventies can be described in many ways. Within the conventional society, the most common term was "permissiveness" and it was related primarily to sex, and secondarily to attitudes to work. Members of the counter-culture focused on ways of best understanding the self and one's relation to the world. In particular they spoke of putting

> the person first by giving power to the person; power that enables us to become increasingly independent of our institutional structures, and gives us the energy to begin to create our own joy and to relate to each other as persons.
> (Smith and Crossley 1975 : 5)

Cock (1979 : 218) expands the term 'power', specifically 'personal power', to include: self-knowledge, power of choice, power to feel and experience, to think and to know, to be as well as to become, to find one's own joy and meaning in life; to develop, to share one's abilities and attributes, and to discover one's unknown and untried potential; "to become a warm, loving human being", "to be honest with myself", "to understand man and myself", "to be independent, self-actualized",to have "peace" and "meaning", be more "creative" and "sensitive". Some counter-culturalists, he suggests, were more narrow in their definitions of "personal power": to them 'power' meant no more than seeking new experiences, trying things out, and following hedonistic impulses. [It is Cock who points out the continuity between Western values of affluence and individualism, and the alternative cultures (Cock 1979 : 228)].

The Growth Movement

The idea of "personal power" was central to the "growth

movement" which appeared in Australia after 1971. The "growth movement" presented itself as a "third psychology", placed between Freudianism which emphasised the unconscious, and behaviourism with its exclusive focus on external action. Some important names associated with the theories of the growth movement were Carl Rogers (1969), A. Maslow (1964), Fritz Perls (1951), R.D. Laing (1967) and Rollo May (1953). In the early seventies the most common tool of the movement was the "encounter group".

The structure of an encounter group was very simple. A number of people spent a length of time together in a room, usually at least two hours, and were encouraged to communicate honestly with each other about their feelings (not their thoughts). Each person was "responsible" for his or her feelings and actions, now and in the past; blame could not be passed on to anyone else. Perls, in particular, liked the method because it could be used with many people at once, it avoided the long tedious rationalisations common in psychoanalysis and was supposed to lead to rapid and deep emotional release. He was also a skilful manipulator and provocateur, who led groups by seeming not to lead.

Cooper (Smith and Crossley 1975 : 54-55), who participated in one of the first encounter groups held in Australia (at the University of New England in Armidale) describes the results he witnessed in this way:

> From this true speaking, I saw miracles occur. People who had been buried in childhood pains relived them and were, for the moment, released from the burden they had carried for years. A face that was tensed and forcing a smile all the time relaxed and really smiled. A girl found that the role she had been playing all her life was not what she really wanted to do. Another lass who was normally timid was able to speak with such truth that I listened to her with awe.

Cooper himself realised that:

> all my life I had been living in my head more than in my body. That, in spite of preaching in the favour of living with nature, I had preferred to sit back safely in my intellectual fortress and not get involved. This eased the pain in me, but

I was left isolated from the group. It was with the help of the group that I was able to contact my feelings which kept changing all the time, from deep sorrow to deep joy. I felt freer and more spontaneous.

Within two weeks after the group, he had lost a stone in weight, decided to sell many of his books, changed from reading philosophy to personal stories, no longer felt the need to write, no longer used a *mantra* when he meditated and found it easier to say "no" when he didn't want to do something. (He also feared, however, that the effect was rapidly wearing off!)

Drugs and "Eastern Mysticism"

There are legal drugs in Australia which are widespread: in particular, tobacco, alcohol and medical analgesics. There are also illegal drugs. Studies of the use of illegal drugs and their relationship to the alternative culture are rare, although assertions of the virtual identity of "the drug culture" and "hippy culture" are not. On the basis of attitude surveys and public opinion polls, Hasleton (Smith and Crossley 1975 : 43) estimated that the "present user population" in 1975 was somewhere between three hundred thousand and six hundred thousand persons. Marijuana offences made up about 56 per cent of all drug charges in 1971; although use tended to be the greatest among middle and upper middle class youth, those arrested were most likely, by a factor of thirty to one, to be from working class and semi-skilled youth (Smith and Crossley 1975 : 42). In Jacubowicz' opinion (Smith and Crossley 1975 : 45), the early use in the late sixties of marijuana, together with LSD, by the counter-culture, was part of a "growing trend amongst people to break free of the oppressive constraints of industrial capitalist society". J. Young describes drug-users as a highly organised bohemian community of psychologically stable individuals, with clear-cut values such as hedonism, spontaneity, expressivity, disdain for work etc. He suggests that drug taking was irregular, mildly euphoric and of mainly symbolic value. Those who used marijuana disdained heroine addicts and suffered few psychotic effects (Cited in Atkinson 1990 : 171).

One of the attractions of illegal drugs in the period under consideration was their alleged ability to allow access to a more vivid reality and greater sensory awareness (See especially Leary

1973). This reality apparently had no place in conventional Christian experience but seemed to match what is spoken of in some Asian religions (especially Hinduism and Tibetan Buddhism). Lawton (1988), notes Frederick Bird and William Reimer's (1982) "impressive study of new religious and para-religious groups" in Canada which concluded that "cult members" have extensively experimented with psychedelic drugs, as well as with astrology and divination. He then suggests:

> Each represents an attempt to discover meaning through a non-rational process, (Bird and Reimer's) conclusion being that the common factor between participants in New Religious Movements, the users of psychedelic drugs and practitioners of divination is the need to gain 'specific, non-ordinary experiences' through experimentation.
>
> (Lawton 1988 : 93)

Lawton also conceded the movements a more positive perspective, not necessarily related to drugs at all:

> The New Religions' eastern mysticism placed humanity in a broad relation to the universe and cosmic power. They were religions of experience; they were not based on reasoned definitions and doctrines, or on what we might call 'rational reflection'. Theology, as understood in the Western world, was irrelevant to their rise to prominence. Neither the moment of conversion nor allegiance to the sect had anything to do with intellectual or rational processes. Members found their authentic moment, or their encounter with the divine, through direct experience (Lawton 1988 : 62).

There can be little doubt that drugs played some part in encouraging membership of the New Religious Movements. Ross (1983 : 418) found that thirty-two of the forty-two members of the ISKCON temple in Melbourne had a history of "fairly extensive drug experimentation", including addictive and hallucinogenic drugs and marijuana. O'Brien in her earlier study of the Hare Krishna movement in Melbourne (1983), also found that:

> a high proportion of members of the movement to be ex-hippies who had been dependent on the psychedelic experience for expressions of inner cognitive urges and

perceived ultimate concerns and who, moreover, appear to have discovered that drugs produce a temporary state of transcendence whilst living in Vrindavan (close Communion) with Krishna is a permanent high (O'Brien 1983 :142).

Judah's study (1974) of the San Francisco temple in the early seventies found that 91 per cent of devotees had smoked marijuana, three-fourths regularly, and argued that there was "a direct link between the counter culture and the growth of the Krishna movement in America" (Rochford 1985 : 62). However, as we shall see, few Australian *sannyasins* claimed that the use of drugs was the major, or only, cause of their turning to Asian Religions.

The Ageing of the Counter-Culture

Craig McGregor has argued (Smith and Crossley 1975 : 15-17) that there were many counter-cultures in Australia, drawing on the attitudes and patterns of behaviour sketched above in different ways and to different degrees. Individuals may have accepted some of the attitudes described above (example, feminism, eastern mysticism) without necessarily subscribing to the whole. To have accepted even a part of the counter-culture, however, was to have begun to question the materialist and authoritarian structures of the whole dominant society.

From the perspective of the 1990s, the sixties are almost a quarter of a century away. The counter-culture has aged and passed into history. Knott discovered in her study of the British Hare Krishna movement (1986) that many of the movement's early "hippy" members were now into their thirties and forties, with homes and children of their own. She sensed that:

> They still adhere to the same philosophy, the same principles and the same basic life-style, but their social position has changed. They have matured, their skills and talents have developed, and their approach to their mission has changed accordingly (Knott 1986 : 17).

Some of today's *sannyasins* were undoubtedly "hippies"; others are their children or people who never fully dropped-out at all. The next chapter is concerned with the definition of the relationship of *sannyasins* to the counter-culture of the sixties and the seventies, and beyond.

CHAPTER EIGHT

BACKGROUNDS TO SANNYASA

We now turn to the individual backgrounds of the Australian *sannyasin* disciples of Swami Satyananda and Osho, and their relationships to the counter-culture sketched above. As it seems inappropriate to describe the followers of Rajneesh as "renunciates", the general term "disciples" will henceforth be used to refer to the members of the various movements. While recognising that all disciples are often termed *sannyasins*, a distinction will be made for the sake of convenience to "Full Sannyasin" and "Karma Sannyasin" initiates of Swami Satyananda, and to the "Neo-Sannyasin" initiated disciples of Osho Rajneesh. The names which will be used for individuals, unless quoted from published material, are consistent with those used within the particular movement but are pseudonyms adopted herein to protect confidentiality.

The study of the background of the Australian disciples will proceed in two stages. The first will be concerned with the simple demographic categories of gender, age, place of birth and upbringing, religion, education and marital status. The second stage will be concerned with personal involvement, or otherwise, with aspects of the counter-culture, in particular radical politics, feminism, the growth movement and yoga. The date of taking *sannyasa*, and age of the disciple at that time, will follow the demographic data and be later related to the various degrees of involvement in the counter-culture.

I: DEMOGRAPHIC BACKGROUND

Gender

Vivekananda's desire to extend *sannyasa* to both men and

women has been very successful among the two groups. Replies to the questionnaire on *Sannyasa* were received from eight female Full Sannyasins and twelve male Full Sannyasins; seventeen female Karma Sannyasins and five male Karma Sannyasins; sixteen female Neo-Sannyasins and eight male Neo-Sannyasins.

It is not true, in Australia at least, that the followers of these particular movements are "mostly young, single, middle-class females" (Lawton 1988 : 89). There is, nevertheless, a preponderance of female members among Karma Sannyasins and, to a lesser extent, among Neo-Sannyasins. The figures for initiation into Karma Sannyasa following the 1983 "Karma Sannyasa Course" at Mangrove Mountain show that eighty-six females were initiated, but only forty-three males, with five names being gender-nonspecific (*Satyananda Ashram Newsletter*, January 1984). Latkin's study of Rajneeshpuram, Oregon, in 1983, suggested that 54 per cent, slightly over half of those attracted to the movement, are women (Thompson and Heelas 1986 : 72). The *Rajneesh Times* noted that among those coming to Poona in June 1988, the number of men and women were almost equal (*Rajneesh Times*, 1 November 1988), which may agree with Latkin's figures. The "faculty" of the *Osho Multiversity* Handbook for 1990 included the names of sixty-eight females and sixty-four males.

Age

The average present age of Full Sannyasins in 1990 was 41.8 years; of Karma Sannyasins was 39.4 years; and Neo-Sannyasins, 36.6 years. The distribution of ages was as follows:

Table 1: *Ages of Renunciates in 1990*

	Full Sannyasins		Karma Sannyasins		Neo-Sannyasins	
	M	F	M	F	M	F
25-29	-	2	1	1	-	1
3-34	-	1	2	3	3	6
35-39	6	2	2	5	1	5
4-44	1	1	-	3	3	2
45-49	3	1	-	3	1	2
5-54	-	1	-	-	-	-
55-59	1	-	-	1	-	-
6-64	-	-	-	-	-	-
65-69	1	-	-	1	-	-
Total	12	8	5	17	8	16

(*Source* : Questionnaries on Sannyasa)

The data supports the findings of Bird and Reimer (1982 : 6) in Montreal in 1980 that yoga groups *now* attract their most significant membership from among the thirty to fifty age range, and appeal less to the under-thirties. One needs to note, however, that most of those who currently have the greatest commitment to yoga were less than thirty when they first became involved with Satyananda.

The relative youthfulness of Neo-Sannyasins is confirmed in the figures available for visitors to Poona in 1988 and 1989:

Table 2 : *Ages of Visitors to Poona Ashram,*
Expressed in Percentages

	1988	1989
Under 21	2	2.9
21 - 25	2	11.0
26 - 30	15	19.2
31 - 35	25	28.1
36 - 40	30	20.6
41 - 50	22	14.1
50 +	4	4.1

(*Source* : *Rajneesh Times*, 1 November 1988, 16 December 1989).

Place of Origin

All but three Full Sannyasins were born and raised in Australia. Two Full Sannyasins had been born and raised in England: one in a small, semi-industrialised city, the other in a small town near the Lakes District. The third foreign-born respondent had been raised in Calcutta and in Perth. A majority derived from capital cities: Sydney (eight), Adelaide (two), Melbourne (one), Perth (one) and Canberra (one). Four *sannyasins* came from country Australian towns: Townsville, Toowoomba, the mid-north coast of New South Wales, and a dairy town in Northern Victoria. *Sannyasins* tended to be raised where they had been born, with one respondent moving from Adelaide to Sydney, and another from Sydney to the Adelaide hills.

Seven of the twenty-two Karma Sannyasins had not been born in Australia; four were from the United Kingdom, two from New Zealand, and one from Germany. Karma Sannyasins derived from a mixture of large and small cities: Sydney (three), Melbourne (two), Adelaide (one), Hobart (one), Ipswich (one), Snowtown S.A. (one),Temora (one), Forbes (one), Morwell (one), Ararat (one), Launceston (one) and Burnie (one). Despite their greater mobility, Karma Sannyasins also tended to be raised where they were born, one respondent moving from Ipswich to Melbourne and another from Melbourne to Moe.

Eight of the Neo-Sannyasins also had immigrant backgrounds. Three Neo-Sannyasins were born and raised in Germany. (Germans currently form the largest group in Poona, being 22.5 per cent of all new arrivals in 1989 and 30 per cent in 1988 (*Rajneesh Times*, 1 November 1988 and 16 December 1989.) Two Neo-Sannyasins were born in England, one migrating to South Australia as a child; one in Scotland; one in Denmark; and one in New Zealand. Again, Australian-born Neo-Sannyasins derived from a mixture of capital cities—Melbourne (four), Perth (three), Sydney (one) and Adelaide (one)—and country towns: Tallangatta (one), Kaniva (one), Cootamundra (one), "South Australia" (one) and "the South Australia country" (one). Neo-Sannyasins had tended to be slightly less settled in childhood than the Karma Sannyasins: individuals had moved from South Australia to Victoria, from Cootamundra to Queensland, from Perth to Kalgoorlie and "a dozen places, from New South Wales to Western Australia.

Overall, we may conclude that disciples derived from stable city and small town settings in Australia and Northern Europe. Although Rajneesh, Swami Satyananda and the former Director of Satyananda Ashrams, Swami Akhandananda, were all Asians, none of their disciples had a non-European background.

Religion

The childhood religious allegiances claimed by most disciples were related the mainline denominations in the Australian society:

Full Sannyasins tended to indicate the most positive response to religion. Catholicism was the most common religious background, according to one respondent, and discussions on religion were frequent among Full Sannyasins. One Full Sannyasin described herself as "quite devout" to the age of thirteen, another as devout until twenty-two, while a third shifted from Catholicism to "universality". One of the Anglicans had been moved to intense religious activity following the Billy Graham crusades,

Table 3: *Early Religious Affiliations of Disciples*

	Full Sannyasins	Karma Sannyasins	Neo-Sannyasins
"Christian"	-	2	1
Anglican	6	8	3
Roman Catholic	5	4	5
Mainline Protestant*	4	8	8
Jewish	2	-	1
None	3	-	5
Total	20	22	23

*Uniting Church, Methodist, Presbyterian, Church of Christ,"Protestant".

after an "unconvinced childhood". A Methodist had been raised in the Christian Science Faith. Another whose father was a minister, later became a teacher.

The comments of the Neo-Sannyasins were surprisingly neutral, in view of Rajneesh's strongly expressed antagonism to orthodox religion. One had a grandfather who was a minister; another had considered going into ministry himself at the age of twenty. Expressed dislike was moderate: "mother Presbyterian, father atheist", "CE- parents' choice", "Church of Christ to eleven- disliked it."

The most negative comments on religion came from the Karma Sannyasins, at least half of whom explicitly claimed "no religion" or "atheism" as adults.

No disciple indicated previous membership of the Eastern European orthodox churches, or of more radical Christian groups. The number of the Jews was very small, although not out of proportion to the general community.

From both their places of origin and types of religious upbringing, it is clear that no disciple could have had (at best) more than a passing knowledge of the Indian religious tradition or its practitioners. Only one disciple, a Neo-Sannyasin, indicated any adult interest in another Asian religion, Zen Buddhism, following a twelve-year commitment to the Transcendental Meditation technique of Maharishi Mahesh Yogi. Charles Wright (1985 : 68), himself a disillusioned Neo-Sannyasin, puts the matter strongly when he states:

Immersed in the spiritual fiction of Carlos Castaneda, and with no background in the tradition of Eastern religions, Westerners were easily misled. They engaged in meditation as they would in glue-sniffing—seeking sensations that they mistook for cosmic experiences. They abandoned their families, their careers, and in many cases their children, and were committed to living life like the fabled grasshoppers, pausing frequently to scoff at the ants. They had been induced to part with their cash, their confidence, and the means of coping in normal society.

Wright's views are perhaps harsh but it is certainly true that most disciples had no means of discriminating in their search between the genuine and the bogus, the virtuous and the fraudulent, other than their good will and commonsense. Some learned painfully the intense cost of renunciation, practised the spiritual techniques taught to them, and developed close ties with other more experienced practitioners, including the Master himself. Others, as Wright states, never did.

Education

Naive the disciples may have been, uneducated they were not (as all the research on New Religious Movements continuously shows). Pichaske (1989 : 100) amusingly captures some of these contradictory qualities:

Sixties people would go anywhere, do anything, fill themselves full of (almost) any chemical, explore any argument, try any living arrangement, take any class, read (at least ten pages of) any book, look at any movie, listen to any song, talk to any individual, tolerate the most unbelievable bullshit or pain for the sake of doing more. They were the most open-minded people in the world, even to the point of not being able to draw any distinctions at all. It is not true you couldn't tell sixties people anything; you could tell them everything. . .

Thirteen of the Full Sannyasins had studied at the tertiary level. Three men had qualified in medicine, one adding specialist qualifications in psychiatry. Two held the B.Sc. degree, one in Mathematics. One held the Bachelor of Engineering. One was a

Chiropractor, another completed a five-year apprenticeship in Lithographic Camera Operating and Platemaking. The emphasis among the male Full Sannyasins on "hard disciplines" is striking. Women Full Sannyasins, on the other hand, tended to enrol in Arts courses, with a bent towards Theatre or Fine Arts, and in Teacher Training. Two of the women had completed only high school.

This commitment to education continued after the *sannyasins* had returned to Australia from *ashram* life in India. One of the physicians had added an M.Sc. to his qualifications; the engineer had completed a Master's degree in Biomedical Engineering, and one of the women was engaged in completing a Diploma of Applied Science in Nursing.

Karma Sannyasins showed the same practical training as Full Sannyasins, and an orientation which may be related to the practical, scientific and medical approach to Yoga taken by Satyananda and his Master, Swami Sivananda, himself a trained medical practitioner. One woman held an M.Sc.; two a B.A. (one in Psychology); three the B.Sc. degree. Three were trained teachers. One held a Diploma in Visual Arts, plus the Diploma in Education and the Graduate Diploma in Graphic Communication Education. One was a trained nurse. Only three of the seventeen women Karma Sannyasins had completed or almost completed high school and gone no further. Of the men, one held a B.Eng., another a B.A., while a third had studied at the Undergraduate level. One held a Diploma in Visual Arts, another the Basic Electrician's Certificate. Here too was the same disciplined commitment to the realisation of practical educational goals which characterised the Full Sannyasins.

The educational experience of the Neo-Sannyasins was the most disparate and the most broken. One male held an M.A. and the equivalent of the M.D. in the area of Psychiatry, another the B.Eng., while two others respectively held Diplomas in Nursing and Teaching. One had discontinued a Master's degree in History, then in Education, while another had dropped out of the second year of the Bachelor of Music degree. Three of the eight men had taken the Matriculation exam or its equivalent but nothing more.

One of the female Neo-Sannyasins had recently completed a Ph.D. in Medicine, although her major contemporary interest was

THE LAUGHING SWAMIS

in Acupuncture. One had taken a "tertiary degree", another a B.A. in Fine Art, two others were trained teachers. One had dropped out of the first year of the B.Sc., another of the second year of the B.Ed. Seven of the sixteen women had studied at the high school level, two to only the third year. One had subsequently undertaken an apprenticeship as a "restorer". One gave no answer. The last simply stated: "My education stopped when school began". The Neo-Sannyasin women were not only younger than their sisters, they were also distinctly less educated and perhaps less employable in any but routine jobs.

The situation of Australian Neo-Sannyasins contrasts with that of Rajneeshpuram, Oregon, where 83 per cent of disciples had attended college; two-thirds had first degrees and 12 per cent had doctorates. In addition, 11 per cent of commune members had post-graduate degrees in Psychology or Psychiatry; and another 11 per cent Bachelor degrees in the field (Fitzgerald 1987: 264, 274). Of the new arrivals in Poona in 1988, 61 per cent had university degrees; and an additional 20 per cent had some other higher education (*Rajneesh Times*, 1 November 1988). In 1989, 51.1 per cent of the new arrivals held university degrees (*Rajneesh Times*, 16 December 1989).

Marriage

In their Study of Recruitment to Asian-based Meditation Groups in North America, Gussner and Berkowitz (1988 : 152) noted that more of their respondents were single or divorced and fewer widowed, than would be expected from a comparable sample of the general population. Such independence of ties allows easier transfer to new, and perhaps more mobile statuses.

Eleven of the twenty Full Sannyasins had, indeed, never married. They were among the younger Full Sannyasins, with an average age of 38.2 years for the men (ranging thirty-six to forty-two years now) and 35.6 years for the women (twenty-eight to forty-nine years now). They were part of a generation itself reluctant to marry, and among the youngest members to take *sannyasa*.

Those who had married were older: the men being now of an average age of 50.4 years (range: thirty-six to sixty-five), the women 41.7 (thirty-five to forty-eight). Two Full Sannyasin couples had been married over thirty years each. They had entered the *ashram* in, or close to, their forties, raised their children there, abstained from sexual relations, and, once living in the *ashram* ceased to be an acceptable option, resumed living together again. In this way they were similar to many other couples of their age, who had chosen to enter well-structured, secure alternative communities for the personal opportunities for growth which the lifestyle could add to the strength of their relationship (Cock 1979: 143). A third Full Sannyasin couple, never long term residents either in India or in the official Australian *ashram* system, had lived together for seven years, given birth to a child, married, then divorced within two years, and were still living contentedly together. Having no sense of the centrality of celibacy to the tradition of *sannyasa*, most members of the Australian community apparently accept it as natural that *sannyasins* might be "allowed" to be married, as ministers of the Protestant churches are.

On returning to Australia and non-communal life, many Full Sannyasins, who had not previously been married, entered into partner-relationships as readily as they resumed their education and careers. Only four of the eleven *sannyasins* who had not been married were not in a relationship now: one of these had worked through "marriage, divorce, affairs ('his' and 'mine'), children" and probably felt the whole business tiring. Three of those who had not been married also described themselves as not being in a relationship now, although one had just ended a four-year partnership. Three simply wrote "Yes" to the question "Are you in a relationship now?" Two were subsequently married (to each other), and one described an ongoing relationship with a Karma Sannyasin which had extended over the past few years. There is a high degree of community in-pairing among Full Sannyasins, natural enough because of the range of partners available and the common specialised interests and experiences of those following *sannyasa* as a way of life. Being a *sannyasin*—mockingly described by one respondent at "poverty, chastity and obedience"—does not stop bodily urges. One Full Sannyasin, who had spent fifteen years of selfless service in Munger, quit the *ashram* within two days of meeting a woman he considered a suitable life partner and both returned to Australia.

On the other hand, marriage is almost at the heart of the definition of Karma Sannyasa. Thirteen of the seventeen women Karma Sannyasins had been married, two more were in stable *de*

facto relationships of between seven and eleven years respectively, and only two had never married. Two of the five men had
been married, another was in a casual relationship. However, six
of the thirteen women who had been married were not in a
relationship now. It may be that Karma Sannyasa had one function for the settled householder, and another for the newly separated householder who still had responsibilities to her children
and community. Within the Satyananda community of Yoga
Therapy centres today, there often seems to be little difference
between the lives of married Full Sannyasins and married Karma
Sannyasins, or single Full Sannyasins and some single Karma
Sannyasins. Full Sannyasins carry higher status because of their
full initiation, and their time in the *ashram* "near Swamiji", not
because of their commitment to chastity.

Surprisingly, in view of Rajneesh's hostility to marriage as a
contractual rather than a spontaneous arrangement of the heart,
the answers to the question on marriage by the Neo-Sannyasins
were the most perfunctory. (Admittedly public expression of
Osho's attitude became muted after 1983, when Rajneeshism was
making a bid to be accepted as a conventional religion.) Unlike
Mullan (1983 : 50), who found divorce common, Latkin reported
that most of those coming to Oregon were already married and
that few had been through a divorce (Thompson and Heelas
1986 : 71). In response to the Questionnaire on Sannyasa, six of
the nine males had been married and five were still in a relationship. One who was not in a relationship nevertheless had "a
couple of close friends and was connecting regularly". Nine of
the sixteen women had married, but only four were in a relationship now. One Ma had the good fortune to be in a long-term
relationship with "an extremely intense, loving, open, accepting,
passionate, free" professional person; to share so many things
with him, "including the love of yoga, animals, nature, fresh air,
peace and quiet"; while both lived separately, "each with a son".
Another Ma had the misfortune to be matched with:

> a fat sort of alcoholic that drinks regularly, has hairs up his
> nose and short legs and is a dud root.[1]

The sixties and seventies were hard on relationships, because

---

1 "Dud-root" is Australian slang for a "poor lover".

there was no longer the pressure to "stay together, no matter what". Pichaske (1989 : 100) remarks:

> More than anything, romantics are keen on themselves. It was, in fact, the sanctity of the self which underlay the sixties quest for absolute freedom... The sanctity of self was in constant conflict with the search for community and meaningful relationships, and with the love ethic of the decade; the complexities and paradoxes have yet to be resolved in the heads of many sixties people: me or him? I or us? How much of myself can I trade for the well-being of others, yet still retain my own integrity? My individuality? My identity ?

The disciples' experience of marriage probably varied little from that of their peers. Full Sannyasins who later married probably showed less confusion and hurt than many Roman Catholic former monks and nuns because of the limited time of their commitment to celibacy.

Demographic Background: Conclusion

The backgrounds of those attracted to Full Sannyasa, Karma Sannyasa and Neo-Sannyasa, are similar to those of the disciples of Swami Vishnu Devananda and the devotees of the Hare Krishna movement described in Chapter Three. Australian disciples are now around forty but were then in their twenties. They derive from stable Northern European and Australian urban or semi-urban backgrounds. In childhood they had a loose relationship with the mainline Christian denominations. They were commonly educated to tertiary level. At the time of entering the movements, most were either single or ending a relationship. They do not derive from environments with a strong involvement in Asian cultures and religions.

II: TAKING SANNYASA

Before turning to the disciples' involvement with 'alternative Australia', it is necessary to describe the ages and years in which they took initiation. On this basis it will later become clear that the first disciples tended to have strong backgrounds in the counter-culture, but also that those who took initiation in the eighties experienced the counter-culture in a different way from their predecessors or were even too young to be involved with it at all.

Age of Initiation

Full Sannyasins were initiated at an average age of 30.9 years; Karma Sannyasins at 37.4; while the average age for the initiation of Neo-Sannyasins was 27.4. The spread of ages is as follows:

Table 4: *Age of Initiation into Discipleship*

	Full Sannyasins		Karma Sannyasins		Neo-Sannyasins	
15 - 19	1	1	-	-	-	-
20 - 24	1	2	-	-	3	8
25 - 29	4	1	2	3	-	3
30 - 34	4	-	2	6	2	1
35 - 39	-	2	1	1	2	2
40 - 44	1	1	-	4	1	-
45 - 49	-	-	-	-	-	-
50 - 54	1	-	-	-	-	-
55 - 59	-	-	-	1	-	-
60 - 64	-	-	-	-	-	-
65 - 69	-	-	-	1	-	-
Unknown	-	1	-	1	-	3
Total	12	8	5	17	8	17

The table indicates that the disciples were not always "thirt-yish". Five of the twenty Full Sannyasins had been initiated by the age of twenty-five and ten before the age of thirty. Eleven of the twenty-five Neo-Sannyasins were initiated before twenty-five and fourteen by the age of thirty. This also agrees with the previous research on the Vishnu Devananda and Hare Krishna movements. On the other hand, although the age of all disciples is similar today, no Karma Sannyasin was initiated before twenty-five and only five from twenty-two by the age of thirty. If Full Sannyasa is a philosophy of world renunciation, and Neo-Sannyasa of world affirmation, then Karma Sannyasa is a powerful sanctification of present obligations and responsibilities, which increase with age.

The average period of time since initiation is 11.4 years for Full Sannyasins, 8.2 years for Neo-Sannyasins and only 3.5 years for Karma Sannyasins.

Year of Initiation

Disciples were initiated at a variety of times and places, which are closely related to the histories of the various movements. On this basis, the cohorts within each movement can be described as follows:

(i) *Full Sannyasins*

Year	Place	Number	Ages at Initiation
The First Cohort: 1970 -1979			
1970	Munger	1	29
1973	Mangrove Mountain	1	19
1976	Munger	2	24, 28
1976	Sydney	4	25, 34*, 42, 51
1977	Munger	1	33, 33
1979	Singapore	1	24*
Total		11	
Average Age		31.0 (31.6, 29)	
Male : Female Ratio		9 : 2	
The Second Cohort : 1980 - 1984			
1980	Munger	2	39*, 42*
1980	Mangrove Mountain	2	23*, 28
1983	Mangrove Mountain	1	19*
1984	Paris	1	30
Total		6	
Average Age		31.0 (29.0, 30.7)	
Male : Female Ratio		2:4	
The Third Cohort: After 1984			
1987	Munger	2	26*, 39*
Average Age		32.5	
Plus : Unknown	1	20	

*Figures marked with an asterisk are those of female respondents.

In order to be initiated as a Full Sannyasin, it was necessary
to be in the presence of Swami Satyananda.The first cohort (predominantly male) were prepared to travel to India to do this.
Cheap airfares made this a possibility and the "hippy trail" of the
seventies had its own excitement and lessons to teach. Men,
apparently, travelled more readily than women. The year 1976
was crucial in the foundation of the movement in Australia, as
Satyananda first initiated a large group of both men and women
in Sydney.

The situation, however, for the second cohort changed. By
1980, Mangrove Mountain was a well-established and highly
efficient training centre, sending Full Sannyasins throughout Australia and to India. Full Sannyasins were initiated either in India
or when Swami Satyananda came to Australia. The revaluation of
the dollar made travel more difficult and there seemed less reason to be in India when Satyananda was visiting Australia regularly. More women became attracted to the movement.

Once Swami Styananda stopped coming (after 1983), initiation
could again only be had in India. Few took advantage of this
opportunity, and the third cohort is correspondingly smaller.

Although the ratio of male to female Full Sannyasins changed
completely over the three cohorts, there was little change in the
age of initiation for either males or females, remaining about
thirty to thirty-two years. Two Karma Sannyasins (one male, one
female) had fulfilled the "promise" of their initiation and moved
into Full Sannyasa—one within a year, the other four years later.
One belongs to the second cohort, one to the third.

(ii) Karma Sannyasins

We have seen that Karma Sannyasa is the most recent of the
three traditions and has the greatest appeal to those aged over
thirty years. How recent is it can be seen from the initiation
figures shown on the next page.

Initiation into Karma Sannyasa has been most dependent on
the visit of the *guru* to Australia (Satyananda in 1983-84, and
Niranjananda in 1988 and 1989). Nevertheless, because it is accepted that the mind of an advanced adept can transcend space,
a small number of Karma Sannyasins have received initiation by
post, writing from wherever they were currently located. This

Karma Sannyasins

Year	Place	Number	Ages at Initiation
The First Cohort: 1983-1984			
1983	Mangrove Mountain	2	28, 34*
1984	Rocklyn (Vic.)	4	28*, 31, 37*, 40*
1984	Auckland	1	28*
Total		7	
Average Age		32.2 (29.5, 33.2)	
Male : Female Ratio		2 : 5	
The Second Cohort: 1987			
1987	Munger	3	33*, 34*, 44*
1987	Post	2	26*, 43*
Total		5	
Average Age		36.0	
The Third Cohort (Initiation by Swami Niranjananda):			
1988-1989			
1988	Lottah (Tas)	1	32*
1988	Melbourne	2	31, 44*
1988	Sydney	2	55*, 67*
1988	Post	1	34*
1989	Munger	2	28, 33*
1989	Lottah	1	35
Total		9	
Average Age		39.1 (31.3, 44.1)	
Male: Female Ratio		3 : 6	
Plus : Unknown	1	22	

apparently never happened for Full Sannyasins, who were expected to be completely available to the movement. Only a few persons have made the journey to Munger for Karma Sannyasa.

The rate of initiation into Karma Sannyasa during the middle 1980s confirmed the increasing feminisation of the movement that was also evident among Full Sannyasins.

(iii) Neo-Sannyasins

Few Neo-Sannyasins were initiated personally by Shree Rajneesh. Most wrote to him, asking to be his disciple. The tendency to act "in the moment" may be one of the reasons why taking Neo-Sannyasa by post was so prevalent among these disciples, and the opportunity to take initiation from Rajneesh's own hands tempting but not finally decisive. This later option was, at any rate, not available once Rajneesh "entered silence" in 1981. On the basis of the location of the *ashram*, Neo-Sannyasins may also be divided into three cohorts:

Neo-Sannyasins

Year	Place	Number	Ages at Initiation
The First Cohort: 1976-81			
1976	Poona	1	24*
1977	Perth (?)	1	?*
1977	London	1	21
1979	Perth	2	21*, 25*
1979	Holland	1	21*
1979	Poona	1	20
1980	Perth	1	36*
1980	Poona	1	23
1981	Poona	3	21*, 24*, 32*
Total		12	
Average Age		24.3 (21.3, 25.5)	
Male : Female Ratio		3 : 9	
The Second Cohort : 1981-85			
1982	Fremantle	1	24*
1982	Munich	1	23*
1983	Melbourne	1	33*
1983	Adelaide	1	33
1983	New Zealand	1	24
1984	Fremantle	1	29*
1984	Adelaide	1	?
1984	Melbourne	2	37*, 40
1985	Sydney	1	29*
Total		10	
Average		30.1 (32.3, 29.0)	
Male: Female Ratio		4 : 6	
The Third Cohort : After 1985			
1987	Fremantle	1	38
1988	Poona	1	36
Total		2	
Average Age		37.0	
Plus: Unknown		1, 25	

The recruitment of Neo- Sannyasins was most closely linked to the existence of a nearby Centre, which were many, and did not require the physical presence of the *guru*. The system of initiation by post had the advantage of allowing a continuous recruitment of new members across Australia at all times. As a method of initiation, it is unusual within the Indian tradition (although practised by Swami Sivananda and Satyananda after him); Australian disciples would not have known this. As well, initiation by post had some of the excitement children know when writing away for free gifts by post, especially as one pondered what sort of "name" one might receive (and whether that name would have the prefix "Anand", for intellectuals, "Deva" for people of strong will, or "Prem", for "heart-people"). The seventies were also for Neo-Sannyasins, as they were for Full Sannyasins, a time when cheap air-travel ensured easy access to the central *ashram*: half of the first cohort were initiated in India.

There was little slowing in the rate of recruitment after Rajneesh's departure for America. Thompson and Heelas (1986 : 85) distinguish between two types of Neo-Sannyasins, "disparates" and "incumbents" whom they met in their research in England in 1979. Disparates were easy-going types. They treated Rajneesh as a friend, refused to take anything seriously, did not think in terms of rules, and generally enjoyed "whatever came along, whether it be meat, alcohol, cigarettes, the cinema, or the occasional meditation". Incumbents, on the other hand, led ordered, predictable lives, "following a relatively strictly laid down path towards enlightenment". It is Thomas and Heelas' opinion that the Incumbents won the day after the move to America and that Disparates then became an "endangered species" (Thompson and Heelas 1986 : 112). Certainly the centres and Ma Anand Sheela exercised stricter control over who took initiation after 1981. Again it was likely that there were changes in the type of person attracted to Neo-Sannyasin after 1982.

Finally, the reduction of recruitment to near standstill after the collapse of Rajneeshpuram is evident in the small size of the third cohort, its exclusive masculinity and its older age. The movement may be meeting new needs for those who do join but is otherwise less attractive than before to most uncommitted people.

Taking Sannyasa: Conclusion

A simple summary of recruitment by years shows the following pattern:

Table 5: *Years of Initiation and Cohorts*

	Full Sannyasins		Karma Sannyasins		Neo-Sannyasins	
1970	I	1				
1971						
1972						
1973		1				
1974						
1975						
1976		6			I	1
1977		2				2
1978						
1979		1				4
1980	II	4				2
1981						3
1982					II	2
1983		1	I	2		3
1984		1		5		4
1985						1
1986						
1987	III	2	II	5	III	1
1988			III	6		1
1989				3		

We can conclude that the major years of recruitment to discipleship lay in the decade 1976 to 1985 and that Full Sannyasa and Neo-Sannyasa peaked in their membership between 1983 and 1984. It was at this time that Karma Sannyasa began to establish itself. Karma Sannyasa drew on a population of a similar current age to Full Sannyasa and Neo-Sannyasa, but one less able to "drop-out" for career, family and possible gender reasons.

III: INVOLVEMENT IN THE COUNTER-CULTURE

Politics

None of the respondents indicated any commitment to the Conservative Liberal or Country parties.

Among the Full Sannyasins, an active interest in radical politics was confined to five members of the first cohort and developed at a time when they were still students. Navaratna (as indicated, all personal names used here are pseudonyms) was a Marxist from the eighteenth to twenty-second year of age (about 1962 to 1966) having just finished high school. Yogapadma took part in anti-Vietnam and anti-apartheid demonstrations in 1970 while completing matriculation and—after being initiated in 1973—in demonstrations for nuclear disarmament and the legalisation of marijuana in 1974. During his Degree courses, Devadas was involved "informally with radical politics in the late sixties" and in "the early 70s—Vietnam, etc." Also a student, Usha participated in "a few political demonstrations in the early 70s". One of the first cohort doctors was involved in "medico-political matters only"; another is slowly "becoming more politically aware now", having been, as he jokes,"slightly retarded before".

From the second cohort, Anandakanti was the daughter of a father who had been very politically active, particularly in the area of conservation and she was very influenced by him. Her involvement, however, led her into "such depression that it became the catalyst for an inner search and an awakening to the insight that 'I have to work on myself first' ".

An interest in radical politics was more common among Karma Sannyasins. Twelve of the twenty-two Karma Sannyasins had had an active involvement or interest in oppositional politics. This was spread fairly evenly across the three cohorts, who tend to be much the same age, and involved issues such as Vietnam, Women's Electoral Lobby, the Nuclear Disarmament party, Amnesty, the environment and the "green parties", and the bus industry for which one Karma Sannyasin's husband worked. One respondent claimed only to have kissed Andrew Peacock at a Young Lib's party. Interestingly, four of the five men respondents expressed no interest in politics at all. The women who gave a reason for their lack of interest tended to indicate a preference for compassionate inter-personal relationships, as did one of the men.

An active interest in left-wing politics among Neo-Sannyasins was largely confined to the first cohort. One woman "was a member of the Labour party", another was "opposed to Vietnam and conservative politics" but "not actively". Satyamurti took part in the Vietnam Moratorium marches in 1969 and demonstrated in favour of the Tasmanian forests in 1988 and 1989, but did "nothing in between". Ananda, the oldest member of the second cohort, had been involved in the anti-conscription movement and anti-Vietnam politics in the sixties and seventies, was a member of the ALP between 1969 and 1971; and secretary of the local branch, but resigned when Labour Party came to power in 1972. Further, he was involved in teachers' politics during the sixties and throughout most of the seventies. One first cohort Neo-Sannyasin had been a member of the Green Development Party in Western Australia.

It is the overseas born women who showed the strongest interest among Neo-Sannyasins in politics. Ambu was involved in left-wing movements in Denmark and in particular an environmental activist group and an anti-nuclear group. Veena was interested in German political groups from age nineteen to twenty-five (1973 to 1979) and a member for a short time. She left because: "I realised that it is more important to go inside than being involved in structured power struggles". Tushita was involved in feminism and Marxism between the ages of fourteen to seventeen (1973 to 1976).

Overall, disciples seem to have been little concerned with ongoing political issues, apart from Vietnam and feminism in the early seventies, the environment in the late eighties, and "nothing in between". These few issues align them with the early counter-culture; the more general apathy may be typical of the wider community. As Peter Spearitt has remarked, Australia is not (with one exception, the Eureka rebellion of 1856) "a country of the spontaneous barricade" (Lawton 1988 : 96). It is clear overall that most of the "mantra chanters" were not "slogan chanters" in the sixties (compare Kent 1988).

Feminism

Interest in feminism has changed as the movement itself has changed and tended, as one might expect, to be stronger among women than among men.

One of the few very good books on women and Yoga, *Nawa Yogini Tantra* (1983), was written by an early Australian woman Full Sannyasin, whose initiated name, Muktananda, meant "the bliss of liberation". None of the male members of either the first or second cohorts showed much interest in the topic at all. Anantapadma was the one person who "supposed he could be called a feminist", although he was "not sympathetic to extreme feminism". He felt that the *ashram* system had potentially offered equality to women, as the rapid growth of Mangrove Mountain and other *ashram* centres allowed them to move quickly into positions of authority. Even then, he commented, they were always "kept under the thumb".

The support of the women of the second Full Sannyasin cohort for feminism was clear, but also qualified. (The third cohort, both women, showed the barest interest in the idea of feminism and none in the practice.) Madhuprem admitted having been "a bit" interested for a while and still keen to know what is happening, but never actively involved. She was interested:

> the same as I am interested in other social questions, e.g. men's liberation, especially in their part in the birth of their own children and the question of old people; education of the young, etc.

Usha had been,

> *to some extent but not fanatical.* Women have been and still are suppressed which will hopefully change (even in ashrams!!). I hope for equality of the sexes and NOT a reverse. (Emphasis as in the original.)

Anandakanti wrote:

> I think feminism is a very important area for improvement in this society. Not so much feminism *per se* as more an equal balance of qualities within *each* individual and less exploitation of others for the gratification of our own desires (hence : Yoga!) I always thought I would have ended up a raging feminist if I hadn't become so involved in Yoga!

Most women of the first cohort of Karma Sannyasins saw feminism in relation to such issues as the Women's Liberation movement of the sixties, rights in general, and the struggle for abortion rights in particular. Tulsimala raised the issue of "spiritual feminism", which she explained as "the need for both sexes to embrace and value the so-called feminine archetypes, including allowing versus forcing, caring, sharing, etc." No one else, in any group, dealt with the issue of equality and personal integration in this way. Dharmadeva's interest in feminism was a flow-on from his involvement in live theatre and courses at university in philosophy and drama. To another of the men in the group, however, feminism was "the most bizarre phenomenon" he had ever come across.

Few Karma Sannyasins in the second and third cohorts expressed no interest in the topic at all, but their interest was similarly qualified. Chamunda appreciated "the attention that the feminist movement has given to women's causes", and supported efforts to encourage women "to overcome restrictions due to their femaleness"(later changing this to read "attitudes to their femaleness"). She was not, she considered, a strong feminist herself. Harigauri rejected the feminism "that seems to stem from hurts, insecurities, fears and leads to a degree of hate for men", as well as the type that saw no difference between men and women. She preferred a feminism that "strives for equality with the opposite sex and breaks down traditions of female inferiority, degradation". She also found appealing a feminism that highlights "the beauty and wonder of females, motherhood, etc". In some ways this complemented Mutan's opinion that he believed in "equality, work-sharing, *both* parents taking responsibility for children", "but also that women are naturally better at child-rearing, mainly due to their conditioning from birth, but also physiology."

In the third cohort, Ambarupa and Kaivalyananda had both benefited from feminism in the past. The former commented:

> for a number of years I was part of a small group of women who got together as a support group. Some women in that group found (still do) it important, that for certain growth in their life, men need to be excluded. Eventually I left the group as I now live in the country and only keep up with certain social interests.

Devashakti provided the briefest and coarsest answer: "I only fuck men".

Neo-Sannyasin women were the least certain about feminism: eight of seventeen expressing no interest at all in the topic. The interest which did exist belonged almost exclusively to the first cohort and was related to active feminist groups in the early seventies, as experienced during late teenage years. Amiyo, the oldest woman in the second cohort by some eight to thirteen years, considered feminism "an essential part of our evolving society", because it served to provoke people to rethink their attitudes and change. Her approach is more psychological than social. Upachara, of the third cohort, believed in "being the total woman—enjoying all the roles of woman, not being 'liberated' from them". Neo-Sannyasin men expressed a minimal interest in the topic, apart from Satyamurti whose "first wife was a very strong feminist, but I wanted my *freedom from roles also*"—explained in a note below as "not simple role reversal"—"this was tricky but came a bit together".

Feminism and Politics

On the basis of the data presented so far, it is evident that political radicalism and feminism formed a part of the experiences of some, certainly not all, of the first cohorts of disciples—Full Sannyasins, Karma Sannyasins and Neo-Sannyasins alike—but was less relevant and less attractive to the cohorts which followed them. In a conservative, economically constrained environment, such as emerged under Malcolm Fraser, there were no large issues which could be set right by marching in the streets, until the environment again became an important issue in the late eighties. Feminism was redefined as a desire for the equality of all persons, or exaggerated into a fierce hatred for all men; its benefits were accepted, the need for further thought and struggle considered unnecessary.

Yoga and the Growth Movement

Many people protested against the war in Vietnam or the oppression of women by men, and more were politically apathetic, but few became disciples of either Swami Satyananda or Osho. Is there something more immediate in the background of the seventies which may have led to an interest in discipleship?

An obvious factor in the background of disciples of Swami Satyananda was the practice of yoga. Yoga offered a technology for understanding oneself and one's powers in ways which were very congruent with the psychological and philosophical values of the counter-culture. Full Sannyasins had practised yoga for an average of 17.2 years (range eight to thirty-two years), almost six years longer than the average time of initiation. Karma Sannyasins had practised yoga for 9.3 years, also about six years longer than the average time of initiation.

The two major reasons Full Sannyasins gave for beginning yoga related to a search for a meaning in life—mainly among men, and the desire to be healthy—mainly among women. A few men were encouraged to take to yoga by significant others, usually their wives, but also including Swami Venkatesananda and Swami Saraswati (on the TV).

The mind and the body are for men and women, respectively but not exclusively, major ways of self-understanding and self-presentation to others. The male search for meaning tended to be expressed in fairly concise terms: "to find a balance", "to solve the mystery of life", "no external goal has meaning unless the inner purpose/awareness is clear", "the real impetus to start came after the death of my sister", "in search of the meaning of life". None of these phrases were explored in depth. The women's explanations of wanting to keep fit tended to be more expansive, with details of family and work situations and one woman *sannyasin* even talked on the phone while practising the shoulder stand.

Only in a few cases was the search for identity sparked by the taking of drugs. One member of the first cohort, who started yoga about fifteen years ago, wrote:

> I was quite lost in the world—smoking a lot of marijuana and only knew what I did't want to do, marriage, family, etc. No direction—suddenly I discovered the first Manly ashram of Swami Satyananda and went to classes and Satsangs and that was it.

Another began practising yoga in 1971. He had:

> A general interest in magic and mysticism. Desire to get "high" and experience other realities or an expanded reality. Convinced there was more than this. Several friends introduced me to yogic literature and I was convinced that

> this method offered the most effective and simple way to
> "higher consciousness" as well as the most accessible (i.e.
> better than shamanism, Don Juan, drugs or parapsychology/
> rebirthing, etc.)

Similarly, a member of the third cohort, who has practised yoga
for eight years:

> drank a lot, smoke a lot, took a lot of cocaine, was just sick
> of myself. A friend recommended yoga. I loved it straight-
> away.

In each of these cases, practising yoga led to the end of taking
drugs. [This was also claimed to be the case in other similar
movements, e.g., the Divine Light Mission and Transcendental
Meditation, (see Smith and Crossley 1975 : 57.)] A deeper sense
of self-integration had begun.

Karma Sannyasins gave more varied reasons for beginning
yoga. Fully half emphasised health reasons for beginning yoga;
this covered all the cohorts and included three of the five men.
Spiritual reasons were put forward by three persons, all female
(one emphasising the first cohort desire to "learn to meditate";
two from the third cohort); personal distress was emphasised by
two (one in each of the first and third cohorts); and the desire to
meet other people was put forward once (by a third cohort
woman). In two cases (both second cohort), the significant other
who encouraged the practice of yoga was a husband. Again, all
these reasons may be seen as part of a process to establish a more
whole identity. Because, as we shall see, Karma Sannyasins were
also exploring the growth movement, yoga was only one tool
available to them.

Yoga had also been available to Neo-Sannyasins. Eighteen of
the twenty-five respondents had tried it at some time or other (six
of the nine men and twelve of the sixteen women). Most had only
"dabbled briefly" for a few months. Those who persisted enjoyed
the sense of physical well-being and in one case "the intensity" of
it. One found it useful in her preparation for children and continued for the next four years. Of those who soon stopped, Turiya
noted that she had "never had an interest in discipline", while
Sumito undertook one year of strenuous Iyengar Yoga to see if
she was "missing out on anything", and discovered the one thing

missing in her life was "pain!". Only Meera has continued the practice of (Iyengar) Yoga for ten years: she finds it energising and centring. Perhaps significantly, she is the most obvious "Disparate" among the first cohort of Neo-Sannyasins and never visits the *ashram* in her city, believing "sannyasa is between Bhagwan and I". She also had no interest in growth work. In general, Neo-Sannyasins did not accept that the disciplined physical practices of yoga could provide a strong centre for personal self-awareness.

The growth movement almost entirely passed the Full Sannyasins by. (At least two Full Sannyasins did not even recognise the term.) The psychiatrist had, naturally, done many groups as part of his professional training. Brahmarishi had participated in the Inner Peace Movement Courses held in Sydney in early 1970. Usha was interested before joining an *ashram* in the late seventies; since then she had preferred to find "it" within. For a number of Full Sannyasins the *ashram* itself was a continuous ongoing growth experience (although none referred to it as an encounter group). Anandakanti had just naturally found herself forcing herself into new situations (travel, share-houses, relationships, careers) "in order to learn more about myself and others and the interaction between". Shantinath, slow in the area of politics, has only just begun to catch up on courses such as "Money and You" and "Powerful Presentations".

Fitzgerald (1987: 275), on the other hand, noticed that Rajneeshdham, "the ranch", was "awash in the Human Potential Movement", not only in the form of encounter therapies but also "bodywork" groups such as rolfing, primal screaming, bioenergetics and "every kind of New Age specialty from shiatsu to accupuncture to past-life readings". Virtually all the Neo-Sannyasins on the ranch had been through at least one course, either there or at their local Centre. This certainly held true for Australian Neo-Sannyasins as well. Most respondents had done at least five groups, some as many as fifteen to twenty. Over fifty different types of group and course were named. However most of these courses were done after taking Neo-Sannyasa, or just before, and in Rajneesh Centres. This is less surprising when we consider the findings of Wuthnow (1976 : 53) in San Francisco, that, although 33 per cent of those he surveyed said that "spending getting to know your inner self" was of great importance to them, and 28 per cent felt the same way about "learning to be aware of your body", in fact "relatively few persons" actually admitted participating in growth groups or sensitivity training. Hence, despite the fact that taking Neo-Sannyasa commits one (more or less) to an interest in therapy work as a dominant means of transcendence, therapy was never a prerequisite to initiation as a Neo-Sannyasin or even an immediately predisposing factor. (There were also no comments on the effectiveness of the method, apart for Kalpa's deeply depressed remark (characteristic of all her replies) that she was "worse now than before" because all her worst fears about herself "were/are true").

Surprisingly, in contrast to the Full Sannyasins only six of the Karma Sannyasins (three men and three women) had not had any experience of the growth movement. Most people had done two to three courses—in areas as diverse as assertiveness, psycho-drama, rebirthing, dance, conflict, resolution, women's self-defence, rolfing and unconditional love—and participated in various Findhorn programmes and Down to Earth Festivals. Their commitment to these courses seemed stronger than the commitment of Neo-Sannyasins to trying yoga. For Karma-Sannyasins, yoga and the growth movement were both part of their search as a whole, yoga only slowly coming to assume its central significance in their new self-definition.

Conclusion on the Counter-Culture

Contrary to claims of Judah, Mullan and Rochford above (pages 97 and 109-110), there is, in Australia at least, no absolute relationship between participation in the counter-culture and the decision to join an Asian religion or to take initiation into *sannyasa*. The *sannyasins* were not, as they were often caricatured, a bunch of long-haired hippies, down from the hills, intent on smoking drugs and seeing visions of Indian goddesses with lolling tongues. Many *sannyasins* had been, however, less than fully integrated into mainstream society because of their marginal status as young, newly educated and single. Further some members of all three cohorts did subscribe to some of the major attitudes of the counter-culture of the late sixties and early seventies, in particular to radical politics, feminism, and some had used drugs. The relationship of most of the younger members of the second and third cohorts to the counter-culture, was, nevertheless, ambivalent.

What disciples shared in common was the quest for a more complete and integrated self-understanding and identity. To this end, Full Sannyasins and Karma Sannyasins had used the techniques of "eastern mysticism" related to yoga as a means of developing interior awareness for up to six years before initiation. Neo-Sannyasins, on the other hand, were disposed to believe that the answer to personal identity could be found in group psychological procedures. Karma Sannyasins participated in both therapy programmes and yoga but gradually came to feel most at home with yoga. These answers were not available in conventional religion.

Karl Mannheim (1952: 306) has drawn attention to the "generation unit", a coherent societal group which, by nature of its limitation, develops idiosyncratic values, language and a common destiny. The unit reflects the values of an interactive community and is not confined to a particular biological age group. He asserts that:

> To become really assimilated into a group involves more than the mere acceptance of its characteristic values—it involves the ability to see things from a particular 'aspect', to endow concepts with its particular shade of meaning, and to experience psychological and intellectual impulses in the configuration characteristic of the group. It means, further, to absorb those interpretive formative principles which enable the individual to deal with new impressions and events in a fashion broadly pre-determined by the group.

Despite the presence of three cohort levels, disciples may be considered to belong to the one generational unit because of their common value-orientation towards *sannyasa*, as a tool for self-discovery and a means of providing a strong personal identity, in the face of wider social situations characterised by uncertainty.

CHAPTER NINE

THE FULL SANNYASIN DISCIPLES OF SWAMI SATYANANDA

From now on, our concern rests much more with the experience of individuals. This chapter opens with a number of "powerful stories", as a way of bringing the human reality of *sannyasa* in Australia to life. Few stories are more striking than that of Ram Giri Baba, an apparently perfect example of the counter-culture renunciate in the traditional Indian style. The stories are given as they were recorded in the research for this study. The chapter then deals with the experience of Full Sannyasins living in the *ashram* of Munger, and with their return to Australian society.

Ram Giri Baba

Ram Giri Baba is a contemporary Australian *sadhu*. His experience with drugs led him into an intense religious search in India and continues to be part of his life-style.

Ram was born in 1953 in the southeast corner of Australia. His mother was a staunch Anglican. After completing school, Ram Giri became heavily involved with the "psychedelic" consciousness of the late sixties. He read Ken Kesey, Timothy Leary and Abey Hoffman, listened to the Grateful Dead and began experimenting with drugs. Later he married, had three children and managed the family property of over four thousand head of cattle.

When his family broke up three years ago, he was "pissed off" with everything here and headed for Asia. From Bangkok he went to Calcutta, where he soon got out of his depth. A Canadian directed him to the *sannyasis* for help. Ram left Calcutta and went to Varanasi (Benares), where he was impressed by "the living religion" of the *sadhus*. Then he went to Agra, was disillusioned with the tourists, and moved on again to Rajasthan, where he began staying with *babas* of the Giri order. Just being in their presence made him feel uplifted. He decided that this was a good way to live and began to learn their habits. (The customs of most *babas* include the devotional smoking of *ganja*.)

Then he moved on again and spent some time sitting with *sadhus* at a particular railway station. They were "primitive" and he felt as though he had been taken right back in time. Eventually they got sick of him because he couldn't speak their language and he left. He met another *sadhu*, a "crooked man", who poisoned him for a whole day. He didn't know whether he was in heaven or hell, or where he was. When he recovered he went back and scolded the man.

Finally he met Krishna Giri, who allowed Ram to stay in his *ashram* as long as he desired, providing he was prepared to work. Krishna Giri was an awesome man, as thin as a skeleton. Krishna Giri also offered to teach Ram. A month later Ram was initiated as a *Naga Baba*. Ram Giri remained another two months at the *ashram*, rising each day at four, drinking water, vomitting it up again, worshipping the *Shivalingam*, chanting the *mantra* "Om Namo Sivaya" and generally sitting for most of the day with Krishna Giri and the few other (mostly Western) *sadhus* in the *ashram*. *Sadhu* means "free"; in his opinion, the only genuine *sadhus* are the naked *Naga Babas*. He was proud to have been with them and not be "a tourist *Sadhu*". Being a *sadhu* taught him strength of mind and the need to root out negativity and desire.

About two years ago Ram returned to Australia. He now lives with Robyn, an old friend, in a fairly inaccessible part of the hills, although Robyn works in a regular job as a typist. Ram Giri "grows food". Despite the cold, he wears a single orange *dhoti*, no shoes and his hair is tangled and knotted. One of his reasons for living with Robyn is that "they persecute you here if you are celibate".

I : TAKING FULL SANNYASA: SWAMI HARIBHAKTI SARASWATI

Ram Giri's story has some striking similarities to and differences from that one of Swami Haribhakti, one of Swami Satyananda's first Australian disciples. It is the differences which are most important.

Haribhakti was born in Sydney in 1941. His parents were Jews. After completing a Bachelor of Science degree in 1963, he started work as a trainee executive, which he found very dull. Searching for more satisfying pursuits in life, he began taking courses in archaeology. He tried to be "arty:" taking LSD, reading philosophical works and starting to ask his own questions about the mystery of life. He participated in politics; that could not sustain his interest either. Then, in 1967, he discovered yoga, studying with one of the first teachers to have trained under Satyananda in India.

He was fascinated by the various postures and became fully absorbed in the practice of meditation. Through meditation it seemed as though he could transcend all his worldly dissatisfactions, his disappointments and woes. Soon he discovered that in India they not only have yoga classes but also enlightened guides called *gurus*, who could lift the veil of ignorance and let the truth be revealed. Within a few more weeks, he found his employment being regretfully terminated, with six months pay in compensation. He was jubilant; now he had the chance (and the money) to search for a *guru*.

At his yoga school he had noticed a poster and brochures for a Training Course to be held in Munger for the purpose of preparing Full Sannyasins. The course commenced on the 8th September 1970, Swami Sivananda's birthday. By this date Haribhakti had left his wife, found his *guru* in Swami Satyananda and been initiated into Full Sannyasa on Basant Panchmi day in February, well over half a year before the course started. One hundred and eight Full Sannyasins enrolled in the course, which was to be free and run for three years. The first month of the course was spent learning to chant the *Taittiriya Upanishad*, the second in silence and *mantra* recitation, the third learning yoga postures, the fourth learning control of breath techniques. Further months of *mantra* recitation and Kriya Yoga (learning about the energy in the body) followed. Most of the teaching was done by Swami Satyananda, who continued to run the *ashram* as well; some *swamis* knowledgeable about physiology also gave classes. The basic training was followed by the construction of an *ashram*

at Rajnandgoan and then a two hundred and fifty mile walk,
begging for food all the way, and staying wherever each pair of
Full Sannyasins could.

Life in the *ashram* was difficult. The food was tasteless and
everything was taken mixed together in buckets. He had no
friends, no comfort, no privacy and worked endlessly. Personal
possessions such as suitcases, emergency supplies of biscuits,
street clothing, and razor blades were handed in at the very
beginning of the course. It was a lonely life, in foreign surround-
ings. The Hindi-speaking *sannyasins* took notes in English; he had
to take notes in Hindi. In time Haribhakti was promoted and put
in charge of a big department conducting courses and seminars,
or another for cleaning, or cooking, or carrying coal. He was
demoted as often as he was promoted. Swamiji intensified every
human weakness, be it fear, guilt, ambition, self doubt, or whatever. By 1978 the *ashram* was so crowded that it became necessary
to stop accepting new applicants. A start was made on a new
ashram and in 1986 a new seven storey Ashram and Yoga Centre
was opened. By then Haribhakti had left.

For a very long time Haribhakti's life had great meaning.
Swamiji was not only a man, he was also an inner form of God
to whom Haribhakti could relate in meditation; he would dance
with the *Guru* and Satyananda's eyes lifted him to the greatest
heights. Everything was fine, except for one thing. Haribhakti
was a *swami*, a monk, and he wanted a woman. Celibacy had
always been a problem and he had reluctantly decided to accept
that sexual passion was an overwhelming desire in him. He fell
in love with someone and he left the *ashram* immediately.

Back in Australia, Haribhakti started a yoga school and then,
learning the economics of yoga, began teaching Science in a high
school. Soon he was teaching morning and evening yoga classes
at a school to both the teachers and the students. Tiring of teaching, he turned to driving taxis and sales work, where there was
still time to talk to people of yoga philosophy and practice. The
relationship came to an end, but there is still the opportunity to
meet women while teaching yoga. It helps to be interested in
feminism.

Some of Haribhakti's story, at the beginning of the generation,
resembles that of Giri Baba's, at the end. Both experimented with
drugs, explored the counter-culture, left comfortable careers and

difficult marriages and went to India to make sense of themselves and what had been happening to them. Both came back, in time, to be with a partner, earn a living at the edge of society, and continue, on an individual basis, putting into practice what had been learnt in India. In as far as there are probably no other *Naga Babas* in Australia, Ram Giri's story is unique. Haribhakti's is not. When the Indian government changed its visa regulations for Commmonwealth citizens in 1984, at least twenty Australian *sannyasins* eventually returned home. (Ratnadevi insisted in her Questionnaire that there have been "many more than twenty returning over the years" and there were also "countless numbers of Swamis who had lived in the Munger Ashram around the world".) These Full Sannyasins had a strong background in yoga practice before leaving for India. They already knew of Swami Satyananda and his Bihar School of Yoga. They experienced the tight structure and discipline of the *ashram* together. They returned to Australia determined to remain outside the Australian *ashrams* and began to create their own network. They have eagerly begun new careers, relationships and educational courses trying to catch up with as much as they could of what they have missed. And yet they remain outsiders to mainstream society. An average of ten years spent in an *ashram* is hard to explain on a job application, especially to large corporations. They have lived and shared experiences others around them will never understand. Externally the robes gave way to street clothes, the hair grew longer. Full Sannyasa is, however, something internal. "I left my Guru in Munger," Haribhakti wrote, "but I still had him in the streets of Sydney. My resolution to serve, love and obey him for the rest of my life remains. I still serve, love and obey him and will for the Rest of My Life. "

The First Full Sannyasin Cohort

As always, Full Sannyasins came to Satyananda in a variety of ways and for a variety of reasons.

Shantinath met Swami Satyananda in 1974. He had been practising yoga since 1971, in search of "higher consciousness". He went to India because he thought "that's where yoga is and that's where you get it." Also, he had been reading books like Carlos Castaneda and *The Autobiography of a Yogi* by Yogananda Paramahamsa. Besides his quest for spiritual answers, Shantinath was not well: he had chronic asthma and a lot of problems with his health. Satyananda taught him how to cure his asthma, showed him that many of his ideas were fantasies, that the reality of yoga was hard work and discipline, and encouraged him to do "research".

The next year Shantinath returned to Munger with a close friend. As medical students, they had arranged to spend the three month elective term before the final year's training studying the therapeutic applications of yoga practices. The friend had received *mantra* initiation from Swami Amritananda, Satyananda's senior woman disciple, during her visit to Australia in 1974. On Basant Panchami day in 1976, they were both initiated into Full Sannyasa.

The life appealed to Shantinath. It seemed a natural step after being with Swamiji for two to three years, thinking about the possibility of initiation and not being interested in much else. Also since he had been doing yoga since 1971, initiation seemed like the culmination of his life.

The friend, Bhadrinath, had begun yoga in 1973 and found the practices helped to balance his mind and emotions, helped his capacity to concentrate and study and improved his personal health as well. Bhadrinath found the Bihar School of Yoga approach to health and yoga to be practical and scientific. He was also impressed by the nobility and radiance of the disciples he met in November 1975. For him initiation was a way of overhauling his personality and misconceptions, so that he could see the light within.

Shantinath found living in the *ashram* a natural extension of all he had ever believed in. It provided him with a structure for living and an endless source of lessons. He spent nine or so years working on and off in India and finally came back to Sydney in 1985 to pursue a post-graduate degree which could equip him with the necessary skills for yoga research. Shantinath has since developed a reasonably strong Human Potential awareness. His asthma was finally cured by being able to relate his most severe attacks to a way of coping (badly) which he had learnt as a child. His post-graduate research was on physiology of the body-work process known as the Feldenkreis method.

Bhadrinath on the other hand, found the limited space of the *ashram*—with so many people living, working, singing and practising yoga in such a confined space—mentally and emotionally difficult. In time he adjusted to the lifestyle though he remained a rather traciturn and diffident individual. He returned to Australia in 1982 to complete his RMO obligations in hospital service. Both have visited Munger several times since for research purposes.

For some, Swami Satyananda's visit to Australia in 1976 was, consciously or unconsciously, the opportunity they had been waiting for to change the direction of their lives. Brahmarishi had been practising yoga since 1967; *sannyasa* was her "state of mind" and she was inwardly prepared for it. On the ninth of October 1976, "Swamiji just gave sannyasa to me—I did not ask him for it". For her husband too, who had been practising yoga since 1968 under Swami Satyananda's influence, "Sannyasa just evolved until it was the only thing to do". He returned to India with Satyananda and worked there for six years. She stayed in the Australian *ashram* with her three Full Sannyasin children.

Anantapadma described the step of taking Full Sannyasa as "no great drama". Everything led logically to it. He had studied yoga since the mid-sixties; from the early seventies in the first Satyananda *ashram* in Australia, under a highly gifted *sannyasin* teacher. Previously he had been informally interested in a number of things: Rosicrucianism, the Theosophical Society and the teachings of J. Krishnamurti. When Satyananda arrived at Sydney Airport in 1976, Anantapadma stood well away from "the mob". According to another disciple, Satyananda's appearance at the airport was like "a golden glow which filtered through that huge terminai" and "his tiny but huge figure was soon enveloped in flowers of all hues and perfumes"(Sambuddhananda, in *Yogakanti* 1989 : 77). Anantapadma immediately fell on his knees and touched the Master's feet in reverence. Satyananda looked at him and said:"You must take sannyasa". He said the same thing to Anantapadma's wife. On the 9th of October 1976 they did. They moved into the Australian *ashram*, separated and worked full time in the cause of yoga.

Satyananda's direct style could be hard to refuse. Navaratna suffered a series of intense psychic experiences during the death of his first wife. He had been pushed past the point of his personal resources after remaining awake with her for four and a half days and asked: "What more can I do?" A voice responded, telling him

to contact a particular *swami* (the same *swami* who had earlier
been Anantapadma's yoga teacher). Navaratna contacted the
man and found him to be a disciple of Swami Satyananda. The
swami came to the hospital and he too was thrown into the
psychic maelstrom of Navaratna's parting with his wife. Because
of the *sannyasin's* presence, the wife became totally centred and
later went into death with complete awareness and love.

In 1976 Navaratna began investigating yoga theoretically while
in Assam, following conversations with a member of the government who was staying at the same hotel. Navaratna took the
practices up in earnest later in the year while in the United States.
The next year he met Swami Satyananda on the 4th July in
Australia. Satyananda told him, "You come to India and take
sannyasa with me!" He did. Navaratna left Australia, went to
Munger and on the 1st December 1977 was initiated into Full
Sannyasa.

Adinatha had a dream in which Swamiji told her to come to
India with him. She resigned from work and joined a group
which was going to Mangrove Mountain to meet Swami
Satyananda, taking with her enough money for a one-way plane
ticket to India. The moment she set eyes on Satyananda, "she
knew". He asked her to come to India. She went and four days
later on the way, she was initiated. Her life had changed dramati-
cally from the moment she started yoga twelve months previously; now "*sannyasa* was inevitable".

Vinayakam's response was made on a similar intuitive level.
He began hatha yoga practices in 1971, "in search for my inner
self". The search took him to the Third World as well and in 1974
he settled into Swamiji's *ashram*. There life involved constant
hard work. The conditions were overcrowded, the food terrible
and too little, there was too little time to sleep and the climate was
awful. This brought a lot of his mind's impurities to the surface;
and acted to cleanse him. The relationship between Vinayakam
and Satyananda was unspoken: "when I first saw Swamiji, his
being answered all my questions without one word being spoken
between us". Satyananda radiated enormous peace and a sense
of oneness. Inwardly Vinayakam knew that Swamiji could guide
him to places he could never reach alone or ever know how to.
Without thinking about it, he found himself one day standing in

front of Satyananda asking to take Full Sannyasa, which he did on the 5th February 1976. It was a most simple occasion, sowing the seed of total change in his life, "though basically I remain the same". Vinayakam followed a five-year Sannyasa Training Course, from 1976 to 1980, remaining in India a total of eight and a quarter years.

Yogapadma took Full Sannyasa at Mangrove Mountain in 1973, the year after he finished high school. He had attended a few demonstrations and taken a spiritual name while still a student. His recollection was simple. Why had he taken *sannyasa*? "Why not?" What led to the actual step? "Nothing".

The Second Cohort

With the firm establishment of Mangrove Mountain in 1976 as the major Australian *ashram* under the strict guidance of the director, the continued spread of the system across Australia and indeed throughout the world, the regular offering of *sannyasa* training and other courses in India, and Swami Satyananda's frequent visits to Australia, taking Full Sannyasa was much less of a plunge into the unknown in 1980 than it had been earlier in the previous decade.

Madhuvidya took Full Sannyasa in 1980 after contact with other *sannyasins*, reading, observing, studying, questioning, visiting Mangrove Mountain for short courses and then spending nine months in full time residence. He liked the aims, the ideals, the lifestyle, attitudes and the philosophy he saw exemplified at the ashram. After initiation, Madhuvidya spent seven intense years in Australian branch *ashrams*. He is one of the only alternative Satyananda stream in Australia never to have visited Munger.

Swahananda started yoga in 1978. She too spent eighteen months at Mangrove Mountain before deciding to take Full Sannyasa during an interview with Satyananda. Her motive was devotional: "Swamiji is my guru, I want to live in his heart".

Anandakanti began yoga at the beginning of 1980, when she was seventeen and a half. She had left her art studies temporarily behind her to discover more about life and was working as a waitress. One of her work-mates was a vegetarian, as she was, and attending weekly yoga classes. The friend invited Anandakanti to join her. After the first class Anandakanti was "high for a whole week" and hasn't stopped practising since. A couple of years later she had her first *swami* teacher, Navaratna, and learned from him about Full Sannyasa. This was the lifestyle she had been trying to lead on her own for years. Here was an organisation of people thinking the way she thought. She had enjoyed learning about herself through forcing herself into new situations in her work, her accommodation, her relationships and travel in general and she jumped right into this new situation. Logically, she decided that it was more relevant for her in this day and age to teach yoga than it was to spend her life perfecting her expression through sculpture. Yoga could become a medium for communicating with and helping far more people than would her creations which only appealed to such a limited audience. ("if any at all!"). It would also be a way of "perfecting" her own life as a human being. That was the end of her B.A. in Fine Arts and the beginning of her commitment to renunciation.

At the end of 1983, Anandakanti went to Mangrove Mountain."Something indescribable" happened when she first met Satyananda that led her in the direction of *sannyasa*. It was so strong that she had no doubt that initiation was the next thing she must do, the next step in her evolution. Anandakanti took Full Sannyasa in order to learn more about " herself and her self" and as a gesture of devotion to the *Guru*'s mission of spreading yoga" "from door to door and shore to shore". For four years she lived in various Australian *ashram*s. In 1989 Anandakanti had the opportunity to return to Munger for a lengthy stay. Instead, she decided to experience a "long-term" intimate relationship, with another Full Sannyasa initiate. Her heart "led her back to Australia".

These three disciples were initiated in Australia. It had become less common to go to Munger seeking initiation, but some still did.

Religion had been integral to Madhuprem's life since birth. She had been raised in a solemn but benevolent Protestantism, which she abandoned as "useless and destructive' after her marriage. She had met her husband at university and dropped out at the end of the second year of her studies to get married. The marriage itself was not easy: there were affairs, his and hers, and eventually they were divorced, the children going to live with her ex-husband and his new wife. Madhuprem felt lonely living by herself but was unable to relate to other people. She needed to resolve the conflicts she had experienced over the past eight to ten years and the only way she knew which would give her peace was inner spiritual growth.

Madhuprem began yoga at the end of 1978, having just left the Women's Electoral Lobby and needing something to fill a gap in her life. Navaratna was a good teacher. After a weekend seminar she realised that yoga practice could solve physical problems she had experienced for years. Even though her Protestantism was now "on the shelf", "a big question mark in her life", she felt some guilt at her new commitment.

In November 1979, Madhuprem set out to travel to India and later on to London. She took a Kriya Yoga course in Munger, then spent time in Kathmandu, before returning to Bihar for a further four week stay in the *ashram*. The possibility of taking Full Sannyasa had crossed her mind in Australia, but when Swamiji sent a messenger around, asking whom among the visitors wished to take initiation, she hesitated for several days. During this time she talked with a few of the *swamis* there. She decided that a link with the *Guru* would offer her the support she needed to keep growing. She also decided that "a swami can do anything and is not limited by the conventions even of sannyasa itself, the wearing of saffron (*geru*) robes and so on". Madhuprem was initiated in early 1980. She continued on to London and too weary to be on her own, stayed with her sister and family. They found her robes and short hair strange; she found talking to them difficult. Later she returned to Australia and settled into *ashram* life, where she would be able to absorb yoga as a daily practice and be with others who were doing the same thing.

Ratnadevi was a teacher. Education was important to her. She completed a first degree and teacher training in 1962, a B.A. almost ten years after that and Honours some time later again. While teaching in the country, she discovered that the physical flexibility she had gained from long years of calisthenics was gradually fading, so she began yoga, amateurishly at first and then properly in 1972-73. Yoga "provided all the answers she'd been looking for".

For many years subsequently she put off the decision to take initiation into Full Sannyasa, knowing nevertheless it was inevitable. She didn't feel ready—too much ego, too many desires and so on. (Madhuprem has never married, perhaps for the same reasons.) In 1980 she was in Munger, "doing research on Swamiji". Because Satyananda had begun his mission on Basant Panchmi day, she extended her stay to be there for it. She decided that she had "been everywhere and done everything", worldly things had lost their appeal, and there was still much more she wanted to achieve ("experience?", "understand?"). Full Sannyasa was the way to do this. The idea of being initiated on Basant Panchmi appealed, "because my ego had always demanded that nothing less than 'the full bit' would satisfy me". The ceremony of that day was especially ritually complete, including a fire-sacrifice and other traditional rites. A few weeks later, she was sent back to Australia to complete a Ph.D. on Yoga (which she never finished) and then to study Tantra. A few years ago she was instructed to study Vedanta. Ratnadevi is one of the very few Full Sannyasins who has never lived any length of time in any *ashram*, either in India or in Australia.

Finally, a few of the second cohort were initiated by Satyananda in *ashram*s in Europe. Trilochana had started yoga in 1982 to help with his sore back. He found yoga filled a spiritual void. Somehow he fell in with Satyananda while travelling around Europe in 1982 and continued to follow him, taking Karma Sannyasa at Mangrove Mountain, December 1983, and full initiation in Paris four months later. Trilochana asked Swamiji about it was told "Good idea". The initiation was simple: Satyananda explained how to meditate using beads and instructed him "Go to Munger". (Initiation could be so simple that some disciples spent years thinking a stray remark had meant that they were now initiated, when, in fact, they were not). Usha, who had started yoga at the age of eight, lived in the Satyananda Ashram in Athens for three years in the late seventies, teaching English. While recognising that Full Sannyasa might provide an answer to the emptiness she felt in her life, she avoided any conscious decision about it, even though Satyananda visited the Athens *ashram* several times during those years. Feeling a strong pull to him, Usha finally went to visit Satyananda in the northern countryside of Denmark, having decided that she might just take Karma Sannyasa. Satyananda suggested Full Sannyasa; feeling unworthy, a product of her Catholic childhood, Usha fought against the idea but was unable to say "no".

The Third Cohort

The third cohort was small. The two women, who coincidentally have qualifications in Fine Arts, were both initiated in Munger.

Shripadma finished her degree in 1986 and had been drawn into working for Satyananda *ashram*s, Australia, but outside the *ashram* structure. Once controversy began to gather around the Director, she moved in to Mangrove Mountain, only to find herself in Munger twelve days later for the Guru Purnima festival. A month later, in August 1987, she took initiation. "There was nothing else to do but take sannyasa", she commented, "I'm not particularly ambitious (I think)".

Nandan was married for seventeen years. Her days were luxurious; she had a nice home, many successful jobs, a high income, two lovely children, a solid relationship, a good social life, and so on. But her life was empty. She tried to fill it with possessions, alcohol, even drugs, but only began to find some direction in her longing for "something else" after commencing yoga 1981. In late 1983 she took Karma Sannyasa at Mangrove Mountain. In a personal interview with Swami Satyananda in Munger in 1987, she asked about *sannyasa*. He replied that one should always try to aim high in the spiritual life and she was initiated into Full Sannyasa the following day. After three months, she was sent back to Australia to open an *ashram*. Currently Nandan works as a freelance graphic designer during the day, runs a small *ashram* in an inner city subrub and assists at the Yoga Therapy Centre, teaching and doing the art work.

II : LIVING IN THE ASHRAM

For these Australians, initiation had the Janus-like effect of closing off the past and opening the future to a new identity. The Full Sannyasins were younger than their Indian counterparts described by Tripathi, better educated, from more prosperous backgrounds ana uprooted from the wider society in which they had been raised. They had come from the margins—having just finished school, left an uninteresting career, were finished with a marriage or still single, with a little religion in childhood but not much, and wanted to find a new meaning for their life and new inner strength. Yoga gave them a glimpse of this new path.

Through Satyananda they were admitted to a new status and way of life, which centred on residence in the overcrowded but self-contained space of an *ashram*, or in the more comfortable but still rugged setting of Mangrove Mountain or one of the branch *ashrams* in Australia. In the *ashram*, they learnt more yoga. They chanted devotional hymns and songs (*kirtan*) in Sanskrit and Hindi. They were vegetarians, celibate and owned virtually nothing. They lived as the Indian renunciates with them did and met the qualities essential to a good renunciate. They were "acculturated to a pious version of a certain Indian life-style" (Miller and Wertz 1976: 28), wherever they were and whatever they did. Outwardly, they were true "Swamis".

Most of all, they worked. When he was in Sydney in 1976, Satyananda described an *ashram* as:

> a place where disciples and inmates would live in community with their guru and express their mental, intellectual, emotional and physical energies in the form of work.
>
> (Satyananda 1979 : 38)

Work was of two kinds : physical—the manual, the kitchen, the toilet, the building, the carpentry, the press, the bank, the post office and so on—and the spiritual (Satyananda 1979 : 142). The physical work took prominence:

> Ashram life is an aid to illumination. This life is designed in such a way that it reminds you of illumination at every moment. In an ashram, you do not meditate the whole day. You see the glory of divinity while you graze the cows, work as a carpenter, cut and boil the vegetables in the kitchen, look after the bank accounts, cash and cheques, see to the cleaning of the premises and take care of the premises, from dawn to dusk. When the sun rises, you see the ashram humming with activity like a bee-hive and when the sun sets, it is still very active.
>
> (Satyananda 1984 : 286)

The spiritual work was expressed through personal yoga practices, mantra recitation, tantric techniques, *kirtan* and occasional lectures. Only in a loose way was the *ashram* organised around the systematic conduct of religious worship, with an explicit, commonly agreed, supernatural meaning. Yoga practices focused on the individual body; meditation techniques were directed towards internal realities; *kirtan* was considered primarily a form of emotional release. The emphasis on work, the body and a personal, non-dogmatic religion based on a reverence for life, were very much in accordance with the Australian Myth sketched in Chapter Six above. Inwardly, the *swami*s had not become Hindus in any but in a loose sense.

The counter-culture had given the Australian myth a focus on personal power as the way of conquering personal despair and relentless struggle. In the *ashram*, power was understood to be the result of the transcendence of one's ordinary consciousness as an individual self, through detachment from personal desires and material attachments. Work was a part of spiritual discipline, as were diet, eating and sleeping. It was a way of achieving a higher consciousness (Muktananda n.d. : 3).

When asked to define the significance of *sannyasa* for themselves at the end of the 1980s, it was this development of interior awareness which most Full Sannyasins tended to emphasise. Only a few mentioned the link with the *Guru*. (Anantapadma appreciated the discipline Akhandananda had been able to teach aspirants when he was at the peak of his abilities, because it made yoga an all-consuming passion. Madhuprem valued "the support of the guru".) *Sannyasa* was not primarily a system of *guru* worship. Nor was it a means of social service. (Nandan mentioned "selfless service and teaching yoga" as part of the meaning of "*sannyasa*" for her, but only as ways of "learning about myself and others".)

We may see the focus on inner psychological processes in the following definitions of *sannyasa*. For Shantinath, *sannyasa* was:

> The renunciation of neurotic obsession with material security and the transcient, in order to place awareness and energy on the Self, the central core of being which is permanent and in the last analysis, the last step, is all that we ultimately have. It is also a way of thinking so that we can do what we want with our lives, so that we are our own masters.

For Gyanraksha:

> Sannyasa to me means finding my true self, whatever that may be. Being myself, relaxing with myself and living yoga.

Treating each life situation as an opportunity to develop
naturally, spiritually, emotionally. Expanding my awareness
of my own mind and helping others in any way I can to
expand awareness of themselves. Living either in the ashram
or the world with this attitude. (In a nutshell, evolving the
mind.)

Nandan's full definition was:

Taking sannyasa to me meant learning to become sannyasin
by learning about myself and others, through selfless service,
teaching yoga and developing awareness in everything I do
in everyday life. I hope to increase the devotional aspect of
myself so that I may know and understand my true purpose
in life not just on an intellectual basis but to feel it fully!

And Vinayakam's observation was :

Sannyasa means everything from total bullshit to total
freedom of the self. It can mean total discipline and tapasya
in order to strengthen the mind and somehow though I
don't understand how, to purify the mind.

And very slowly over the many years the inner light
glows more strongly, the heart and mind remaining more
constant, though the obstacles throw themselves in your
path constantly. Sannyasa or rather the outcome gives one
a contact with the self, an *ancorage*. In this ever changing
world around us.

Its a letting go of all our perconceived ideas and prejiduces,
please excuse my spelling. And maybe to many these answers
come to all just through the process of ageing, though I have
only trodden this path, maybe life's answers would have
come anyway.

The *ashram*, as Muktananda explained (in Ajanananda 1990 :
6), provided many things: a unique opportunity to step out of the
world, food and shelter, the opportunity of not only learning
about yoga but living it. Most importantly:

It provides for interactions with our teacher and other
ashramites which challenge our conditioning and self-
centeredness. These relationships illuminate our

psychological blind-spots and accelerate growth. In the ashram we are free from decisions and responsibilities. All we have to take care of is our own mind! Most important, we have the freedom and safety to let go of limiting ways of being. We do not have to keep ourselves together to cope with the necessities of survival—we can fall apart completely, if necessary, so that our authentic self can grow through.

Living in the *ashram*, especially in the seventies in Munger, could never have been easy. As we have seen, the life was austere, lonely, the food tasteless, the climate harsh, the language and surrounding culture strange, work relentless and unending. Yet most (fifteen out of twenty) insisted that adjustment to the life of *sannyasa* had been easy. Swadhyaya, having followed Satyananda back to India in 1976, found "some cultural problems", but was "generally O.K.". Gyanraksa took to *ashram* life quickly and also to India and the culture. Vinayakam knew "instinctively" that *sannyasa* life was good for him, that the environment of India felt good in every aspect of his being and that living with Swamiji's energy activated the "dross" of the mind, made him aware of the impurity of the mind, and encouraged him not to rest in himself.

Those who acknowledged problems ("Is it easy for anyone?" Ratnadevi wondered), located these problems in the same area of personal psychology. For Shripadma, adjustment to the life of *sannyasa* was:

horrendous! The first year must have been the very worst time of my life. Major problems: relationships with people and self confidence.

Nandan listed the problems of adjustment as:

Initially the concept of sannyasa and my own conditioned way of thinking. The idea of surrender, I couldn't understand it. I could't feel it. Purification, Anger especially, 'phew'so much, I was awful and can still be a pain.

Perhaps significantly, these third cohort *sannyasin*s had no long-term experience of living in Munger and took Full Sannyasa after the Australian *ashram* system began to fall apart. They thus had few role models and little support for their socialisation into the status of *"Swami"*.

"Surrender" was Adinatha's one word definition of *sannyasa*. There were two areas in which Full Sannyasins found it difficult to resign themselves to what might be happening around them.

The first of these related to authority. Usha found adjustment to the life generally very easy, as her life outside the *ashram* had been quite simple too (although she did, at first, miss raw foods and fruit). What she found most difficult were "orders, regular meals and a hierarchy within the ashram". Muktananda reflected (Ajnananda 1990; 6-7):

> there are also serious limitations to the structure of traditional ashrams, where power and control are concentrated at the top. The traditional ashram fosters a reliance on an external source for all decisions: not only spiritual ones, but ordinary daily ones. We can develop difficulty in taking responsibility, that is, our ability to assess a situation and respond with appropriate action. Yoga encourages us to find our ishta devata, or inner guru, the source of our own answers within. Yet this was not given practical expression in our communal ashram life and decision making. In BSY this went along with a poverty of cooperative skills. During the inevitable disagreements matters were settled 'from above' by Swamiji, or whoever he put in charge: "Swamiji says". We had no examples of, nor experience in, group problem solving or conflict resolution.

Muktananda also noted (Ajnananda 1990 : 7) that the further one moved up the hierarchy, the more one became out of touch with "the reality of other peoples' needs and feeling". Errors easily arose when there was little or no "feedback for correction" from others, and the interpretation of inner guidance might become distorted.

The authoritarian, hierarchical pattern of decision-making is an important part of Indian culture. It is not unknown in Australia, but the pretence is usually otherwise. Within the counter-culture, there was a valuing of mutual decision-making, based on consultation and discussion. To do otherwise was to infringe on the other person's area of personal power. "Surrender" meant giving up one's power, in situations in which one had in fact no power anyway, in order to conserve that power for other situations. It was sometimes a necessary step but not normally one an individual could feel proud of.

Yogapadma found adjustment to Full Sannyasa easy and noted only one problem: "sex". Despite the Australian *ashram*'s reluctance to distribute The Questionnaire on *sannyasa* because of its questions of a "personal" nature, it has been this researcher's experience, both in Canada and Australia, that all respondents have been willing to write answers in this area and were not the least embarrassed. Sex was the second area in which most *Sannyasins* had difficulty in the *ashram*. Like authority, intimacy relates to personal power and control over the expression of one's body.

Devadas was aware of the faltering legitimacy of the Australian leadership prior to his transfer to Munger in 1983 and even more after his return in 1987 when the issue could no longer be covered over. Originally intending to take initiation in India, he had become a Full Sannyasin 1976 when Swami Satyananda came to Australia. One of his reasons for taking Full Sannyasa was a commitment to the ideals of the yogic philosophy and *sannyasa* and the perspective they gave him on life and his place in it. Another reason was his wanting to help start a *sannyasa* tradition in Australia. Three of his ongoing difficulties of life as a *Sannyasin* related to authority:

— not having the freedom to make my own decisions
— accepting orders from someone I had lost respect for
— trying to understand what the hell was going on.

The fourth related to sex:

— trying to determine whether I was meant to be celibate or not (finally deciding I did't have to be).

Celibacy has been an element of much of the Indian renunciate tradition from the beginning. Allen and Mukherjee (1984 : 4) describe *sadhus* as "a numerous, prestigious and predominantly male segment of the Hindu population", noting Tripathi's finding that 71 per cent of the orthodox *sadhus* he studied either claimed to hate or be indifferent towards women. A different part of the tradition, however, has shown a strong interest in the power associated with controlled sexuality and sexual relationships.

(See, for example, the discussion on *yati* ascetics and the *kapaladharin*s in Part Two above). Among orthodox Hindus, there would seem to have been little public discussion of the psycho-social dimensions of celibacy and their place in the life of the renunciate. Such matters were implicit and it was easier instead to talk glowingly of the "glories of *brahmacharya*".

Satyananda too spoke little on the issue. Many Full Sannyasins apparently assumed, with Anantapadma, that *sannyasa* was about "poverty, chastity and obedience". Anantapadma took Sannyasa in his fifties and felt that celibacy wasn't a problem for him, nor for his former wife as far as he was aware. Swadhyaya, aged forty-two, did not find celibacy a problem at the time and now states: "there is no need for me to be a celibate now because the attachment has gone". Brahmarishi did not find celibacy a problem either as she worked fifteen to eighteen hours a day. Other, younger *sannyasin*s found the problem remained. They did lots of spiritual practice (*sadhana*), ate less, slept less, worked harder, used more energy in *kirtan*, focused their awareness on the *guru*, or sometimes masturbated and had wet dreams.

In the confined spaces of Munger, there was little opportunity for satisfactory sexual intimacy (although it was not impossible, especially outside the *ashram* itself). The wider open spaces of the Australian *ashram*s and the less strict norms of Australian culture and the counter-culture, would certainly have allowed for greater closeness. (Most members of the public did not know whether *Swami*s are supposed to be married or not.) Couples who came into the *ashram* together usually experienced some ongoing sense of togetherness for at least the first year, even if they lived separately, or at least until they were sent to different branch *ashram*s. Among the various responses to the question, "Was/is celibacy a problem for you? How did/do you deal with?", were:

— Partly celibate for ten years. It was a difficult experience and transitory. I do not believe that it is healthy long term for most people but it is something all of us should experience to understand sex and its potency.

— Not a big problem. I managed to score something now and then. So I have never been totally celibate for more than a year.

— At first celibacy wasn't a problem for me. After two years in the ashram I found it difficult and finally broke it because I couldn't supress it anymore and it was abnormal. There was a certain amount of guilt feeling at first.

and the breathtakingly simple:

—Yes. I fucked.

For those living outside the *ashram* system, celibacy was not a problem. "It was never enforced on me," says one respondent.

The "message" Devadas "finally got from Satyananda" was "make up your own mind—there are no rules". This would seem to be an accurate perception. Satyananda (1986 : 189) describes his own first tantric initiation in this way:

When I was eighteen, a tantric yogini came to live in our family. She was an expert in tantra and she initiated me into the actual tantric practices. I was eighteen and she was thirty-five. I was educated and she was illiterate. She stayed with us for six months and during that time she trained me in every tantric practice. There was nothing which I did not learn from her.

He subsequently studied for six to eight months "with a venerable holy man who was maybe eighty or ninety at that time", near Udaipur. He learnt a lot about the classical texts from the old man, but was asked to leave when it became clear that Satyananda knew more about the actual practices than his teacher. Satyananda's later reluctance to speak at length on sexuality may have been more due to his belief that there are "secret practices which can only be given to those who are prepared for them" (Satyananda 1979: 23), and his fear of being misunderstood by a prudish public, than to any desire to encourage continence. (Reference should also be made to Satyananda's talk on "Vama Marga", published in *Yoga*, March 1981.)

Leaving the Ashram

If *sannyasa* is about inner transformation and an inner relationship with the *guru*, then it would seem to follow that is not necessary for the *sannyasin* to live always in the *ashram*. Shripadma wrote:

> Geru robes and shaved heads and living in an ashram with
> your guru are not Sannyasa. I crave for all that but real
> Sannyasa is an attitude inside. It's a thing that grows and
> unfolds. It's not paraphenalia and rules. Renunciation,
> celibacy, vegetarianism, Ahimsa (non-violence) come
> naturally from within, eventually.

Usha agreed:

> Sannyasa used to mean living a so-called "spiritual life" in
> an ashram. Now it means to be totally aware and free within
> everyday living.

As Anandakanti firmly insisted, the *ashram* provides a structure and a support for renunciation but the two should not be confused.

None of the twenty respondents is presently committed to returning to live on a long-term basis in the *ashram* in Munger. None joined the Australian *ashram* system on returning home. (After 1986, the system began to shrink from twenty-five *ashrams* to less than four.) Instead, they became a separate stream within the Australian Satyananda movement, loosely referred to as "the Munger Swamis". (Even those one or two who never went to India or stayed any length of time there are classified in this way.) Some set up their own *ashrams*, although these were usually no more than one person, a couple, or a few couples. The spiritual community, one of the options for commune dwellers in the seventies and a reason for the popularity of the *ashram* system as a whole, had shrunk to an option for a particular style of family living. "It is important for me to live with one sannyasin", wrote Swadhyaya, "my wife".

Why did people leave the *ashrams*?

Some were never involved, or only briefly. Others were instructed by Swami Satyananda to set up their own *ashrams* and understood this to mean that they were to remain independent of all systems. Navaratna says very firmly:

> I was given direct and personal instruction by Swami
> Satyananda in 1979 in front of (the senior leaders of the
> Australian Ashram system) to under no circumstances have
> any affiliation with "these people" (indicating the

abovementioned with a dismissive wave of the hand)—you must remain completely independent. He later said: "You will establish your own ashram in the jungle".

(Some years later in a radio interview, Satyananda justified the existence of two *ashram*s in the same state, one "official" and one "unofficial" with the words: "Why two? You mean not more than two? Good idea. . .") Usha's visa expired in 1986 and she had no choice but to return to Australia from India.

Many had reached the point in their lives where they felt that it was now time to do other things. Haribhakti, Gyanraksha and Anandakanti chose to set up relationships with other Full Sannyasins. Devadas was tired of the restrictions of *ashram* life and wanted to test himself in the wider world. He felt the *ashram* had helped him mature in many areas, but it had also retarded his development in dealing with society and the outside world. He needed greater intellectual stimulation. Madhuprem too felt "institutionalised" and needing more challenge. She was keen to see if her yogic training equiped her for "the average life and the tensions of living". Fortunately, she decided when she tried it that she was well prepared for this step.

Shantinath saw the *ashram* as a "stepping stone". For others again, the institution had broadened to include the world. There was still regular contact with other Full Sannyasins, who acted as peers to provide emotional support and a means of checking on one's feelings and sense of self-importance.

III : LIVING IN AUSTRALIA

In resuming employment in Australian society, *sannyasin*s tended to opt for small-scale self-employment. Some of the men are doctors, psychiatrists and medical researchers. Others are taxi-drivers, carpenters and market gardeners. The women work as freelance graphic designers, teachers, part-time in a health food shop, selling bread and designing stained-glass windows. Paid child-care appeals to both men and women. Almost all are involved in teaching yoga. Five are involved in administering *ashram*s and Yoga Therapy Centres.

With food and shelter no longer provided by the *ashram*, all must fend for themselves. Most claim to live simple lives, with few needs. Devadas regretted that many things had passed him

by while he was working selflessly in the *ashram* and could never
be regained. Those who do yearn for a few decent things—like a
nice, well-equipped house, a stereo, a car, decent clothes, tend to
justify these things as being potentially useful for enabling them
to work more freely in the world of yoga. Some operate on the
magical principle that everything they need "seems to come",
sooner or later.

Saraswati (1988 : 5) has proposed that:

> the values espoused in spiritual communities are congruent
> with the requirements of conventional social roles. A respect
> for personal discipline and acceptance of authority could
> make work routines and authority structures easier to bear.
> Striving for inner detachment potentially makes the
> impersonality and repetition of most jobs less oppressive,
> while the redefinition of work roles imbues them with new,
> intrinsic value.

However, on the data presented above, it is evident that Full
Sannyasins have avoided employment in large public and private
corporations, and that their drives to ambition and self-aggran-
disement are few. They have accepted the need for self-sustaining
employment and couples relationships, but do not measure their
success or identity in terms of material achievement as conventional society does. Vinayakam lives with his *de facto* wife in a
comfortable mud brick hut, tending a vast garden of vegetables
and fruit trees, which he sells at a local market on two days a
week, and teaches yoga at home. He belongs more to the ongoing
counter-culture. Madhuvidya is glad to have time for surfing;
overtime is not an issue for him.

Being self-employed has as one of its benefits the freeing of the
individual to continue yoga practices, which all the Full Sannyasins do, regularly and extensively. One of Satyananda's more
poignant comments is that: "In yoga it is not necessary to do very
much, but it has to be done for a long time" (Satyananda 1979:
137). *Sannyasa* has given these individuals the benefit of a guide
on their spiritual journey, peace, inner tranquillity and strength.
These are not qualities they would readily forego. Their latest
idea is a creative transformation of that conferred in their initiation.

CHAPTER TEN

HOUSEHOLDER SANNYASINS

Karma Sannyasins are about the same age as Full Sannyasins, and have the same levels of education in the same practical areas. Whereas Full Sannyasins have spent two decades practising yoga and have lived in an *ashram* context for at least half of that time, Karma Sannyasins have practised yoga for about nine years, been initiated less than four years, and have spent little, if any, time living in *ashram*s. On the other hand Full Sannyasins are only now struggling to establish the homes, families and careers which will hopefully see them through to the end of their lives. Karma Sannyasins know all these areas intimately through long experience, and have no choice but to regard the world as their sphere of growth. Living in the world as a *sannyasin* with obligations and responsibilities is not a new adventure but a necessity they have always endured.

This chapter, like the last, begins with the life of a typical Karma Sannyasin. It then studies the processes leading to the initiations of the various cohorts, the meaning of Karma Sannyasa for them, and the nature of their current lifestyle. The chapter concludes with a consideration of some of the relationships which exist between Full and Karma Sannyasin disciples of Swami Satyananda.

I: Taking Karma Sannyasa: Swami Tulsimala Saraswati

Tulsimala was born in 1949. She was raised in a small town in England. As a child she could have been considered a Christian, as an adult she firmly rejected religion. She was a good student, graduating with a Master's degree at the age of twenty-two. She was only moderately interested in politics, slightly more in feminism, but not active in either.

As an adolescent Tulsimala wanted to find her own spirituality, one which would make sense of the world for her. It took her ten years to find the teacher she needed and she began yoga at the age of twenty-five. Over the next few years she developed an interest in the spiritual community at Findhorn, off the north coast of England, and watched with some interest as its rigid governing structure became more open and equal. She also learnt about Jungian psychology and came to value the feminine archetypes both in herself and in those around her, men included. Her academic training started to make room for qualities such as "allowing things to happen", rather than trying to force them to be the way she thought they ought to be. She became a gentler, more caring person.

About eleven years ago she moved to live in the Australian countryside, with her partner, Govinda, who shared her interest in yoga. One day while she was meditating, she received direct guidance from Swami Satyananda that she should seek initiation. After this experience she took the first available opportunity to do so and enrolled in the first and only Karma Sannyasa course ever held at Mangrove Mountain, in December 1983. The training lasted a week. Swamiji had not given Karma Sannyasa at all when he was in Australia the previous April and there were almost one hundred and forty people enrolled in the course. They had filled in the appropriate form, including their astrological sign, and additional forms requesting a *mantra*, a spiritual name and a psychic symbol for meditation purposes if they did not already have these. They contributed forty dollars towards the cost of the initiation (for the cloth and beads, in particular) and paid for their accommodation. Many had counted their finances carefully before coming and found the extra forty dollars a burden. During the week they practised yoga, listened to lectures, heard Swami Satyananda speak several times and worked hard around the dam at the top of the hill. At other times they tended the extensive vegetable gardens on the hill slopes or swam in the river. Once, late in the week, they had relaxed by swimming in the dam itself, only to be sent scurrying for their clothes as Swami Satyananda drove up to inspect the work. He had laughed.

The initiation took place at the end of the week. Some wore all orange, others did not. A few had shaved their heads, most had not. They were to return to their homes afterwards and the initiation meant different things to each of them. As their old names were called out in the large hall, each person went forward, bowed to Satyananda Paramahamsa as he sat at the front of the raised stage and received from him a *geru dhoti*, a set of beads for meditation and a card with their Karma Sannyasa name. It was the same style of name as used by Full Sannyasins, bearing the prefix *swami*, for men and women alike, and the family name *Saraswati*. Most received back their old spiritual names. A few had new names. Some had old names altered by the addition of the affix *ananda*; these were the most prestigious. Satyananda spoke of their initiation as being a death to a life lived "amidst flowers, pleasures, sensualities, desires, 'haves' and 'have nots' ", and a new birth, in which the value of everything they would henceforth do had now substantially altered because of their commitment to growth and the daily practice of yoga. Because it was near Christmas, Swami reminded them that the Christ-consciousness was being born in them, wished them "Happy Birthday", and sent them out to find their "true mother". (The talk is recorded in Satyananda 1984 : 144-48). Outside they celebrated, embraced, compared names and felt enormous delight.

Tulsimala was now a *sannyasin*. She decided that she should stay as much as she could at the *ashram* and follow the advice of the *swami* in charge. For her, she notes looking back, this was entirely the wrong decision to make. The *ashram* was beginning to change: as Anantapadma recalled, the early message had been "Look within yourself, find yourself"; it was now "Listen to what I say, then go away and do it". Tulsimala grew thinner, weaker and was desperately unhappy. Then, as she says, "bang! I rebelled".

The process of the year had been a painful one but it taught her a lot. She recognised and came to terms with many of her old habits, especially her tendency to give away power over her own life to other people. Previously she had been driven by "shoulds and oughts", and the conditioning that "you're no good unless . . ." As she came to understand what was happening to her, she was freed from many of her own "top dogs" and guilty feelings.

Today, as a *sannyasin*, she sees her life as an adventure, a mystery journey in which each new section reveals itself in due course, in a way she knows she will be able to deal with, without needing to live up to the expectations of other people. Because no restrictions are placed on Karma Sannyasins with regard to material things, she has no yearning for them. Nor is she celibate. She works at woodcraft, participates in dancing and singing and spends lots of time in nature, exploring her inner link with the wild places. From time to time people seek her out for informal counselling. Tulsimala feels she has developed an inner link with the *Guru*. It is important for her to be part of a community of spiritual aspirants (for which she uses the Buddhist word *sangham*), and she meets with other Karma Sannyasins often, phones them up and works with them on various projects. She and Govinda are enrolled in a Yoga Teacher Training Course and regularly attend residential training programmes together. However, Tulsimala feels no need to live with any other *sannyasins*. She is at home with herself and peaceful.

The First Cohort

Tulsimala is one of the first cohort of Karma Sannyasins, those initiated by Swami Satyananda during his visit to Australia and New Zealand in late 1983 to early 1984.

Kriyatmananda was another who took Karma Sannyasa the same day as Tulsimala. Tulsimala was thirty-four and held a postgraduate degree; he was just twenty-eight and a qualified electrician. He had begun yoga the year before, for his bad back and to get fit, and had soon gone on to complete a Teacher Training Course. He was impressed with the quality of life exhibited by the *sannyasins* at Mangrove Mountain and dissatisfied with his own conventional existence. During a dream, Satyananda came to him and said "you will be a swami". By being initiated, he had accepted the inevitable.

Devachittam, Kumarimurti and Gyansindhu were initiated by Satyananda at a country *ashram* together. For Devachittam, the decision was a conscious one. She had begun yoga during a time of personal and family crisis in her early twenties, having seen a class on television. Within twelve months she was teaching yoga herself in her home town, often finding it difficult to maintain a distance as a teacher and preferring to be regarded as one of the group. For five years she thought of taking *sannyasa* but continually deferred the decision for fear of it being "an ego trip". Although suppressing the thought frustrated her, she was able to simplify her lifestyle during this time. When Satyananda arrived at the *ashram*, she knew that the moment for initiation was at last right.

She was grateful for the extra connection initiation would give her with him and saw it as a stepping stone to deeper states of awareness. Her friends and students went to the *ashram* with her. Kumarimurti had no reason to take Karma Sannyasa and did not understand the concept. She had been practising yoga for twelve years, having originally fractured her back in a fall and needing to straighten it out. She assumes that "Ha! Swamiji must have drawn me. . .", to take initiation from him. Gyansindhu, heavily involved with anti-nuclear politics, conservation issues, abortion law reform, Friends of the Earth and Down to Earth Festivals took up yoga in 1981, hoping (mistakenly, she now sadly realises) to stay young forever. She knew nothing of Karma Sannyasa but on the day it was offered, she thought: "Well, of course, do it!" Although she had no money, a stranger lent her the required forty dollars. There was no great decision, but like all she has ever done in connection with yoga, it was fine, made sense and seemed right.

The Second Cohort

Like the first cohort of Full Sannyasins, the first cohort of Karma Sannyasins entered their new status as an adventure, with not too much sense of knowing with what they were getting involved. Their innocence ensured that they captured something of the radical "otherness" of renunciation and this quality has remained with them over the years. For the second and third generations of Karma Sannyasins, as for later Full Sannyasins, the *ashrams* were established fixed entities, role models were sufficiently plentiful, and the books explaining what they were doing were available for previous study and consideration.

Kaivalyananda took Karma Sannyasa by post from Swami Satyananda in early 1987. She had begun yoga in 1984, following the break-up of her marriage. A seminar by Anantapadma's wife helped her to learn to relax and be more accepting of what she was undergoing. In January 1987, she spent some time at Mangrove Mountain and was very impressed by hearing one of the senior staff members talk of his feelings for Swami Satyananda. Feeling lost and without must sense of direction in her own life, she decided that it "felt right" to apply for Karma Sannyasa. Kaivalyananda admits that she doesn't always think things through, she usually acts on the basis of her feelings; this decision has subsequently proven to have given her a steadying influence in her life.

The *Guru*-disciple relationship is not one that has ever greatly appealed to her, but she cannot deny having felt guided and cared for many times since her initiation.

Harigauri, too, took initiation by post. She met her husband in 1983: he had been practising yoga for several years. He was a steady and constant man, who amazed her with his perceptions and intuitions (which she considered uncharacteristic of men in general), and his calmness; and all these qualities he attributed to yoga. Harigauri took a Beginners Course at Mangrove Mountain in 1984, to see if yoga was really in conflict with her strong Pentacostalist Christian beliefs. (Harigauri was converted at fifteen in the Anglican Church and joined the Assemblies of God at twenty). She decided that God (not necessarily the God of the churches, whom she subsequently renounced) was stronger than the devil (whom her Christian friends told her was behind yoga). As her spiritual understanding broadened, she took Karma Sannyasa in 1987, writing from Mangrove Mountain a few months after the birth of her first child. Harigauri felt that Karma Sannyasa would help her further along the path in her spiritual journey.

Suparnananda, Chamunda and Om Murti all took Karma Sannyasa in Munger from Swami Satyananda during 1987. Suparnananda had begun a Bechelor of Education degree after the age of thirty-five. She developed an interest in feminism. During her course she did a lot of humanistic psychology and was introduced to yoga by someone running a particular group. It seemed a good form of exercise which wasn't too difficult. She also felt a strong connection with Swami Satyananda. Following these, and other, major changes in her life, she went to the local *ashram* and never returned home again. After staying for six months, she left for India to take initiation.

Chamunda and Om Murti both followed a special Yoga Kriya course in Munger which their local Yoga Therapy Centre had arranged. Chamunda had been practising yoga regularly for seven years; initiation felt like a natural progression along the path she had chosen, the opportunity was there, so she did. Om Murti began yoga in 1984, because of insomnia and the need to learn relaxation. As she progressed, she felt that a lot of her questions about health, the body and the mind, were answered and that she was undergoing "incredible personal growth". She took Karma Sannyasa to intensify this growth. Initiation also provided her with a close connection to Swami Satyananda, whom she was sure was her *guru*, as she believed she needed his guidance in her life.

The Third Cohort

The Yoga Therapy Centres are also crucial to the stories of the third cohort, but not by their sending people to India. From May to June 1988, Swami Niranjananda visited Australia "to discuss the research program of the Yoga Research Foundation with doctors and research students " (*Yogakanti* 1989 : 158). He may also have been sent by Satyananda to investigate what was happening to the Australian *ashram* system, now in a state of major crisis, but if so was remarkably ineffective against his older and more wily foe. He visited the mainstream *ashram*s in Melbourne and perhaps elsewhere; the Yoga Therapy Centres in Brisbane, Sydney, Melbourne and Hobart; and some of the country centres run by Karma Sannyasins associated with the Yoga Therapy Centres. It is likely that his visit strengthened the Therapy Centres' claim to be the legitimate extension of Munger in Australia and served to further isolate the Australian system.

Mangalananda decided to take Karma Sannyasa after being in Niranjananda's presence for the first time. She had practised yoga intermittently from 1978 and regularly from 1987. Rationally, initiation was a way of being closer to the *guru*'s energy; intuitively, it "just felt right". Shankarananda, too, was overwhelmed by Niranjananda's presence. Initiation seemed to offer a link with the *guru*, direction and stability to his life, the state of mind he had seen in some *sannyasins* (detachment, calmness and compassion), and membership of that same extended family. His wife had been a Karma Sannyasin since 1983.

For Brahma, who had practised yoga for five years and Jamuna, who had been practising for thirty-five years, initiation was a means of further commitment to yoga and a natural development from it. Yogalata, who had practised yoga for five years after looking for a philosophy "which fitted into my beliefs of growth and development through self awareness", also saw Karma Sannyasa as a further commitment to yoga and "just felt drawn to it."

Those members of the third cohort who took initiation in Munger did not go to India solely for this purpose but included the Bihar School of Yoga as a very important part of their itinerary. Mutan was in Asia for five and a half months. He had started some yoga practices while learning Transcendental Meditation and then became more regular after discovering a Satyananda Ashram in his capital city in 1983. As an engineer, he liked the structured, careful presentation of the teaching. Karma Sannyasa later seemed a way of consolidating what he had been doing, of combining 'normal' life with 'spiritual life', and an orderly way of ensuring that all the steps, processes and interactions of his existence could become part of a learning process. He visited Munger at the end of his travels in 1989 and was impressed by the effect it had on him. Initiations were being held and Karma Sannyasa seemed "the right thing" (intuitively) to do at the time.

Ambarupa started yoga after one of the Down to Earth festivals but did not become serious about it until a few years ago. In the middle of 1988, she became close friends with a man at her work who had taken *sannyasa* recently. She observed him carefully and appreciated his strong sense of peace and joy. In July, on her birthday, she sensed that strong changes were coming in her life and decided to visit India in order to take Karma Sannyasa. After visiting her parents in Germany, where she had been born, she stopped over in India for five days on her return flight to Australia. By the time she had organised her travel from Delhi, she was only able to stay two days at the *ashram*. Ambarupa was eager for an intensive link with Swami Satyananda, ready for total transformation, curious to know her name and the personal practice which would be prescribed for her, and wanting to open new channels in her life. Two days were short enough but have changed, she says, the rest of her life.

Devashakti, always her own person, took Karma Sannyasa once by post and once in person from Swami Niranjan, because she happened to be in Munger when he was initiating people. She says she took initiation because she felt devotion towards Swami Satyananda and liked the *geru* colour. She also disliked the first name she had been given.

The Meanings of Initiation

For Full Sannyasins initiation into *sannyasa* meant, as they now perceive it, a commitment to inner growth. Karma Sannyasins tend to see their initiation in slightly different terms, two of which may be considered institutional, one of which is personal.

In the stories of coming to Karma Sannyasa presented above,

there is a much greater focus on the person of Swami Satyananda than in the stories of the Full Sannyasins. His influence is felt both on a psychic and religious level. The first meaning of Karma Sannyasa relates to the establishment of a link with the Master. Devachittam stated that initiation provided her with "a subtle but stronger connection to the *guru*"; it placed her on a spiritual path "with a psychic connection with a master whose guidance is there to help you find the master within". Chamunda, too, commented on "a commitment to a spiritual path, and a connection with *guru* while being in the world".

The relationship between *guru* and disciple forms an important theme in the teachings of Swami Satyananda in the book *Karma Sannyasa*. There he insists: "for Karma Sannyasa, the *guru*-disciple relationship is not only most important, it is the only important thing" (1984 : 116). The role of the *guru* is to discern the present stage of spiritual evolution of the aspirant, to find out to what degree he (or she) is attached to earthly things and to what degree he can transcend them and then to suggest to the aspirant what he should do with his life (1984 : 115). Because the two will not always be in close physical proximity, this guidance will need to be done on a psychic level. There are two ways in which the disciple may withdraw his ego so that the *guru* can penetrate further into the disciple's understanding. The first is through meditation, the disciple changing his consciousness into "voidness". There are no distances in the void, so "a link is automatically established between you and the *guru*". The other way is the path of extreme devotion, *bhakti yoga*:

> When your mind is completely devoted to your guru and for you he means not only something but everything, then the link is very easy; even with your eyes open you can maintain a link with him.
>
> (Satyananda 1984 : 293)

There is a traditional psychological explanation for this process, which Satyananda also gives:

> When you begin to look within your own self, you must have a concept or symbol upon which to focus and steady the mind and that concept is God, guru or ishta devata. God is formless and nameless, so the next best representative is the ishta devata—a divine form you have chosen for yourself. The

concept of the ishta devata may be a hypothesis; it doesn't matter. Even the word God, the concept of God, is also a hypothesis, because you don't know whether what you have understood from the books, is correct or not.

The ishta devata which you have chosen, is one concept of the inner life. Another concept is the guru. When you draw yourself within, you have to base your consciousness on either one of these two, or even both, if possible. And as you become more and more aware of the ishta devata and the guru, you begin to develop a rapport between yourself and him. That unity, that totality of consciousness in which you can experience yourself and him as one—that is called bhakti or bhakti yoga.

(Satyananda 1984 : 83)

But it is also significant that in the explanations of some of the Karma Sannyasins, the link between the *guru* and disciple has some strong similarities to the type of relationship which is encouraged in some Christian churches between the believer and the anthropomorphic person of Jesus. This is, as one would expect, most obvious in Harigauri's response:

Sannyasa is a commitment to furthering my spiritual journey. I do not profess a great understanding of sannyasa other than reading the book "Karma Sannyasin" and Swami Satyananda's initiation speech in 1983 at Mangrove Mountain. . .

(This 1983 speech is one of the few places where Satyananda speaks on "Inner Christ consciousness".)

. . .Like the stage when Christians talk about being "saved" or accepting Jesus into their life, to me, sannyasa is similarly a point in my life when I say yes I would like to further my evolution. I am unclear about Guru/discipleship. I still look to Jesus as my "guru" (I suppose) or my devotional example, however Satyananda's teachings are wonderful and much clearer than the bible. He is my teaching "Guru".

Kaivalyananda spoke of *sannyasa* as meaning:

I am part of a big link to God through a very special man called Swami Satyananda. . .

It is also a way of being committed to developing an awareness and understanding of her spirituality through daily yoga and meditation, and of trying "to live a good life of loving and caring for the people I come in contact with". Gyansindhu wrote of a "connection with a highly evolved being—whether I really know it or not", and of his role in "exploding" the unevolved brain centres.

Coming from a background in which there is a strong religious stress on a personal interior relationship with human images of the divine, it is not surprising that Karma Sannyasins, with little experience of highly abstract Indian religious discourse should tend to cast their experience into this more familiar conversion experience pattern.

If the first institutional understanding of Karma Sannyasa was vertical and eternal, the second was horizontal and contemporary. Through their initiation, Karma Sannyasins felt that they were part of a rather undefined community of like-minded persons, on whom they could count for help and with whom they could be friends. Mangalananda wrote:

> It is important to be with like-minded persons working towards a common goal with a degree of discipline, commitment, honesty and openness and responsibility. Sannyasins are more sensitive, attuned to these qualities, have a more intellectual approach to life.

Yogalata stated:

> I live not with, but in close contact with other sannyasins. I feel that the contact, sharing of common goals, interests, experiences, knowledge, is very important for deeper knowledge and self awareness through yoga.

None of the Karma Sannyasins spoke of their fellows as though they were part of a religious group or even a club (although some had been accused by others of joining a sect and reacted with amusement to this suggestion). The limits of the group as a whole are so vague, membership so uncertain, that there could be no sense of belonging to a known and defined society.

The third meaning of initiation for Karma Sannyasins was similar to the Full Sannyasin's commitment to inner growth. Karma Sannyasins tended to express this, however, not in psychological terms but through metaphysical biological images. The idea of evolution, a growth towards a specific goal, was prominent, although the nature of the goal was never stated. Brahma saw Karma Sannyasa as "an inner commitment to spiritual growth". For Kumarimurti, it was "a way of life, a means of personal evolution". For Om Murti, Karma Sannyasa meant "being able to develop in the quickest, safest way". Within this process of evolution, the individual was understood to be following a particular personal path. His or her greatest need was to understand "life" participate in it fully, to make the most of one's own life.

II : LIVING IN THE WORLD

One of the greatest advantages of Karma Sannyasa for many was that one could make this commitment to the *guru* and to personal evolution while living an "ordinary life". Karma Sannyasins live as individuals dispersed throughout the community. Despite their vague sense of relationship with each other, none expressed the wish to actually live with other Karma Sannyasins or to move into an *ashram*. There are obvious reasons for this. Karma Sannyasins have their own families and friends. The *ashram* in Munger is too far away and unfamiliar for residence there to be a meaningful possibility. The Australian *ashram* system was spoiled by its moral dereliction towards children, one of the most repugnant of offences for householders. The Yoga Therapy Centres, with which some Karma Sannyasins are heavily involved, are usually non-residential. The attitudes expressed towards the possibility of living with other *sannyasins* included the following:

> It is beneficial to associate with other sannyasins but not ultimately important. I like to associate with others of similar interests, not necessarily swamis.
>
> (Poornima)

> I have never wanted to spend long periods of time in an ashram. It leads to dependency.
>
> (Devachittam)

> My relationship with the guru is primary. I don't need the buildings or other sannyasins. It is nice to share the things we have in common.
>
> (Om Murti)

> It is very important to associate with other sannyasins but I
> couldn't live with them . . . they are all half fucking mad.
>
> (Devashakti)

Such independence of spirit also served to stop the Karma
Sannyasins becoming an inward looking exclusive group.

The Karma Sannyasins' involvement in the normal day-to-day
life of their society is, in fact, very strong. Although many have
children, few have the leisure to be "just a wife and mother". Karma
Sannyasins maintain careers. Some are similar to those upon which
Full Sannyasins have recently entered: yoga teaching (although
less than half of the respondents), running plant nurseries, carpentry, building maintenance work, childminding, physiotherapy,
community nursing, and free-lance journalism. These are forms of
small-scale, self-directed employment, in contact with the earth, or
with people and their physical well-being. A few operate in larger
organisations: one is an electrical engineer, another a civil servant,
and some are teachers and school office workers. One man is an
assistant pre-school teacher. Some operate on a large scale, although within the parameters of the ongoing counter-culture
commune movement. Poornima is a member of a cooperative
which has thirty beneficiaries, owns one hundred and fifty acres of
land and operates four businesses—desktop publishing; building
and painting contracts; crystals, gems and rocks; fruit and vegetables. Ambarupa is a member and Director of one of the longest
established bourgeois rural communes. She runs the childcare
centre for children up to the age of six, employs six full-time and
part-time teachers, manages the finances, carefully monitors the
changes which she regularly introduces to improve the teaching
and learning environment, and deals with the parents and their
materialistic concerns. One Karma Sannyasin woman has been a
professional musician for fifteen years. These careers have often
taken many years to build. They are individual and personally
fulfilling. For Karma Sannyasins, initiation serves to enhance their
work (not to replace it), by giving it added meaning. Sannyasins
learnt to honour work but not to care what work they did; for
Karma Sannyasins with families to support and houses to maintain, this is not a practical attitude. There was almost no magical
thinking among Karma Sannyasins that anything they wanted
would, somehow, come. They claimed to live simply, as those with
limited possessions must, but saw no conflict with their spiritual

aims in working as hard as they could to get what they wanted.

Just as material possessions were not a significant issue for Karma Sannyasins because of the ideology they espoused, neither was celibacy. Nevertheless, over half the respondents are currently not in partner relationships. Some of these found that hard work and yoga helped them cope with being single. The attitude they expressed towards their sexuality was, however, positive. A few described sexual relations as an important part of intimacy and love. Others wondered if sex might be useful as a means of attaining greater spiritual awareness, as Tantra taught. One considered celibacy a problem only when she "wasn't getting enough of the other". One man, not yet thirty, saw celibacy as not much of a problem since he had "started sex later in life", but anyhow he had recently discovered something of the Chinese "Tao of Sex" and was busy finding out about the energy centres in the body. Those respondents who were married or in a relationship simply stated that celibacy was "not applicable" to them.

Given this freedom to accept life as it is, without guilt, without needing to change anything, most Karma Sannyasins found adjustment to their new role easy. As Jamuna wrote: "Karma Sannyasa is ideal as I still have a husband and find I can still abide by my yoga sadhana and not neglect my home life".

The greatest difficulties seem to have been with immediate families who did not "understand the yoga philosophy" and had trouble with some of the external marks of the *sannyasins*, in particular the use of a spiritual name. Those who adopted all the marks had the worst time. (This is not something Satyananda insists on: see Satyananda 1976: 74). Poornima caused herself a lot of pain by leaving her daughter behind when she moved into an *ashram*. Given the nature of the particular *ashram*, this decision was probably something she chose rather than something which was imposed upon her. Devachittam has found that:

> Over the years my main problem is with other people who expect me to be some strange unrealistic goddess. When they see me shopping, dancing, or hugging a male etc., they go into shock.

Gyansindhu had trouble with people who thought she had joined some weird cult. Ambarupa learnt to cope with public disapproval by keeping a low profile:

> I have not insisted on anybody calling me by my spiritual name, liking my geru clothes and short hair cut, or respecting my withdrawals from many social or sensational happenings, but people are telling me how they like it, how they see it is good for me.

The more subtle problems took place internally. Despite their busy lives, almost all Karma Sannyasins practise at least an hour a day of yoga postures, breath control and meditation. For some it was difficult in the beginning to overcome laziness and lack of discipline. While most recognised the interior dimensions to spiritual evolution, only Mangalananda listed her adjustment problems in the language of growth psychology:

> I consider myself to be constantly adjusting to the life of sannyasa—that this is problematic shows areas where my personal responsibilities and commitments need addressing.
>
> Main problems for me—
>
> * areas of ego—separation, illusion
> * direction of personal desire
> * interpersonal conflict
> * ignorance, pain and suffering.

Om Murti noticed that her increasing strength and independence was tending to bring her more and more into conflict with her husband; she learnt to compromise with him and keep a balance by "not harping too much on yoga". Karma Sannyasa works as an eminently practical philosophy, and has served to confirm the personal worth of these individuals.

All Sannyasins Together

There are a number of different ways of structuring the relationships which can occur when Full Sannyasins and Karma Sannyasins are together.

A common first cohort Karma Sannyasin way of relating is to see all initiated disciples of Swami Satyananda as equal. This may become distorted by the sense that Karma Sannyasa life is superior to that of full Sannyasa because of the greater struggle involved in maintaining a spiritual way of life in the face of the temptations of everyday living without the security of the *ashram* and the facilities provided there.(Swami Satyananda seemed to offer some support for this view in Auckland 1984 when he stated that: "Karma Sannyasa is much more difficult than Full Sannyasa, because you have to maintain a very careful balance between the external life and the inner expiation, without rejecting anything ", *Teachings*, Vol. 5, 1986 : 504.) A second and third cohort temptation is to see the Full Sannyasins, struggling to establish homes and careers, as children.

On the other hand, a common Full Sannyasa perspective is to see the Full Sannyasins as superior by virtue of their higher initiation and time spent in an *ashram*. The natural role of the Sannyasin then becomes the creation of a centre that is as like one of the former *ashram*s as possible, with a full range of yoga courses, Kriya Yoga and internal cleansing programmes, and regular *satsang* evenings spent singing *kirtan*, in which *swami* sits on the platform at the front. In this exaggerated perspective, Karma Sannyasins (like everyone else) become students, congregation and, at worse, clients in a difficult economic world.

A relationship of mutual respect has been shown in the various Teacher Training Courses, Celebrations of Yoga, and Karma Sannyasa programmes. In most centres, it is recognised that the total number of disciples is so small, and their skills so diverse, that cooperation is essential, as well as pleasant.

Because of the personal, physical nature of initiation in the Satyananda tradition, the number of *sannyasins* is likely to increase only slowly in the future, if at all. The lifestyles of Full Sannyasins and Karma Sannyasins are already becoming increasingly indistinguishable. Convergence is likely to continue. It is also possible that both groups may blend with other groups of Non-Sannyasins. Poornima has suggested.

> The sannyasa attitude is being developed in many people, all in the process of growing in awareness, through whatever method they choose. In many ways there is increasingly less and less "need" to formally make a commitment by taking sannyasa. People are heading for enlightenment in many different ways.

Evolution is not always a straightforward line.

CHAPTER ELEVEN

THE NEW SANNYASA

Swami Satyananda was raised as a Hindu. He experienced nine years' residence in Sivananda's *ashram* and has spent his life among Hindu *sadhus*. In initiating European men and women into Full Sannyasa, he was doing no more than his Master had done before him. The understanding of *sannyasa* he encouraged is a recognisable type within Hinduism. Rajneesh, on the other hand, has been described as "a Jain with Buddhist sympathies" (Gussner 1986: 311). His creation of Hindu-like *sannyasins*, dressed in orange robes and *malas*, was quite an extraordinary decision, the more so as Neo-Sannyasa was intended not to complement but to exist in opposition to the traditional renunciate orders. The order prospered. World-wide there were perhaps three hundred thousand Neo-Sannyasins at the beginning of the eighties (Mullan 1983 : 94), with one tenth of that number visiting the Shree Rajneesh Ashram in Poona in any one year (Thompson and Heelas 1986 : 19). For Australians, Satyananda offered a firm sense of identity, respect for the grace and capacities of the body, a non-theistic spirituality, and a sense of community. In this chapter we explore the perception of Rajneesh, his message, and their relationship with him, which is to be found among Australian based Neo-Sannyasins. As in the previous two chapters, our focus is on the process and meaning of coming to discipleship, and on aspects of daily lifestyles as lived out both in the main *ashram* and/or in the wider society. Again we begin by describing the life of a representative disciple, in this case with a strong emphasis on his wife who is also a Neo-Sannyasin.

I: TAKING NEO-SANNYASA: SWAMI ANANDA

Swami Ananda was born in 1944 and raised in a major Australian provincial city. The closeness of his working-class family was intensified by their commitment to the Baptist Church. When he finished high school, Ananda went to the university in the state capital and took an Arts degree in English and History. At the age of twenty, he considered a call to the ministry of his Church. Instead he married the next year and began a career in teaching. He continued his association with the Church for another two to three years.

The moral confusion of the churches over the war, the 'death of God' movement within theological thought, the petty self-preoccupation of the denominations, together with his own growth away from fundamentalist thinking, all led to his decision to turn away from religion. In 1967 he joined the Labor Party. Because he could write and keep records, he was made Secretary of his local branch. He became involved in the activities of his teaching union. He joined in the protests against Australia's involvement in Vietnam. The variety and demands of his political activities led him in 1969 to resign from the Master's course he was pursuing in History. When the Labor Party came to power in 1972, he dropped out of party politics as well.

Ananda began to study yoga in 1974. He had reached the age of thirty; physically and emotionally, he felt he was "falling apart". Yoga appealed at once, with its combination of physical exercises, breath control techniques and meditation practices. After the first lesson he felt he had come home. He studied the teachings behind yoga, "esoteric yoga" as it was still called following the theosophical tradition. His teacher maintained a fierce independence from other schools; there were no pictures of Indian swamis on the wall here! Ananda started to develop an interest in New Age thought; he attended various "workshops", and in particular those of Paul Solomon and of the Findhorn group. In 1977 his first marriage came to an end.

Ananda continued to practise yoga until 1979. In that year he moved to an interest in the thought of Wilhelm Reich, a controversial German Freudian, who emphasised the ability of the body to hold itself in pain as a response to stressful situations and for this tension to continue to exist long after the painful situation had passed into the subconscious. Ananda undertook Neo-

Reichian Therapy courses in 1979 and 1980, Breath Therapy training in 1980, and Postural Integration training in 1981. The aim of Postural Integration is "to loosen the connective tissue throughout the body, release the joints and then restore the bones to their natural places" through the use of massage. In this way, the many tensions which may be traced to "mental and emotional factors" can also be released, along with the fears and tensions which accompany them (*Osho Multiversity* 1990: 84.) Ananda also studied Rebirthing (another breath technique, aimed at reliving, and thus releasing, the traumas association with the time of one's birth) and Gestalt Encounter work. With Amiyo, Ananda began offering Rebirthing to the public in 1983, through their "Rebirthing Centre".

Ananda began living with Prem Amiyo in 1982. They shared much in common. Amiyo had been a devout Catholic as a child, was a trained Primary Teacher, had begun yoga in 1975 in preparation for the conception of her son and continued practising until 1979, and also had an interest in growth work. Amiyo also had an interest in the teachings of Bhagwan Shree Rajneesh, based on the reading of his books. "Through the books", as she has said:

> I connected with someone who said the things I had been saying and feeling for years. It was a coming home—such a deep and wonderful experience. To read his books and feel as if I was there as the words were being said—a YES, YES, YES, from my heart, my mind, every cell jumping for joy—a feeling of oneness in purpose—a wanting to be part of this fun, this love, this wisdom. Life becoming richer and richer and the possibility of more.

For two years Amiyo procrastinated about taking Neo-Sannyasa, feeling "not good enough", the feelings she had learnt towards herself from the nuns as a child. Finally she decided to jump in. She notified her intention to the leaders of the Rajneesh Meditation Centre, a three storey pink and purple building in the city, with a nearby restaurant, and attended a couple of meditations. Then she filled in the form, giving her name, address, educational qualifications, skills and hobbies, asked for a completely new name (rather than keeping part of her original name in her *sannyasa* name), included a photograph of herself, and wrote a letter to Bhagwan.

Ananda fought taking Neo-Sannyasa all the way. But after listening to a tape on the Master-disciple relationship, his heart started "to burst apart" and he felt such love being poured into him from Rajneesh that there was nothing for him to do but to take *sannyasa* too. He and Amiyo received their names a few weeks later and were given their *mala*s by the Centre leader in late 1984. For Ananda, initiation was "a way of linking with Bhagwan and receiving from him". For Amiyo, it was" a love affair with a most wonderful human being and a true friend", and a way of becoming "one of his people". Amiyo's initiation was followed by a number of powerful psychic experiences.

They were still living in a small country town. Ananda suffered from the judgements, opinions and rumours which went around after his initiation, as he wore red clothes and the *mala* to school each day. Amiyo was at first self-conscious wearing the *mala*, but gradually relaxed as people came up to her in shopping centres and said how much they liked Bhagwan. Otherwise her life was as it had been for the past five years. The next year, 1985, they closed their small "Rebirthing Centre", Ananda resigned from teaching and they visited the Ranch for more training, then moved to a small Neo-Sannyasin commune in the countryside near the city. They became Directors of the community in 1987, after the original founder had decided to move back to the city, and established a breath therapy training centre. Although they used many Rajneesh techniques and meditations in their training, it was not good business to give too much prominence to their connection with this controversial *guru*.

They still live in the commune with five other Neo-Sannyasins. Ananda would like to live in a house and have a few more comforts, like a new car, a bulldozer to put in roads and dams, and a really good stereo system. He quotes Bhagwan approvingly: "If you have the choice between living richly and living poorly—live richly". Amiyo simply says: "I think material possessions, acquisition, power, etc., are great—and I'll have whatever comes along". Celibacy is not an issue. Ananda practices "High Tech" meditations at least once a day, using tapes such as "Ultra Intelligence", "Maximum Immunity" and "Genesis". They come together for Tantra Yoga once or twice a week.

Coming to the Master

The heavy stress on Rajneesh as an Enlightened Master, the emphasis on therapy as a means of self-knowledge, the affirmation of possessions and sexuality, as well as the relative indifference to disciplined "spiritual practices" including meditation, are all features which distinguish Neo-Sannyasins from other *sannyasins*. These distinctive features occur constantly in the stories of coming to initiation.

The First Cohort

In his study of an English Neo-Sannyasin community, Mullan (1983 : 50-79) suggests that disciples came to Rajneesh for basically one of four reasons:

(i)   through "seekership", exploration of the counter-culture in search of an alternative style of life with a new meaning;

(ii) through "personal distress", some difficult turning point in life;

(iii) through "his charisma", Rajneesh's extraordinary qualities, special gifts, etc.; or

(iv) through seeing the world as a "rat race", that is, by being disenchanted with success.

These categories are moderately applicable to Australian Neo-Sannyasins but they are not the whole story.

Seekership is a factor in the following stories. Sagarpriya spent "years of trying different life styles, travel, meditation, drugs, reading" and some feminism. When she met the Master in Poona in 1976, there was no need to decide, initiation was "inevitable". For her, "sannyasa is the only thing that matters". Nityanando left university at the end of his second year of music studies and went to Poona "to do some groups and find out more about who I am". He was afraid, but keen to "go beyond the mind and its chattering, and to open my heart". He too did not decide but simply said "YES to what was happening". For him, *sannyasa* is "being here and relaxed". Turiya had read some books on Zen, including Allan Watts, and later Rajneesh, and wanted to find someone who could teach her how to "be here now". Having the idea that India was the place where one was likely to find such a person, she planned a trip there. Even before she arrived, she met some Neo-Sannyasins and was immediately attracted by them. She went to the *ashram*, liked the commu-

nity, saw Rajneesh and knew that "he was the one who could teach
me what I needed". She started doing the meditations and took
initiation soon afterwards. Neo-Sannyasa to her means wanting to
become enlightened, and having Rajneesh as her "beloved Master".

"Charisma" and "the rat race" overlap in the following stories,
with the former being very much more important. Shradda took
initiation in Perth in 1980. She had "nowhere else to go", as she
felt she had "done everything". Her reason for taking Neo-
Sannyasa was that she "fell in love with the Master!". He is the
air she breathes and "the breath of life". Bodhi Pravino had spent
a few days in the country with a *sannyasin* woman and her five
sannyasin children. She appreciated the love and acceptance she
received and having "nothing to lose", Pravino took Neo-Sannyasa
in Perth in 1979, finding in it the "totality" she had always been
searching for. For her, Neo-Sannyasa is "awareness, meditation
and doing what feels right for me in the moment", as well as
accepting Rajneesh as her Master and taking in "his love, presence and insights like a very thirsty person drinking pure cool
water—with love and gratitude". Abhiyana took initiation in
Poona in 1981 from Swami Anand Teertha, after Osho had entered into silence. She decided to take Neo-Sannyasa because of
her "love for my Master"; "his silence" led to the "actual step";
Neo-Sannyasa means "Everything. Life feels like fluid sunlight".

A crucial factor for Australian Neo-Sannyasins does not occur
in Mullan's list. Fully half of the Neo-Sannyasins decided to take
initiation after practising one of the strenuous meditations devised by Osho or following a weekend group. Meditations and
groups require, as Gussner (1986:302) technically states, "authen-
ticity and cathartic release of repressions at the outset and a de-
focal expressive mode of meditation further on". Tushita found
out for the first time after the dancing meditation, Nataraj, that
"you can celebrate life". She wanted to know more about herself
and the world around her. Meera did the *kundalini* meditation:
she didn't want all "this *outer* jumping, shaking, etc.", but by the
end of the meditation she was "very much IN", and had "glimpsed
my inner self, the stillness and peace and harmony of my real
self". She took initiation because she felt she could totally trust
him to be her guide and friend. Ambu had started travelling once
her boyfriend had gone off with another woman. After half a year
of meditations and groups at her own centre, she went to a nearby

centre, did the most demanding of all the Rajneesh meditations, Dynamic Meditation, and suddenly:

> I couldn't help it.
> I couldn't keep up the fight against it.
> I drowned myself in an ocean of love: Bhagwan.

Dynamic Meditation, too, caught Premartha; after that he had run out of reasons "not to". A group opened up a whole new world of meditation for Purna, turning her illusions upside down. She was another who "did not decide! It happened."

Despite the apparent passivity of their decisions, these Neo-Sannyasins subsequently defined their understanding of Neo-Sannyasa in active, and lengthy, terms. Summarising, Neo-Sannyasa is turning one's energy inwards, away from prestige, possessions and emotional bondages, towards the self and one's true nature. A consequence is "awareness", living each moment totally and affirming life ("saying YES"). Through this awareness, one strips off the old layers of self-defence and becomes expanded, more in harmony with "all people, things, nature, the earth". In Premartha's one word answer (the same as the Full Sannyasin Navaratna's), Neo-Sannyasa means 'Life !!!'.

The Second Cohort

The second cohort of Neo-Sannyasins too came into a situation where there were books available easily, centres within easy access and many other Neo-Sannyasins. It made no difference to them that Rajneesh had withdrawn into silence on the Ranch in America. His image drew them to Neo-Sannyasa.

Sumito and Satyam Chaitanyo both felt that Rajneesh said what they had always felt. Chaitanyo felt Bhagwan was like an old friend. She was stunned by the "aliveness" of Neo-Sannyasins and their celebrations, their sheer delight in being alive and knew that this was what she "wanted and deserved".

Yogendra spent three and a half years "around sannyasins and around Bhagwan" before coming to the point of "WHY NOT!". In a rare and honest moment, working with his father, Yogendra heard himself saying he could keep on doing groups and meditations without becoming a *sannyasin* and "corrected myself there and then". Mukti finished a group and thought "What the heck!", put his application in, "And it wasn't such a big deal after all (in some ways) apart from totally changing my life". Bhadra followed a friend who had taken Neo-Sannyasa: "I loved the spirit of the sannyasins I associated with through her; I learnt to hear what Bhagwan was saying and feel the love that was available through opening myself to his presence". Ragini was searching for something better than the way she was living. She met some Neo-Sannyasins:

> It looked like a great way to live, at the time, everyone seemed so happy and lived out everything they wanted to live out with no repressions. It was wild, so much energy in people who were already sannyasins. I also wanted to live like that. I didn't really know much about anything else at the time (Inner growth, etc.)

Ragini's decision to take initiation happened easily, with hardly a thought or a fear". Satyamurti, on the other hand:

> was totally freaked out. What if it's not real, just some clever trick, etc., but finally—if one per cent chance of truth—what choice do you have? Fuck all I say.

Upachara was caught up in the fuss surrounding the end of Rancho Rajneesh, felt tremendous attraction to Bhagwan, went to her present Master, was formally released by him, and took Neo-Sannyasa immediately.

In essence, the second cohort also described Neo-Sannyasa as a way of living life with awareness and spontaneity, through contact with one's "true feelings . . . Buddha nature, consciousness, awareness, nothingness". To this typical first cohort response, the second Neo-Sannyasin cohort also typically added the link with Bhagwan as an important part of their understanding: "My Master is a reminder of my centre and my possibilities. I become so thrilled to see him. . ." (Satyamurti); "The Master guides me" (Yogendra); "I feel a very small, silent connection to the source—whatever that is, or whatever that means. Being with Bhagwan has helped me to connect with that. If I wasn't with him right now I wouldn't lose that connection—it is of great strength to me" (Mukti); "Devotion to the Master and his teachings" (Upachara). Unlike Karma Sannyasins, Neo-Sannyasins did not put this personal devotional tie into a larger evolutionary or metaphysical context.

The Third Cohort

Members of the third cohort, as one might expect in a time of flux and lack of definition, tended to describe their coming to initiation and their understanding of Neo-Sannyasa, in the most personal terms. Kamaal had been heavily involved with Zen Buddhism after a Catholic upbringing. (During the eighties it seemed to be the Jesuits who were most active in promoting Zen in the west.) Kamaal heard of Rajneesh and within twelve days went to Poona in 1988. He took Neo-Sannyasa from "Zorba the Buddha" (as Osho was briefly known at that time), "out of deep gratitude and love", and with the aim of spreading the living Buddha's message of love, goodwill and celebration.

Mahasattva had what he described as a " 'conversion' type experience", in which he saw visions of Bhagwan and experienced various psychic sensations ("spinal/kundalini experiences"), "in the presence of a Ma with whom I had an intense (non-sexual) contact". This experience led to the practical follow-up of immediately applying for initiation. For Mahasattva, *sannyasa* is "commitment to a spiritual path which I had suspected (but avoided) for some years", and in particular "Its applications to global issues which I have felt concerned about and committed in trying to help". The apocalyptic strain in Rajneesh's teaching (see, for example Rajneesh 1975: 56) emerged with particular force in 1988, the year Mahasattva took initiation, coinciding with his own strong interest in the environment.

The depressive Kalpa (it is impossible to tell her cohort) provided the only concrete, object-oriented answers to these questions about initiation and the meaning of Neo-Sannyasa. She took Neo-Sannyasa to "grease" (flatter) her therapist. The actual step came about because she had "nowhere else to go and the Hare Krishna food is awful". Neo-Sannyasa meant "Papa Luigi's" (a spaghetti bar where Neo-Sannyasins "hang out"), "Baggy pants, 'Bhagwan' in a funny tone" and "Fremantle" (where the Centre is). The therapy culture requires one be constantly articulate about one's feelings. Most Neo-Sannyasins, like their Master, love words. Kalpa was unusual in her attachment to specific things.

Sex

Individuals took Neo-Sannyasa because of their desire to find personal meaning, their exhaustion with the rat-race, because

they fell in love with Bhagwan, as the result of doing his meditations, under the influence of friends and Neo-Sannyasins they
met, and for other personal reasons.

In the public press, Osho was often referred to as "the sex
guru". Hugh Milne, Bhagwan's bodyguard for over a decade,
wrote a bitter book, *Bhagwan—The God That Failed* (1986), in
which he suggests young Westerners were attracted to Rajneesh
because of the freedom he offered, particularly in the area of sex.
To this licence, Rajneesh added "meaning, a purpose in life". It
was:

> the complete package: permission to engage in transcendent
> sex, indulged in with the idea that it would lead to spirituality
> and enlightenment.
>
> (Milne 1986 : 26)

Further, according to Milne, the women around Rajneesh were
highly attractive and dressed in a very provocative way. Set
against the prudish attitude of Indian society towards sex and
nakedness, this was a volatile and exciting mixture.

With the possible exception of Ragini, attracted by the way that
Neo-Sannyasins "lived out everything they wanted to with no
repressions", none of the respondents suggested unbridled sexual
freedom as the major (or even a minor) reason for their attraction
to Shree Rajneesh. The seventies was a "permissive" decade in its
own right. And Rajneesh's insistence on awareness meant that,
sooner or later, the disciple would learn that "licentiousness is
not freedom", that:

> Freedom can exist only according to a certain behaviour
> pattern which you have accepted consciously, knowing all
> its implications.
>
> (*Rajneesh Times International*, 16 June 1989)

II : THE BUDDHA FIELD

It is difficult to describe the average "life-style" of the Neo-
Sannyasin. For the Full Sannyasin and Karma Sannyasin, there
were more or less clear rules: yoga and meditation, in the morning and at night; work as a dedicated activity; celibacy or not, as
one understood the situation; simple material possessions; living
in the *ashram*, or treating the world as one's *ashram*. This was not

Rajneesh's way; it could not be when the disciple was encouraged
to live and act from "moment to moment", with no predeter-
mined plan (Rajneesh 1976: 41-42). Before 1987, there were four
commitments which each Neo-Sannyasin accepted: to dress in
clothes which were the colours of the sunrise; to wear the *mala*
outside the clothes so that it was plainly visible; to use the new
name given at initiation; and to meditate at least one hour each
day (*Rajneeshism* 1983 : 33). In late January 1987, the first three of
these four "vows" were withdrawn, allegedly to stop the public
harassment of Neo-Sannyasins; Neo-Sannyasa went "under-
ground" (*Rajneesh Times of Australia*, 3 March 1987 : 4). None of
the four commitments had ever structured how one lived the
day.

The most meaningful factor was the proximity of the individual to Rajneesh. Lifestyles differed according to whether one
was living in, working in, visiting or hoping to visit the *ashram* in
Poona (or Oregon). Those not near Bhagwan were usually either
residents of their local Rajneesh Meditation Centres or regular
visitors to it. The central *ashram* operated under different rules
between 1974 (the move to Poona) and 1981 (the move from
Poona); 1981 to 1986 (the opening and the closing of the Oregon
period); and after 1987 (back in Poona). The centres changed
much less over this time. Individual Neo-Sannyasins outside the
ashram or centres lived singly, with their family, in couples, or in
other shared arrangements. The term "the buddhafield", meaning more or less an energy field in which the Buddha assists
beings to engage in rapid spiritual growth, was sometimes used
with reference to the whole community of Neo-Sannyasins, sometimes only with reference to "the commune" around the physical
presence of the Master.

Shree Rajneesh Ashram
The *ashram* at Poona consisted of "six acres on the residential
outskirts of the city of Poona" (Mullan 1983 : 14), a former hill
station cantonment to the east of Bombay. Mullan estimates
(1983 : 23) that:

> At any one time there were about six thousand Rajneeshees
> in Poona, some visiting for weeks or months to do groups
> or meditations, with about two thousand working and living
> on a permanent basis in or around the *ashram*.

Bernard Gunther (1979 : 2) more poetically describes the *ashram* as:

> a cosmic combination
> of crazy house
> college campus
> church
> carnival
> and cloister
> an intense immense
> heterogenous conglomeration
> of buildings
> gardens halls
> huts and tents.

The daily programme began at six o'clock in the morning, with Dynamic Meditation. Rajneesh gave his discourse each morning from eight to approximately nine thirty. From ten to eleven there was another period where one could either meditate formally, sing *kirtan* (predominantly attended by Indians), or join in Sufi dancing (a form of Rajneesh square-dancing and a good place to meet people).

In the afternoon, a taped discourse was played in the main auditorium area. *Nadabrahma* (a humming meditation) followed at four, *Kundalini* at five thirty; and *Gourishankar* (a dancing meditation) in the evening. *Kundalini* was the most popular form of meditation; *Gourishankar* has some of the feel of a "singles' bar", the last chance to meet someone before the day closed.

There were three circles of people in and around the *ashram*. The inner circle worked in the *ashram*: tending Bhagwan, running the administration, editing books and newspapers, translating, selling books, running the boutique, guarding closed-off areas, doing maintenance and garden work, cooking, gardening and so on. Some workers also lived in the *ashram*; the closer to Bhagwan, the higher one's status. Workers had their own line which went into discourse before everyone else and took the front places. They were also provided with meals. Work was well organised, a form of "selfless service", and holidays were few. Here one did not do as one pleased.

Among the workers, a high status was accorded to the group leaders. In 1976, there were ten groups: Primal Therapy, Hypno-

therapy, Enlightenment Intensive (three days with the question
"Who am I?"), five forms of Encounter Group and two forms of
massage, including Rolfing. Over the next few years the number
of groups increased to about eighty. Neo-Sannyasins were as-
signed groups by Rajneesh during *darshan* or sometimes chose for
themselves. One paid to participate in the groups, as one did to
attend the meditations and the morning discourse. (By Indian
standards the costs were high.) Some groups were quiet and
meditative, the Vipassana group for example; others were violent
and had a strong sexual component, for example the Encounter
and the Tantra groups. (Hence the famous lines in Sally Belfrage's
book, *Flowers of Emptiness*, (1981: 198), "But didn't you get laid?. . .
Well for God's sake, baby, what do you think the groups are for?
You mean to tell me you haven't got laid? At all?") For the time
that they were "doing groups", visitors had the privileges of the
workers: passage through reserved areas in the *ashram*, food,
accommodation within the *ashram* area, but not front positions at
discourse. (The most graphic insider account of groups is Bharti
1980.)

Those who were purely and simply visitors could wander
around the small public area of the *ashram*, do the meditations (or
not), join in Sufi dancing, buy books and eat at the restaurant.
Non-Sannyasin visitors were allowed to do the groups and to
meet Rajneesh in *darshan*.

Oregon
"Big Muddy Ranch" in Oregon, officially renamed
Rajneeshpuram (Rajneesh City) included one hundred square
miles of empty, neglected land, close to the adjoining town of
Antelope (population forty), over which the "Rajneeshees" soon
gained control (Mullan 1983 :127). The land was extensively
cultivated. By the end of 1984, houses had been built for most of
the two thousand residents (Thompson and Heelas 1986: 90);
during the World Celebrations, the population grew briefly to as
many as fifteen thousand (Milne 1986 : 348). The Rajneesh Institute for Therapy and the Rajneesh Institute for Meditation and
Inner Growth were established to provide groups for the summer
visitors. (See Fitzgerald 1987 : 275-76, for a wry account of these
groups; and Carter 1987:159 for a useful general description of
the Ranch's geography.)

In 1983, Rajneeshism was proclaimed a "religion", with its own systems of meditation, worship and education; ministers; religious practices; and celebration days. Life at the Ranch was strictly regulated and supervised; work was renamed "worship" and was the major focus of most residents' lives. What had formerly been an extremely sexually vigorous community became almost puritanical as stringent regulations were introduced relating to the use of condoms, rubber gloves, jellies, the avoidance of kissing (and blowing out birthday candles), and extreme patterns of hygiene (Palmer 1990:141). As Satya Bharti later wrote (1992 : 274):

> We could make to love to anyone we wanted, but we couldn't live where we wanted, work at the jobs we wanted, or even be sick when we were sick. It was a strange freedom.

The Centres
Living as a Neo-Sannyasin meant working near Rajneesh for a few; visiting him, for those affluent enough; and for most regular participation in one's local "Neo-Sannyasa Commune". There were centres in all major Australian capitals and many country towns.

The actual functions of the centres changed little from 1974 to 1985. Typically, the centres housed a small community, ran regular meditations during the week and, especially, at the weekend; and arranged groups as often as possible, usually encounter groups and Enlightenment Intensives. Centres processed applications for Neo-Sannyasa, sold books and generally administered as necessary, increasingly in strict response to directives from Oregon.

During the eighties, life in and around the centres became subject to more stringent controls. Sheela ruled from Oregon with ruthless efficiency. Great emphasis was placed on "surrender" to her directives, the raising of funds to support the Ranch, on participation in groups and the development of appropriate attitudes and behaviours. Violation of the four commitments led to immediate expulsion. Despite the discipline, the centres in general, and Oregon in particular, were felt to be "beautiful places" because of Bhagwan's intense presence there.

Headlong into the Temple of Ruin

By 1984, the Neo-Sannyasa movement was well established in
its dual character as a *Guru* cult, focused on Rajneesh, his wisdom, insight and special love for his followers; and also as psycho-
religious movement, in which growth activities were promoted
as a whole way of life within a framework of spiritual devotion
and a community of like-minded persons (Hummel and Hardin
1983 : 24-27, Mullan 1983 : 26). Then in late 1985, as we have seen
above, the movement went terribly wrong. Sheela was sentenced
to four years gaol for fraud and other offences. Rajneesh escaped
the charges against him by "plea-bargaining". The Oregon *ashram*
closed, the Rolls-Royces were sold, and centres all around the
world found themselves in immediate difficulty.

Almost all of the respondents experienced the upsets of that
time of collapse; the two who took initiation later may be said to
have become disciples despite the reports of what happened in
Oregon. None of the Neo-Sannyasins chose to speak of the impact
that this testing time had on them, nor were they asked to. We
must put together the responses as best we can from reports in
the Rajneesh and popular press.

One reaction was that of pain, bitterness and anger. Most of the
one hundred and twenty to one hundred and fifty Neo-Sannyasin
residents in the Sydney commune left the movement. Some spent
months in Buddhist retreats, or joined other therapy groups such
as Est. More were absorbed into the mainstream, many resuming
their old professions. Some who stayed refused to work, stole
and generally took advantage of the others. A few took the
various business enterprises in hand and struggled to pay off the
enormous debts of over one hundred thousand dollars. (*The Good
Weekend*, 12 December 1986, 16-21.) The story was the same in
Perth and among the other remaining communities.

The opposite reaction to anger and panic was to refuse to
admit that anything was happening. The Western Australian
Centre stated on the 2nd December 1985:

> Things are moving fast here and we have gone through a lot
> of changes in the communal life-styles as well as in ourselves
> the last few months. It is beautiful to know that Bhagwan is
> well and resting. In his last discourses Bhagwan talked a lot
> about freedom and responsibilities and the message gets

clearer and stronger. It is beautiful to see and hear him.
Even in jail clothes He looked so beautiful!

(Letter to the Author)

In the press release from India dated 8th December 1985:

Bhagwan denied that His movement is falling apart. Through
what has happened in the last month, the sannyasa
movement has become even stronger. Those who have left
Him have come back again. "They have started again to love
me."

He said that Sheela isolated Him for three and one-half
years. She had the power and represented Him. As He
started to talk she became what she was before, a nobody.
"Who was she anyway? A secretary—we did't have any
other relationship but at that time I needed such people for
my commune, so to say, unpolished stones. I knew that
sooner or later I would have to do something to improve
her.

Somewhere in the middle of these responses the resolution of
the cognitive dissonance began, as Neo-Sannyasins increasingly
turned their anger back on themselves. Swami Prem Arvind, the
first Australian to take initiation in 1973 at Mt. Abu, said in
Sydney in early 1986:

A lot of times we really said "yes" when we really meant to
say "no", because on the ranch if we disagreed with anything
we were told to leave.

We were doing things out of fear.

And we compromised because we wanted to be on the
ranch, and we wanted to be with Bhagwan. We all trusted
that what was happening was him. We didn't have enough
intelligence to what was really going on. We saw it, but we
compromised because otherwise if we voiced our opinion
we would be on the next bus. Twice I was asked to leave...

We've all grown through it ... We're much stronger
through this.

Melbourne born Sue Appleton, now a senior administrator at
the *ashram* in Poona said, with what *The Western Australian Maga-*
zine described as "disarming candour":

> We stuffed it up. He talked about sex being a basic energy
> that could be transformed to find super-consciousness, but
> we jumped on the sex bit and fucked our brains out. He told
> us to meditate, but a lot of people never did. He had a vision
> of creating a beautiful experiment in Oregon, but we blew
> it (20-26 May 1989:10).

With this adjustment, those who had decided to stay in the
movement absolved Rajneesh of any involvement in the debacle,
and committed themselves to working intensely for his sake.

The Return to Poona

The collapse of the *ashram* in Oregon led to an outpouring of
therapists to the remaining centres throughout the world. For a
while groups were the only positive activities taking place at the
local level, as Rajneesh continued to tour the world uncertainly
looking for somewhere to settle. In early 1987, the wearing of
orange and the *mala* were abandoned. When Rajneesh finally
denounced groups at the end of 1987 as a distraction from meditation, even the last fixed point of the lifestyle seemed to slip
away. Senior Neo-Sannyasins, however, decided otherwise, for
the denouncement of groups was not unequivocal and may have
been motivated by Rajneesh's antagonism to a few specific therapists. He said:

> A few idiot therapists from this commune have become
> masters. They know nothing about their own being, they
> know nothing about any mystery of existence. All that they
> know is a certain mind game. That mind game can be of
> help, if ultimately you are under the guidance of a man who
> has arrived.
>
> A little clarity, a little less confusion, a therapy group can
> certainly create.
>
> But a therapy group is not the end.
>
> It is only the beginning.
>
> It is a preparation for meditation, just as meditation is a
> preparation for enlightenment.

[The Poona Programme, (*Rajneesh Times*, 21 March 1988 : 2)]

With this let-out, courses began once more to proliferate and
the focus of the movement again settled on the revitalised *ashram*

in Poona. Previous programmes were updated and adjusted to the changed consciousness of the late eighties. Opening the recent handbook for the *Osho Multiversity* (1990: 130-31) at random, for example, we find courses for "Osho Zen Witches", "Osho Tantric Yoga", "The Osho Island Experience: A Journey to Inner Space", the "Osho Co-dependency Group", "Trusting the Impossible before Breakfast", and "Osho Magic Touch". The last course uses "theater, music, hypnosis and therapeutic processes to unmask our true beauty". Then: "As a final magic touch, experts in skin and hair care and many beauty processes, clothes design and colour selection show easy ways to enhance our beauty and let it shine outwardly". The course is for "men and women seeking to reach their full potential". Neo-Sannyasins were obviously taking seriously the Master's desire "to create the biggest and most beautiful 'spiritual health club' in the world—a Club Meditation" (*Osho Now!* brochure, 1989 : 8).

Within the Meditation Hall, Rajneesh added his own new touches to his discourses, now held at night. In early 1988, he introduced the greeting "Yaa Hoo!", the new "sannyasin salute", with both hands raised, based originally on a dirty joke (*Rajneesh Times*, 16 April 1988). He then extended this greeting into a meditation stretching over three weeks, involving three hours of laughter everyday for a week, followed by a week of weeping for three hours each day, and finally a week of silent Vipassana meditation mixed with dancing. The *Rajneesh Times* hailed this "Mystic Rose Meditation" as "the first major break-through in meditation" since the time of Buddha (16 June 1988). To follow his discourses the new "Let Go" meditation of gibberish followed by complete relaxation was begun (*Rajneesh Times*, 16 May 1988). Finally, the common wearing of robes, only while on the *ashram* premises, was re-introduced: red robes for daily wear, black robes for group leaders, and white for meditation (*Rajneesh Times*, 16 August 1989). *Malas* were not worn.

When Osho died on the 19 January 1990, his body was taken to the ghats by red-robed Neo-Sannyasins. It was as if nothing had ever changed. Some, indeed, claim that the feeling of his energy at the *ashram* is stronger than it has ever been. (See the reports in *Yes Osho!*, The Melbourne Osho Meditation Centre Newsletter.) They are possibly fighting a losing battle, as the number of overseas' visitors to the *ashram* has been declining since 1988 (*Rajneesh Times,* December 16, 1989), and without the physical presence of the Master the *ashram* is unlikely to continue to attract younger Western seekers in the future.

III : LIVING AT THE END OF THE EIGHTIES AS A NON-SERIOUS NEO-SANNYASIN

In *I Am The Gate* (1975: 39) Rajneesh said:

> To me Sannyasa is not something very serious. Life itself is not very serious, and one who is serious is always dead. Life is just an overflowing energy without any purpose, and to me Sannyasa is to live life purposelessly. . . If you can take this whole life just as a dream, a dream act, then you are a sannyasin.

Neo-Sannyasins do indeed lead more playful lives than other *sannyasins.*

Work

Neo-Sannyasin respondents were engaged in a smaller and less remunerative range of occupations than other *sannyasins.* Half of the respondents saw their local Osho Centre as the major focus for their energy. Involvement ranged from full-time management, typing and taking care of the reception desk, to offering occasional sessions of different types of massage. "Bodyworkers" supported themselves by other work such as cleaning and bartending. One respondent was a landscape gardener, "playing with rocks"

Of those others not focussed on their centre to pass the time, one was a "Holistic medical practitioner and counsellor", one a project engineer. One was a teacher in "mainly government schools", presumably a supply teacher. There were two enrolled nurses and one office-worker. One woman was a student of naturopathy.

Bodhi Pravino was the most committed to work; her attitude was similar to that of the Karma Sannyasins; work was important as a means of self-support and for furthering one's spiritual activities:

> I run a painting business with a partner, working three to four days a week and making enough money to live as I like

and also save to go to the ashram in Poona for at least three months of the year.

Bhadra tended to savour his leisure:

I wake in the morning, usually have tea and toast for breakfast. I might then do any number of things from fence building, moving a goat, being present with a body session, boiling jam, picking plums, driving tractors, cutting grass—lunch is around 1-1.30 p.m., usually soup and salad, afternoon until 4 p.m. a quiet time, stop, sit, smoke a cigarette —then again some work until tea time, dinner if you like, around 7.30 p.m., then sitting with friends laughing, reading, writing. Bed around 11 p.m. to 12 p.m.

This sounded decidedly more healthy than the way Kalpa spent her day: "Lying in my bed imagining I'm killing all the people I hate".

The relaxed attitude towards work these days extends all the way to Poona. Sue Appleton is reported as saying:

Nowadays people just say, "Fuck you, I don't want to clean toilets. I want to write novels." If we think they can write novels we let them.

(*The West Australian Magazine*, 20-26 May 1989:10)

Possessions

In view of their relaxed attitude to labour and the limited range of usually poorly paid jobs in which Neo-Sannyasins are engaged, it cannot be expected that most disciples would live in the "Club Med" style to which the Poona *ashram* now aspires. Few expressed a desire for anything beyond the essential necessities of food, shelter and some basic items (including a good "sound system"). What was valued, however, was not simplicity, but comfort and beauty. Bhadra, for example, wanted "a porsche, a house near the beach, perfect waves for surfing" and much more, but was content to "just wake up tomorrow with fresh air and a cup of tea". When Satyamurti has money, he lives "beautifully with money things"; when he has no money, he lives beautifully without. The disciples have accepted Rajneesh's aesthetic attitude to the world and reject, as he did, the "virtue" of poverty..

Celibacy

Celibacy was not "a problem" for Neo-Sannyasins. (A few professed not to understand the word, as some Sannyasins did not understand the term "the growth movement".) Some were highly critical of the concept, calling it "a crime", "a disease", "a joke" and "totally foreign to me". Because sex was accepted as natural, healthy and a means of creative self-expression, celibacy tended to be considered the state of waiting for a partner. (One woman thought it a type of contraception and preferred condoms.)

Rajneesh's attitude to sexuality was complex, as the title of his infamous *From Sex to Super-Consciousness* (1973) suggests. The premise of the book is, in fact, a common one in Indian religious discourse: the transformation of sexual energy can lead to spiritual awareness. Most Indians, however, focus only on the other end of the equation. Rajneesh chose to honour the beginning of the journey as well as the end and it was this which caused so much distress to his audience and critics, then and ever since. He argued that sex is a basic human energy, life's expression of its desire to continue and develop itself. At the time of intercourse, the ego is transcended and time ceases to exist: at that moment, more than any other, we are close to God, both because of our self-transcendence and our openness to the creation of new life. This energy may be despised (as it has been despised by conventional religion and public morality), or it may be transformed through love into contentment and self-acceptance and an attitude of peace towards the whole world. While sexual experience in itself cannot lead us completely to God, it can be the beginning, a first glimpse. The fuller understanding is reached when love becomes meditation. Rajneesh's argument is summarised in these words (*samadhi* may be translated as "spiritual bliss"):

> A long way there is between sex and *samadhi*. *Samadhi* is the eternal end of which sex is the first step. I want to point out that those who refuse to recognise the first step, those who censure the first step cannot reach the second step; cannot progress. It is imperative to take the first step with consciousness, knowledge and awareness. But, be warned that it is not the end in itself, it is the beginning. We have to take more and more steps to progress further. . . (Rajneesh 1973:131).

Neo-Sannyasins have accepted the need to accept and exhaust the sexual drive, they do not consider the need for sublimation meaningful for themselves.

Meditation

Neo-Sannyasins are less likely than other *sannyasins* to spend regular time in the practice of a consistent form of meditation, despite this being the only one of the four commitments now in force. The most common practice was the Buddhist form of Vipassana meditation. Kamaal, with his strong background in Zen Buddhism, spent at least two and a half hours each day "sitting" and sometimes as many as four or five. Three others practised Vipassana everyday, two "now and then". Two practised one of the meditations devised by Rajneesh each day, but not always the same one.

For the others, life itself, lived with awareness, was the meditation they preferred. As Meera wrote:

I live my life ordinarily as simply as possible, and WITH AS MUCH AWARENESS as possible. Continually looking at myself, what I am doing, feeling, thinking, acting, the games I play, the reasons I do things. I watch my health, practice yoga, eat good foods, try to keep my mind healthy also. Sometimes I sit silently in meditation but mostly, just living my life day to day is my meditation; it is continuous, never ending.

Others echoed these sentiments, often emphasising the difficulty of the task:

Remembering this moment. Often enough for the realization that this moment and all moments are one.

(Abhiyana)

Watching my mind, breath, emotions (moods if possible)— whenever I remember, in any moment, situation.
I often do meditations, whatever suits me at the time, whatever I feel like doing.

(Ragini)

Watching—whenever I remember.
Lately—inconsistently, chakra sounds.

(Sumito)

Vipassana encourages an interior awareness of the thoughts and emotions, in an objective manner. It is, therefore, consistent with some of the aims of therapy, although not with those forms which stress spontaneous action. In choosing these apparently different approaches to meditation, Neo-Sannyasins are, in fact, working from a common base. Yoga may argue that in the spiritual life it is not necessary to do much, but that one has to do it often; Neo-Sannyasa suggests one has already done more than enough, it is time to be aware of what one is doing.

Conclusion

While conducting research on *sannyasa* in Canada, the question was asked in one interview: "Are the Rajneeshees real *swamis*?". The respondent, a forty-five-year-old German woman *sannyasin*, was aghast. After a few moments, when she regained her breath, the question was repeated. "No", she finally replied firmly, "they can't be. They enjoy themselves" (Aveling 1988 : 16).

Osho taught a form of renunciation that is strongly opposed to the common contemporary traditionalist understanding of renunciation as world-rejection and regulated self-denial. Neo-Sannyasins meet none of the criteria described by Miller and Wertz (1976 : 2-3) as characteristic of *sadhus*, nor do they wish to. They do not cultivate a holiness which the layman can worship or reverse. They have no knowledge of Hindu religious thought, nor usually of the complexity of their own teacher's thinking. They do not lead ritual performances. They do not follow a distinctive lifestyle, accompanied by austerities, worship, or abstinence from sex, material possessions, or particular items of diet.

In dropping the wearing of the colour orange, the *mala* and the spiritual name, the movement ceased to exist in opposition to traditional *sannyasa*. It may be seen as then having fully internalised renunciation or as merely having become a *guru* and therapy club for Europeans, confined to the few acres in Poona, and fascinated by the fads of the expensive end of the range of New Age culture. The second interpretation seems closer to the truth.

Rajneesh taught, but he left the rate and the nature of the disciples' learning entirely at their own discretion. It would seem that the complex range of his teachings, particularly on the need for meditation, have on the whole been quietly put to one side by most Neo-Sannyasins while they get on with the job of "being here now".

In retrospect, it is clear that Rajneesh failed to transform the old institution to which he stood opposed, or to create a new one in its place. Ironically, with the declining numbers of European visitors to the *ashram*, and the "simply staggering" number of Indian visitors (see Forman 1990 : 423), the *ashram* is likely to become another memorial to a great, dead sage. The tradition has met Rajneesh's challenge by incorporating him into itself.

POSTSCRIPT

I began this book wanting to write an analysis of contemporary Australian *sannyasins*. As the study progressed, it became increasingly obvious that the present could only be understood in terms of the past. Lawton (1988 : 88) predicted that "Asian religions are not a passing phenomena in Western society", and that their followers will continue to grow until they rival some of the major denominations in size. This prediction seems now to be clearly wrong. The age of the "New Religious Movements" has gone. Those who follow these ways are remnants of their former communities.

The two movements described here were destroyed in the second part of the 1980s by the moral failure of some of their most senior leaders. That the two men at the top did not know of, and did not in some way countenance, these failings is difficult to believe.

From another perspective, the movements faded because they could no longer meet the developmental needs of their members. Erik Erikson (1963) has suggested no less than eight developmental stages central to each human life. Successively, these involve the individual's attainment of trust, autonomy, initiative, industry, identity, intimacy, generativity and ego integrity. *Sannyasa* has as its ultimate task the development of two goals which occur late in the life-cycle: compassion (Erikson's seventh stage) and wisdom (the eighth). It is the case that both movements allowed for the development of a strong personal identity, which Erikson considers an early adulthood issue, but may also relate to mid-life. Later, however, Full Sannyasins left their *ashrams* to deal with the matter of intimacy, as Karma Sannyasins were already doing. The Rajneesh movement, on the other hand, tended to encourage a relaxed self-centredness in place of mature identity and to weaken industry and intimacy. Neo-Sannyasins in general were unable to attain the philosophical understanding, subtlety and intensity of purpose characteristic of their Master.

To the extent that the Satyananda movement undoubtedly did succeed in Australia, it succeeded because of its convergence with the Australian values of appreciation for physical grace, religion without God, and an easy community of equals. Rajneeshism appealed because of its easy playfulness and world-affirmation. Both became part of a search for personal identity which had its roots in the marginal status of their members and was first expressed in the language of the counter-cultural psychological and philosophical world-view of the seventies. Neither movement made it into the mainstream, which remained increasingly anxious about material welfare, complacent about personal change and racist.

Satyananda's story of the "Laughing Swamis", presented at the beginning of this work, is an essentially optimistic view of the contributions Australians could, and for a while did, make to the inner renewal of the tradition of sannyasa. It is possible that the laughing swamis may be growing in strength in the jungles and deserts of the Australian community. On the other hand, they may each be dying, with no one to light their bonfire. Time will tell.

CELEBRATION OF YOGA
QUESTIONNAIRE ON SANNYASA

Over the past two decades, an increasing number of Australians have taken *sannyasa*. Yet there is still little understanding of this distinctive lifestyle in the wider community. The Celebration of Yoga gives us all the opportunity to make an assessment of the strenghts of *sannyasa* and yoga in Australia in 1990s.

I am interested in writing a sympathetic and reasonably objective study of Australian *sannyasins*—their backgrounds, way of life, and what *sannyasa* means to them.

To do this, I need first to gather information that will give an overall impression of *sannyasa* in Australia today. This questionnaire is designed to collect that preliminary information. Could you please complete it in as much detail as you wish, and return it to the camp administration or to the address below. The confidentiality of your answers is assured.

I was initiated into Karma Sannyasa in 1983 by Swami Satyananda at Mangrove Mountain. Currently, I am working towards the degree of Master of Education at the University of New England. The study will eventually be the basis for a book.

Thank you for your cooperation.

Sw. Sureshwar Saraswati
17 Longbourne Avenue, Nottinghill, Victoria, 3168.

[This cover-letter was used for the Celebration of Yoga held in Tasmania, 1990. The participants were Full Sannyasins, Karma Sannyasins and lay disciples of Swami Satyananda.]

QUESTIONNAIRE ON SANNYASA

PLEASE EXPAND ANSWERS WHEREVER POSSIBLE.
AVOID ONE WORD ANSWERS WHENEVER POSSIBLE.
FEEL FREE TO WRITE ON THE BACK OF THE PAGES.

1. Sannyasa name (optional):
    Male/female:
    Date of birth:
    Place of birth:
    Place brought up:

2. Religion as a child/adult:

3. Highest level of formal education and year:

4. Have you ever been married?
    Are you in a relationship now?

5. Have you ever been involved in politics? Please detail:

6. Have you been/are interested in feminism?

7. What courses, if any, have you done in the area of 'personal growth'?

8. How long have you practised yoga? Why did you begin yoga?

9. When did you take *sannyasa*?
    Where?
    Who from?

10. What 'Sadhana' or 'meditation' do you do? How often?

11. Why did you decide to take *sannyasa*?

12. What led to the actual step?

13. What does *sannyasa* mean to you?

14. What are the benefits of *sannyasa* for you?

15. Was adjustment to the life of *sannyasa* easy for you? What were the major problems?

16. How much do you yearn, if at all, for such things as material possessions, acquisitions, power, etc.

17. Was/is celibacy a problem to you?
How did/do you deal with it?

18. How important is it for you to live with other *sannyasins*?

19. What are your main activities now? (e.g. teaching, medicine, building a rural commune, working in a library, etc.?

20. How have you changed during your time as a *sannyasin*?

21. Any other comments?

THANK YOU

GLOSSARY

ashram: a residence centred around a teacher and associated community: unlike a Christian monastery, an *ashram* is open to the constant flow of outside human activity.

Australian Ashram System: system of *ashram*s dedicated to the teachings of Swami Satyananda in Australia.

brahmacharya: the life-stage of the celibate student; ideally followed by marriage, withdrawal from secular affairs, and finally *sannyasa*.

Brahman :   The Ground of Being; God.

brahmin :   a member of the Hindu highest caste in society.

guru :   one who teaches, by word and example; one who is qualified to give authentic initiation to a disciple.

Karma Sannyasin :   *sannyasin* disciple of Swami Satyananda who still pursues his / her worldly obligations.

Ma: a female initiate of Bhagwan Shree Rajneesh.

mala :   necklace of 108 wooden beads, used in the practice of meditation.

Mangrove Mountain: central *ashram* of the Australian Ashram System.

Munger (Monghyr) :   northeast Indian town, centre for the major Satyananda Ashram.

Osho :   the Buddhist title assumed by Rajneesh during 1989, meaning "Beloved Master".

sadhu :	general term for an Indian ascetic.
sannyasa:	world renunciation.
sannyasin:	one who practises *sannyasa*.
swami :	master (of the Self), a title given to some renunciates.
Swamiji:	a respectful form of address or reference towards a *'swami'*.
yoga :	the practice of various physical, mental and spiritual disciplines.
vanaprastha:	the third stage of the "ideal of life"; retired householder.
Vedanta:	one of the six orthodox schools of Indian philosophy; its major teaching is the common identity of the inner self (*atman*) with the universe and God (*Brahman*).

BIBLIOGRAPHY

Ackerman, S.E. and Lee, R.L.M. (1990), *Heaven in Transition: Non-Muslim Religious Innovation and Ethnic Identity in Malaysia*, Forum, Kuala Lumpur.

Agehananda Bharati, Swami (1970), *The Ochre Robe: An Autobiography*, Doubleday, New York.

Ajnananda, Swami (1990), *Celebration of Yoga*, Yoga Darshan Ashram, Lottah, Tasmania.

Akhandananda Saraswati, Swami (1983), *Tantra, Yoga and Everyday Life*. Satyananda Ashram, Mangrove Mountain.

Akhandananda Saraswati, Swami (1984), *Mantra Yoga*, Satyananda Ashram, Mangrove Mountain.

Allen, M. and Mukherjee, S.N. (eds.) (1989), *Women in India and Nepal*, Sterling, New Delhi.

Alper, H.P. (ed.) (1989), *Understanding Mantras*, State University of New York Press, Albany.

Amran Kasimin (1985), *Saudara Baru Cina di Wilayah dan Selangor*, Monograph 11, FSKK, Universiti Kebangsaan Malaysia, Selangor.

Ananthanarayanan, N. (1970), *From Man to God-Man: The Inspiring Life of Swami Sivananda*, The Author, Baroda.

Appleton, S. (1987), *Bhagwan Shree Rajneesh: The Most Dangerous Man since Jesus Christ*, Rebel, Zurich.

Atkinson, P. (1990), *The Ethonographic Imagination*, Routledge, London.

Aveling, H. (1986), "Confessions of an Orange Boy", *County Honk (DDIAE)*, July, 15.

Aveling, H. (1988), " Western Renunciates", Unpublished paper, Armidale College of Advanced Education.

Aveling, H. (1989), "Western Renunciates: The Sannyasin Disciples of Swami Vishnu Devananda", *Journal of Inter-cultural Studies*, 10:2, 34-42.

Barthes, R. (1986), *The Rustle of Language*, Basil Blackwell, Oxford.

Beckford, J.A. (1985), *Cult Controversies: The Societal Response to the New Religious Movements*, Tavistock, London.

Belfrage, S. (1981), *Flowers of Emptiness*, Womens Press, London.

Bharti, Ma Satya (1980), *The Ultimate Risk, Encountering Bhagwan Shree Rajneesh*, Wildwood House, London.

Bharti Franklin, Satya (1992), *The Promise of Paradise*, Station Hill, New York.

Bilimoria, P. (1989), *Hinduism in Australia*, Spectrum, Melbourne.

Bird, F. and Reimer, W. (1982), "Participation Rates in New Religious and Pre-Religious Movements", *Journal for the Scientific Study of Religion*, 21:1, 1-14.

Bly, R. (tr.) (1972), *Kabir*, Writers Workshop, Calcutta.

Bouma, G.D. and Dixon, R. (1987), *The Religious Factor in Australian Life*, MARC Australia, Melbourne.

Brady, V. (1981), *A Crucible of Prophets*, ANZEA, Sydney.

Breward, I. (1988), *Australia: "The Most Godless Place Under Heaven?"*, Beacon Hill Books, Melbourne.

Buhler, G. (1969), *The Laws of Manu*, Dover, New York.

Burghart, R. (1983), "Renunciation in the Religious Traditions of South Asia", *Man* (N.S.), 18, 635-53.

Carter, L.F. (1987), " The 'New Renunciates' of the Bhagwan Shree Rajneesh: Observations and Identifications of Problems of Interpreting New Religious Movements", *Journal for the Scientific Study of Religion*, 26:2, 148-72.

Chakraborty, H. (1973), *Asceticism in Ancient India*, Punthi Pustak, Calcutta.

Clifford, J. and Marcus, G.E. (1986), *Writing Culture: The Poetics and Politics of Ethnography*, University of California Press, Berkeley.

Clifford, J. (1986), "On Ethnography Allegory", in Clifford, J. and Marcus, G.E., 98-121.

Clifford, J. and Marcus G.E. (1986), "Introduction" in Clifford J. and Marcus G.E., 2-15.

Coleman, J. and Baum G. (eds.) (1983), *Concilium: New Religious Movements*, T. and T. Clark, Edinburgh.

Cock, P. (1979), *Alternative Australia, Communities of the Future*, Quartet Books, Melbourne.

Croucher, P. (1989), *Buddhism in Australia*, NSW University Press, Sydney.

Crowley, F. (1986), *Tough Times, Australia in the Seventies*, William Heinemann Australia, Melbourne.

Dalton, J. (1973), " Australian Foreign Policy" in Mayer H. and Nelson H. (eds.) *Australian Politics : A Third Reader*, Cheshire, Melbourne.

Daner, P.J. (1975), *The American Children of Krsna*, Holt Rinehart and Nelson, New York.

Dumont, L. (1972), *Homo Hierarchicus*, Paladin, London.

Dutt, S. (1962), *Buddhist Monks and Monasteries of India*, Allen and Unwin, London.

Erikson, E.H. (1983), *Childhood and Society* , Norton, New York.

Feuerstein, G.A. (1974), *Introduction to the Bhagavad Gita*, Rider, London.

Fitzgerald, F. (1986), *Cities on a Hill*, Picador, London.

Forman, J. (1988), *Bhagwan Shree Rajneesh: The Buddha for the Future*, Rebel, Zurich.

Forman, J. (1990), *Bhagwan: One Man Against the Whole Ugly Past of Humanity*, Rebel, Zurich.

Foucault, M. (1972), *The Archaeology of Knowledge*, Tavistock, London.

Foucault, M. (1973), *The Order of Things*, Vintage Books, New York.

French, H.W. (1974), *The Swan's Wide Waters: Ramakrishna and Western Culture*, Kennikat Press, Port Washington, New York.

Ghosal, H.R. (1962), *An Outline History of the Indian People*, Ministry of Information and Broadcasting, New Delhi.

Ghurye, G.S. (1964), *Indian Sadhus*, Popular Prakashan, Bombay.

Goldman, L. (1975), " Dialectical Materialism and Literary History", *New Left Review*, 92, July-August.

Gopalan, S. (1973), *Outlines of Jainism*, Wiley, New Delhi.

Gordon, J.S. (1987), *The Golden Guru*, Stephen Greene Press, Langton Mass.

Griffith R.T.H. (1971), *Hymns of the Rig Veda*, Chowkhamba Sanskrit Series Office, Varanasi.

Gunther, B. (1979), *Dying for Enlightenment: Living with Bhagwan Shree Rajneesh*, Harper and Row, New York.

Gussner, R.E. (1986), "Teachings on Karma and Rebirth: Social and Spiritual Roles in the Rajneesh Neo-Sannyasin Movement", in (ed.) Newfeldt, R.W. *Karma and Rebirth, Post Classical Developments*, State University of New York Press, Albany.

Gussner, R.E. and Berkowitz, S.D. (1988), " Scholars, Sects and Sanghas, I: Recruitment to Asian Based Meditation Groups in North America", *Sociological Analysis*, 49:2, 136-70.

Hogan, M. (1987), *The Sectarian Strand in Australian History*, Penguin, Melbourne.

Hume, R.E. (1968), *The Thirteen Principal Upanishads*, Oxford University Press, London.

Hummel, R. and Hardin, B. (1983), "Asiatic Religions in Europe", *Concilium*, January, 23-28.

"Was Rajneesh Murdered? " *Illustrated Times of India*, February, 11-17, 1990, 10-17.

Joshi, V. (1982), *The Awakened One*, Harper and Row, San Francisco.

Judah, J.S. (1974), *Hare Krishna and the Counterculture*, Wiley, New York.

Jung, C.G. (1971), *Psychological Types*, Princeton University Press, Princeton.

Kelly, T. (1990), *A New Imagining: Towards an Australian Spirituality*, Collins Dove, Melbourne.

Kent, S.A. (1988), "Slogan Chanters to Mantra Chanters: A Mertonian Deviance Analysis of Conversion to Religiously Ideological Organizations in the Early 1970s", *Sociological Analysis*, 49:2, 104-18.

Kidder, L.H. and Judd, C.M. (1986), *Research Methods in Social Relations*, 5th. ed., CBSS Publishing, New York.

Knott, K. (1986), *My Sweet Lord: The Hare Krishna Movement*, Aquarian Press, Wellingborough.

Laing, R.D. (1967), *The Politics of Experience*, Penguin, Middlesex.

Lanoy, R. (1971), *The Speaking Tree*, Oxford University Press, London.

Latkin, C.A. *et al.* (1987), "Who Lives in Utopia? A Brief Report on the Rajneeshpuram Research Project", *Sociological Analysis*, 48:1, 73-81.

Latkin, C.A. (1991), "From Device to Vice : Social Control and Intergroup Conflict At Rajneeshpuram", *Sociological Analysis*, 52:4, 363-78.

Lawton, W. (1988), *Being Christian, Being Australian*, Lancer Books, Sydney.

Leary, T. (1973), "The Religious Experience: Its Production and Interpretation", in (ed.) Heenan E.F., *Mystery, Magic and*

Miracle: Religion in a Post-Aquarian Age, Prentice-Hall, Eaglewood Cliffs, 36-60.

Levi, P. (1983), *On the Frontiers of Paradise*, Collins, London.

Levinson, D.J. (1978), *The Seasons of a Man's Life*, Ballantine, New York.

Lim Hin, Fui (1983), "Ambiguity of Identity: The Case of Muslim Converts in Western Malaysia", *Ilmu Masyarakat*, October-December, 39-47.

Lorenzen, D.N. (1976), "The Life of Sankaracharya", in (ed.) Reynolds, F.E. and Capps, D., *The Biographical Process*, Mouton, The Hague.

Mahadevan, T.M.P. (1967), "Social, Ethical and Spiritual Values in Indian Philosophy" in (ed.) Moore, C.A. *The Indian Mind*, University Press of Hawaii, Honolulu, 152-72.

Mannheim, K. (1952), *Essays in the Sociology of Knowledge*, Routledge and Kegan Paul.

Mascaro, J. (tr.) (1970), *The Bhagavad Gita*, Rider, London.

Maslow, A.H. (1964), *Religions, Values and Peak Experiences*, Ohio State University Press, Columbus.

May, R. (1953), *Man's Search for Himself*, Signet, New York.

Mehta, G. (1990), *Karma Cola*, Minerva, London.

Meredith, G. (1987), *Bhagwan : The Most Godless Man*, Rebel, Poona.

"For or Against", *The Mesto Muse*, November 1986, 10.

Miller, D.M. and Wertz, D.C. (1976), *Hindu Monastic Life: The Monks and Monasteries of Bhubaneswar*, McGill- Queens University Press, Montreal.

Millikan, D. (1981), *The Sunburnt Soul*, Lancer, Sydney.

Milne, H. (1986), *Bhagwan: The God that Failed*, Caliban Books, London.

Mitchiner, J.E. (1989), "Three Contemporary Indian Mystics: Anandamayi, Krishnabai and Rajneesh", (ed.) Werner, K., *The Yogi and the Mystic*, Curzon Press, London, 149-65.

Mol, H. (1972), *Western Religion*, Mouton, The Hague.

Monte, C.F. (1987), *Beneath the Mask: An Introduction to Theories of Personality*, Holt, Rinehart and Winston, New York.

Muktananda, Swami (1983), *Nawa Yogini Tantra*, Bihar School of Yoga, Bihar.

Mullan, B. (1983), *Life as Laughter: Following Bhagwan Shree Rajneesh*, Routledge and Kegan Paul, London.

Murphy, D. (1986), *The Rajneesh Story*, Linwood Press, West Linn Oregon.

Niranjan, Swami (1989), " From the Desk", *Sydney Yoga Therapy Research and Education Centre, Newsletter*, March 1990, 2-3.

O'Brien, L.N. (1983), "A Case Study of the 'Hare Krishna' Movement" in (ed.) Black, A. and Glasner, P., *Practice and Belief: Studies in the Sociology of Australian Religion*, Allen and Unwin, Sydney.

Olivelle, P. (1981), ''Contributions to the Semantic History of Sannyasa", *Journal of the American Oriental Society*, 101:2, 265-274.

Oman, J.C. (1903, repr. 1984), *The Mystics, Ascetics and Saints of India*, Cosmo Publications, New Delhi. ·

"For Love and Money", *The Oregonian*, June 30-July 19, 1985.

"On the Road Again", *The Oregonian*, December 30, 1985. *Osho Multiverstiy* (1990), Rebel, Cologne.

Palmer, S.L. (1990), "Virus as Metaphor: Religious Responses to AIDS", in (ed.) Robbins, T. and Anthony, D., *In Gods We Trust: New Patterns of Religious Pluralism, Transaction*, New Brunswick (USA), 130-50.

Pande, G.C. (1978), *Sramana Tradition* , L.D. Institute of Indology, Ahmedabad.

Pannikar, R. (1982), *Blessed Simplicity*, Seabury Press, New York.

Perls, F., Hefferline, R.E. and Goodman, P. (1951), *Gestalt Therapy*, Delta Books, New York.

Pichaske, D. (1989), *A Generation in Motion, Popular Music and Culture in the Sixties*, Ellis Press, Peoria Illa.

Prasad, R.C. (1978), *Rajneesh: The Mystic of Feeling*, Motilal Banarsidass, Delhi.

Quick, J. and Garran, R.R. (1901), *Annotated Constitution of the Australian Commonwealth*, Angus and Robertson, Sydney.

Rajneesh, Acharya (1971), *The Mysteries of Life and Death*, Motilal Banarsidass, Delhi.

Rajneesh, Bhagwan Shree (1973), *From Sex to Super Consciousness*, Jeevan Jagriti Kendra, Bombay.

Rajneesh, Bhagwan Shree (1975), *I Am the Gate* , Rajneesh Foundation , Poona.

Rajneesh, Bhagwan Shree (1976), *The Grass Grows by Itself*, Rajneesh Foundation, Poona.

Rajneesh, Bhagwan Shree (1976), *Diary 1977*, Rajneesh Foundation, Poona.

Rajneesh, Bhagwan Shree (1978), *Path of Love: Discourses on Songs of Kabir*, Rajneesh Foundation, Poona.

Rajneesh, Bhagwan Shree (1978b), *The Art of Dying*, Rajneesh Foundation, Poona.

Rajneesh, Bhagwan Shree (1978c), *The Discipline of Transcendence*, Rajneesh Foundation, Poona.

Rajneesh, Bhagwan Shree (1984), *The Perfect Way*, Rajneesh Foundation, Rajneeshpuram.

Rajneesh, Bhagwan Shree (1985a), *Krishna:The Man and His Philosophy*, Rajneesh Foundation,Rajneeshpuram.

Rajneesh, Bhagwan Shree (1985b), *Books I Have Loved*, Rajneesh Foundation, Rajneeshpuram.

Rajneeshism (1983), Rajneesh Foundation, Rajneeshpuram.

Ramanathan, A.A. (ed.) (1978), *The Sannyasa Upanishads*, Adyer Library and Research Centre, Madras.

Roe, J. (1986), *Beyond Belief: Theosophy in Australia 1879-1939*, NSW University Press, Sydney.

Rochford, E.B. (1985), *Hare Krishna in America*, Rutgers University Press, New Brunswick.

Rogers, C. (1969), *Freedom to Learn*, Merrill Books, Ohio.

Ross M.W. (1983), "Clinical Profiles of Hare Krishna Devotees", *American Journal of Psychiatry*; 140 : 4, 416-420.

Sadananda Giri, Swami (1976), *Society and Sannyasin*, The Author, Rishikesh.

Saraswati, Meanjin (Muktananda) (1988), Post-Communal Life: Integration or Alienation?, Unpublished paper.

Satyananda Saraswati, Paramahamsa (1969), *Yogasanas, Pranayama, Mudras and Bandhas*, Australian School of Yoga, Melbourne.

Satyananda Saraswati, Paramahamsa (1976), *Sannyasa Tantra*, Bihar School of Yoga, Monghyr.

Satyananda Saraswati, Paramahamsa (1979), *Satyam Speaks*, Satyananda Ashram, Mangrove Mountain.

Satyananda Saraswati, Paramahamsa (1983), *Light on the Guru and Disciple Relationship*, Satyananda Ashram, Mangrove Mountain.

Satyananda Saraswati, Paramahamsa (1984), *Karma Sannyasa*, Satyananda Ashram, Mangrove Mountain.

Satyananda Saraswati, Paramahamsa (1981-1986), *Teachings*, Vols. 1-5, Bihar School of Yoga, Monghyr.

Sivananda, Swami (1963), *The Necessity for Sannyasa,* Divine Light Society, Sivananda Nagar.

Smith, M. and Crossley, D.C. (1975), *The Way Out, Radical Alternatives in Australia,* Lansdowne Press, Melbourne.

Spradley, J.P. (1980), *Participant Observation,* Holt, Rinehart and Winston, New York.

Stark, R. (1987), "How New Religions Succeed: A Theoretical Model", in (ed.) Bromley, D.G. and Hammond, P.E., *The Future of New Religious Movements,* Mercer, Macon Georgia.

Stark, R. and Bainbridge, W.S. (1985), *The Future of Religion,* Universiti of California Press. Berkeley.

Strelley, K. (1987), *The Ultimate Game,* Harper and Row, San Francisco.

Tagore, R. (1915), *One Hundred Poems of Kabir,* MacMillan, Bombay.

Talal, Asad (1986), "The Concept of Cultural Translation in British Social Anthropology", in Clifford, J. and Marcus, G.E., 141-64.

Tamney, J.B. and Riaz Hassan (1987), *Religious Switching in Singapore,* Flinders University of South Australia, Asian Studies Monograph 3, Select Books, Singapore.

Thompson, J. and Heelas, P. (1986), *The Way of the Heart: The Rejneesh Movement,* Aquarius Press, Wellingborough.

Tiwari, K.N. (1977), *Dimensions of Renunciation in Advaita Vedanta,* Motilal Banarsidass, Delhi.

Tripathi, B.D. (1978), *Sadhus of India.* Popular Prakashan, Bombay.

Tyler, S.A. (1986), " Post Modern Ethnography", in Clifford, J. and Marcus G.E., 122-40.

Van Driel, B. and Richardson, J.T. (1988), "Categorization of New Religious Movements in American Print Media", *Sociological Analysis,* 49:2, 171-83.

Vaudeville, C. (1974), *Kabir,* Clarendon Press, Oxford.

Vaus, D.A. (ed.) (1985), *Surveys in Social Research,* Allen and Unwin, Sydney.

Vishnu Devananda, Swami (1960), *Complete Illustrated Book of Yoga,* Pocket Books, New York.

Walker, B.(1969), *The Hindu World,* I-II, Praeger, New York.

Wallis, R. (1984), *The Elementary Forms of the New Religious Life,* Routledge and Kegan Paul, London.

Wallis, R. (1988), "North America", in (ed.) Clarke, P. and

Sutherland, S., *The Study of Religion: Traditional and New Religions*, Routledge, London, 154-166.

Wright, C. (1985), *Oranges and Lemmings*, Greenhouse, Melbourne.

Wuthnow, R. (1976), *The Consciousness Reformation*, University of California Press, Berkeley.

Yogakanti Saraswati, Swami (ed.) (1989), *Past, Present and Future... 25 Years of BSY History*, Bihar School of Yoga, Monghyr.

Zaehner, R.C. (1973), *The Bhagavad Gita*, Oxford University Press, London.

Newsletters Consulted:

Light of Love (Mangrove Mountain), 1980-81.

Melbourne Yoga Therapy Centre Newsletter, 1989-90.

The Mesto Muse, (Sydney), 1985-86.

Osho Times (Poona), 1989-90.

Rajneesh Times Australia (Fremantle) 1986-87.

Rajneesh Times International (Poona/Rajneeshpuram/ Poona), 1973-89.

Sydney Yoga Therapy Research and Education Research Newsletter, 1989-90.

Yoga (Monghyr), 1977-83.